OECD *Economic Surveys* Electronic Books

The OECD, recognising the strategic role of electronic publishing, issues the OECD ***Economic Surveys***, both for the Member countries and for countries of Central and Eastern Europe covered by the Organisation's Centre for Co-operation with Economies in Transition, as electronic books – incorporating the text, tables and figures of the printed version. The information will appear on screen in an identical format, including the use of colour in graphs.

The electronic book, which retains the quality and readability of the printed version throughout, will enable readers to take advantage of the new tools that the ACROBAT software (included with the diskette) provides by offering the following benefits:

- ❑ User-friendly and intuitive interface
- ❑ Comprehensive index for rapid text retrieval, including a table of contents, as well as a list of numbered tables and figures
- ❑ Rapid browse and search facilities
- ❑ Zoom facility for magnifying graphics or for increasing page size for easy readability
- ❑ Cut and paste capabilities
- ❑ Printing facility
- ❑ Reduced volume for easy filing/portability

Working environment: DOS, Windows or Macintosh

Subscription: FF 1 800 US$317 £200 DM 545

Complete 1994/1995 series on CD-ROM:

FF 2 000 US$365 £220 DM 600

Please send your order to OECD Electronic Publications or, preferably, to the Centre or bookshop with whom you placed your initial order for this Economic Survey.

OECD ECONOMIC SURVEYS

1995-1996

GERMANY

ORGANISATION FOR ECONOMIC CO-OPERATION AND DEVELOPMENT

ORGANISATION FOR ECONOMIC CO-OPERATION AND DEVELOPMENT

Pursuant to Article 1 of the Convention signed in Paris on 14th December 1960, and which came into force on 30th September 1961, the Organisation for Economic Co-operation and Development (OECD) shall promote policies designed:

- to achieve the highest sustainable economic growth and employment and a rising standard of living in Member countries, while maintaining financial stability, and thus to contribute to the development of the world economy;
- to contribute to sound economic expansion in Member as well as non-member countries in the process of economic development; and
- to contribute to the expansion of world trade on a multilateral, non-discriminatory basis in accordance with international obligations.

The original Member countries of the OECD are Austria, Belgium, Canada, Denmark, France, Germany, Greece, Iceland, Ireland, Italy, Luxembourg, the Netherlands, Norway, Portugal, Spain, Sweden, Switzerland, Turkey, the United Kingdom and the United States. The following countries became Members subsequently through accession at the dates indicated hereafter: Japan (28th April 1964), Finland (28th January 1969), Australia (7th June 1971), New Zealand (29th May 1973), Mexico (18th May 1994), the Czech Republic (21st December 1995) and Hungary (7th May 1996). The Commission of the European Communities takes part in the work of the OECD (Article 13 of the OECD Convention).

Publié également en français.

Table of contents

Boxes

Tables

Figures

Text

BASIC STATISTICS OF GERMANY

THE LAND

Area, 1993 (thousand sq. km)	357.0
Agricultural area, 1993 (thousand sq. km)	195.3
Forests, 1993 (thousand sq. km)	104.2

Major cities, June 1993 (thousand inhabitants)	
Berlin	3 472
Hamburg	1 702
Munich	1 256
Cologne	962
Frankfurt	664
Essen	625
Dortmund	602
Stuttgart	598
Düsseldorf	578
Bremen	553

THE PEOPLE

Population (thousands), end 1993	81 338
Number of inhabitants per sq. km	228
Net natural increase in population (thousands), 1993	–99
Net migration (thousands) 1993	471

Labour force (thousands), 1995	38 448
Employment (thousands), 1995	34 864
of which:	
Agriculture, forestry, fishing	1 020
Industry (including construction)	12 393
Private services	14 078

PRODUCTION

GDP, 1995 (billions of DM)	3 460
GDP per head, 1995 (US$)	29 682
Gross fixed investment 1995:	
Per cent of GDP	21.7
Per head (US$)	6 444

Origin of GDP, 1995 (per cent)	
Agriculture, forestry, fishing	1.1
Industry (including construction)	33.5
Services	65.5

THE GOVERNMENT

Public consumption, 1995, (per cent of GDP)	19.5
General government current revenue, 1995 (per cent of GDP)	45.9
Public debt, end 1995 (ratio to general government current revenue)	134.2

Composition of Parliament:	Seats
Social Democratic Party (SPD)	252
Christian Democratic Party (CDU)	244
Christian Social Union (CSU)	50
Greens	49
Free Democratic Party (FDP)	47
PSD	30
Last general election: November 1994	
Next general election: 1998	

FOREIGN TRADE

Exports of goods and services, 1995 (per cent of GDP)	23.0
Main exports, 1995 (per cent of total merchandise exports):	
Products of agriculture, forestry and fishing	1.1
Basic materials and semi-finished goods	23.7
Manufactured foods and tobacco	4.3
Other consumer goods	11.3
Investment goods	56.8
End products	2.8
Total	100.0

Imports of goods and services, 1995 (per cent of GDP)	22.0
Main imports, 1995 (per cent of total merchandise imports):	
Food,	10.3
Raw materials and semi-finished goods	14.5
Finished goods	71.7
of which:	
Primary products	13.3
End products	58.4
Other exports	3.5
Total	100.0

THE CURRENCY

Monetary unit: Deutschemark

Currency units per US$, average of daily figures:	
Year 1995	1.433
June 1996	1.527

Note: An international comparison of certain basic statistics is given in an Annex table.

This Survey is based on the Secretariat's study prepared for the annual review of Germany by the Economic and Development Review Committee on 1st July 1996.

•

After revisions in the light of discussions during the review, final approval of the Survey for publication was given by the Committee on 26th July 1996.

•

The previous Survey of Germany was issued in August 1995.

Introduction

The recovery which began in mid-1993 was rather narrowly based on exports and construction, but was expected to broaden to business fixed investment and consumption, according to the traditional pattern of German recoveries. Indeed, this was the projection presented in last year's *Economic Survey of Germany* which consequently raised the possibility that monetary policy might eventually shift to a more neutral stance. In the event, the expansion faltered in 1995. GDP stagnated in the second half of the year, due largely to weak business fixed investment and declining construction, but also to slower growth of export markets. These factors continued to exercise a restraining influence in early 1996. Output is estimated to have fallen in the first quarter, as the IFO indexes of business expectations and of current conditions continued to deteriorate. Bad weather also affected the construction sector. Signs of a resurgence began to appear toward mid-year as export and subsequently domestic orders began to pick up. Moreover, in the face of falling inflation and modest wage settlements, monetary policy has become progressively, if cautiously, expansionary. The exchange rate appreciation of 1995 has been reversed. Tax cuts and automatic stabilisers are making for a more supportive budgetary stance this year although the government remains committed to meeting the Maastricht fiscal consolidation targets, and this will require considerable fiscal restraint in 1997. These factors, with rising export demand, should ensure that a modest recovery takes place during 1996, which should strengthen into 1997.

While macroeconomic policies are expected to underpin output growth in the near term, longer-term growth prospects are more problematic, because of deep-seated structural problems related to the cost structure of German industry, which have contributed to undermining business confidence and could continue to do so. Contrary to past experience, structural rather than cyclical factors seem to be exercising a key dampening role in the current slowdown. Unemployment has risen sharply and on past experience is likely to persist: employment is projected to decline significantly in 1996, due in major part to labour-shedding in the manufacturing sector. One factor behind this trend has been the appreciation of the effective exchange rate, which has put German enterprises under continuing pressure to cut costs, but more fundamental has been the development of wages, taxes and social charges during the 1990s which, together with excessive regulation, have reduced German competitiveness. The low level of inward direct investment in Germany is a symptom of the malaise. These problems demand a structural rather than macroeconomic policy remedy and in response the government is presently implementing a fifty-point programme of deregulation and liberalisation.

The *Survey* begins with a description of recent trends, with particular reference to the reasons for the pause and the prospects for a resumption of the expansion later in the year. Chapter II analyses budgetary and monetary policies, against the background of the need for fiscal consolidation to achieve the Maastricht criteria and the challenges faced by monetary policy in creating the conditions for sustained, non-inflationary growth. Chapter III contains a discussion of the tax and benefit systems in Germany, the reform of the tax and social security system being essential both from the point of view of reducing the future non-wage labour cost burden on the working population, and containing the expansion of public debt. Chapter IV elaborates a broad programme of reforms for Germany in the light of the requirements laid out in the *OECD Jobs Study,* covering not just the labour market *per se* but also initiatives to improve human capital, enhance competition and reduce the burden of taxation. Conclusions and policy recommendations are presented in Chapter V.

I. Recent trends and prospects

Nature of the slowdown

Following the unexpected strength of the 1994 upswing, the expansion began to lose momentum in the first half of 1995, with real GDP growth falling to an annualised rate of 2 per cent. The pace of growth slowed further in the second half, to an annual rate of 0.8 per cent, and for the year as a whole GDP grew by 1.9 per cent (Figure 1). The extent of the slowdown was unclear at the time because of the evident unreliability of some economic statistics such as industrial production, orders and trade volumes.[1] Contrary to the pattern of previous recoveries, gross fixed investment failed to pick up in 1995, while the export impulse slowed. Business fixed investment in machinery and equipment stagnated throughout the year, falling in the last quarter, while other investment sectors were also weak. Public investment was adversely affected by the increasing budgetary pressure on the territorial authorities and construction activity collapsed. Offsetting these negative influences to some extent, import growth slowed, government consumption remained buoyant, as it was throughout 1995, and private consumption also expanded moderately. However, the uncertainty associated with rising wage costs and the appreciation of the currency led to a downward revision of business expectations and to reduced inventory accumulation, aggravating the slowdown (Table 1). Unemployment rose sharply in western Germany, and employment creation in eastern Germany came to a halt.

Declining fixed investment continued into 1996, with GDP estimated to have contracted in the first quarter. Construction was particularly weak (although the underlying weakness was exaggerated by unusually harsh weather in the first quarter, which led to a marked decline in building activity); the IFO indexes of business expectations and of current conditions continued to deteriorate, and business concerns about excess stocks suggest that stockbuilding was a drag on

Figure 1. **MACROECONOMIC PERFORMANCE**[1]

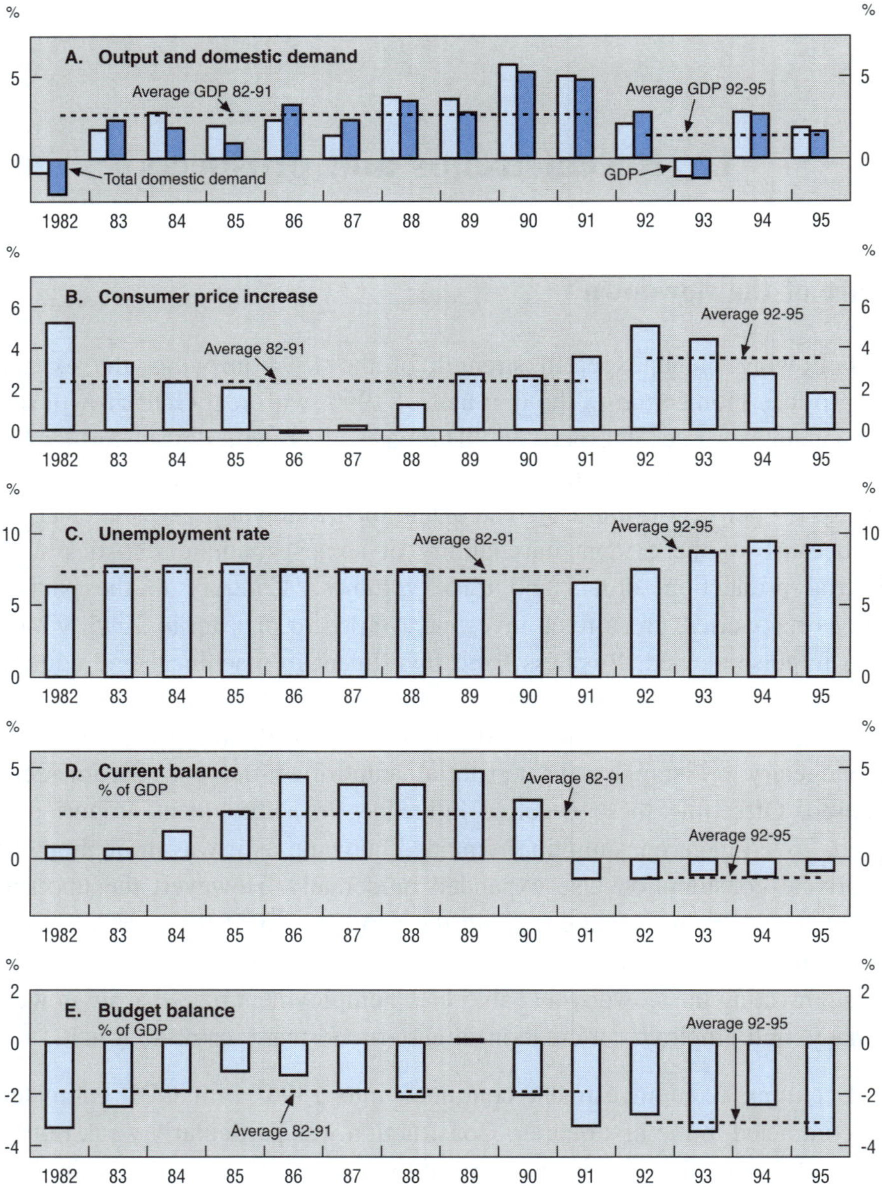

1. Western Germany up to 1991.
Source: OECD.

Table 1. **Demand and output**

Percentage change from previous period, 1991 prices

	1992	1993	1994	1995	1995 S1	1995 S2
Private consumption	2.8	0.5	0.9	1.7	2.5	0.4
Government consumption	5.0	–0.5	0.7	2.1	3.0	2.3
Total fixed investment	3.5	–5.6	4.3	1.5	0.2	–0.9
Construction	9.7	0.9	7.8	1.2	0.2	–1.6
Business	9.4	–1.2	3.0	0.4	–0.2	–1.0
Residential	9.4	3.8	13.1	3.0	–0.1	–0.1
Government	11.1	–3.3	1.8	–2.7	–4.4	–1.2
Machinery and equipment	–3.5	–14.1	–1.2	2.0	0.3	0.2
Final domestic demand	3.4	–1.1	1.6	1.7	2.1	0.5
Stockbuilding [1]	–0.6	–0.2	1.2	0	–0.5	–0.6
Total domestic demand	2.8	–1.3	2.8	1.7	1.6	–0.1
Net exports [1]	–0.6	0.1	0.1	0.3	0.4	0.9
Exports of goods and services	–0.3	–4.7	7.5	3.8	1.0	7.4
Imports of goods and services	2.2	–5.2	7.1	2.7	–0.7	3.8
GDP at market prices	**2.2**	**–1.2**	**2.9**	**1.9**	**2.0**	**0.8**
Memorandum items:						
Total employment	–1.8	–1.8	–0.7	–0.3	–0.5	–0.4
Household savings rate	12.8	12.2	11.6	11.5	11.7	11.4
Relative ULC in manufacturing	6.7	7.3	–0.7	6.3	13.9	–1.9
Export market growth in manufacturing	2.7	1.2	10.4	9.4	9.3	7.2

1. Contributions to changes in GDP (as a percentage of real GDP in the previous period).
Source: Statistisches Bundesamt.

growth. With business sentiment remaining depressed, growth has been dependent to a great extent upon government consumption and the support to private consumption provided by lower inflation and rising disposable income. However, consumer sentiment also deteriorated early in the year and, for the first time in three years, households became more pessimistic about their future income. Western German unemployment surged by 100 000 in the first three months, with construction accounting for about a third of the increase.

Indications of improving economic activity became more widespread during the second quarter. Construction, while still sluggish, recovered strongly from the weather-induced trough of the first quarter and by April this was also reflected in significantly lower unemployment. Abstracting from seasonal factors, manufacturing output appeared to be recovering and foreign and domestic orders began to pick up. Supporting these indicators, the IFO index of business expectations improved in April and May and the index of investment intentions also indicated a potential strengthening in investment in equipment and machinery. The underlying strength of the upturn in growth nevertheless remained unclear: leading indicators for the new *Länder* were weak while the unemployment rate for salaried workers, which is less influenced by seasonal factors, has continued to increase.

Inflation, wage growth and the problem of international competitiveness

Inflation has decelerated sharply. At the beginning of 1995, producer price inflation had been running at an annualised rate of some 2½ per cent, but by the end of the year this had declined to around ¾ per cent and in the first quarter of 1996 prices fell. Construction prices stabilised, and export prices were steady. After falling throughout most of 1995, import prices picked up in the first quarter as a result of a stronger dollar and a jump in oil prices. While this will eventually feed through to consumer prices, year-on-year consumer price inflation has slowed to 1.6 per cent in May, led by slower increases in housing rents and services.

While the achievement of relative price stability is a positive influence for growth, structural factors related to levels of wage and non-wage costs have exercised an important dampening role in the current slowdown. In the manufacturing sector, which is relatively large in Germany, stagnant investment in equipment and declining employment is attributable to high relative wage costs and low rates of return on new investment following the post-reunification investment boom. One factor underlying these trends has been the rapid appreciation of the nominal effective exchange rate with respect to eighteen industrial countries amounting to 4.3 per cent from January to April 1995. Coming on top of the previous appreciation of some 6 per cent between 1991 and 1994, this put German enterprises under continuing pressure to cut costs. Between January and April 1995, the effective exchange rate of the Deutschemark appreciated by 5.3 per cent against the currencies of the EU countries, which account for about 50 per cent in Germany's overall exports, while over the same time span the Deutschemark appreciated against the US dollar by 11 per cent (Figure 2).

Figure 2. **EXCHANGE RATE AGAINST SELECTED CURRENCIES**
Index 1991 = 100

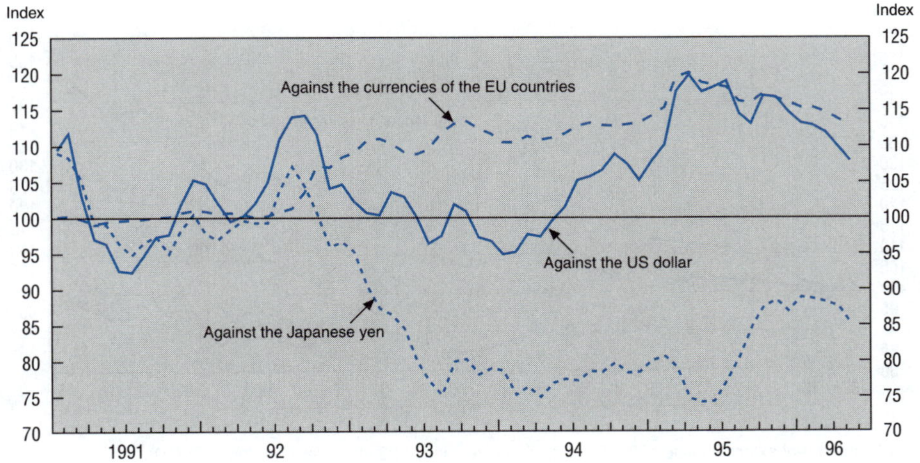

Source: Deutsche Bundesbank.

Reinforcing the pressure arising from the nominal exchange rate has been the development of wages and social charges: relative unit labour costs in manufacturing, expressed in a common currency, have increased by 20 per cent since 1991. Broader indicators of unit labour costs in the total economy and of final demand and consumer prices also indicate an increase in the real exchange rate, though a less substantial one, over this period (Figure 3).[2] With rising unemployment and a negative output gap opening up during the recession, the pressure on unit labour costs eased somewhat in 1994, the average private sector wage rate per employee increasing by only 2.5 per cent, helping profit margins to recover in some sectors. But overall it now appears that the level of profits in relation to capital has remained low both internationally and in comparison with the previous recovery. And wage moderation did not continue in 1995, when unit labour costs started to rise again despite continued rationalisation. The 1995 wage round increased hourly labour costs in manufacturing by around 5.5 per cent and represented a severe negative shock to the economy. As important as the wage increase itself was the signal that a recovery in profitability, such as occurred in 1994, could be quickly bid away in the form of higher wages.

Figure 3. **MEASURES OF THE REAL EFFECTIVE EXCHANGE RATE**

1975 = 100

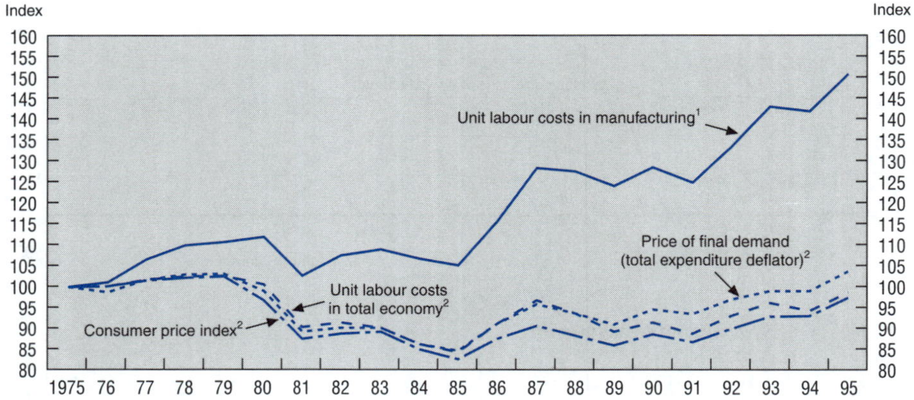

1. Weighted real external value of the DM against currencies of 23 industrial countries (OECD).
2. Weighted real external value of the DM against currencies of 18 industrial countries (Bundesbank).

Source: Deutsche Bundesbank; OECD.

Reduced competitiveness has led to a declining German export share. In 1995 exports of goods and services grew at a real rate of 3.8 per cent after 7.5 per cent in 1994, the slow down in export growth contributing to the interruption of the economic upswing. To some extent the slowdown was attributable to world trade growing less rapidly than in 1994, but German exporters also continued to lose market shares as a result of the appreciation of the Deutschemark, which the unexpectedly high 1995 wage settlement served to amplify.

The rise in the exchange rate that occurred in spring 1995 was associated with weakening export growth which continued into the second semester of 1995, although orders and export expectations picked up towards the end of the year. For the year as a whole, however, Germany experienced a slow down of export growth to both the EU and the United States, where the slow down was particularly pronounced (Table 2). Exports to non-traditional markets in fast growing regions were buoyant, as were exports to the dynamic Asian economies, which were aided by the trend depreciation of the Deutschemark against the yen. Exports to the transition countries in central and eastern Europe also grew

Table 2. **Trade by region**

Percentage changes

	1991	1992	1993	1994	1995	Share of total in 1995
Exports to [1]						
EU	1.8	0.8	–13.3	9.0	3.3	56.7
EFTA	–2.7	–4.3	–5.5	10.1	6.9	6.3
Central and Eastern Europe	–5.3	–4.6	12.0	13.1	13.3	8.6
North America [2]	–10.0	0.3	7.6	16.0	0.6	7.9
Japan	–5.4	–11.2	4.9	14.0	6.3	2.5
Asia [3]	12.3	4.3	15.3	23.3	13.0	5.8
Central and South America	6.2	5.4	6.0	10.7	10.9	2.5
Other	7.0	–7.9	9.2	1.5	4.0	9.7
Total	0.6	0.6	–5.8	10.0	5.3	100.0
Imports from [1]						
EU	15.9	–0.7	–16.2	8.5	0.3	54.4
EFTA	7.6	2.3	–4.0	9.8	6.2	6.0
Central and Eastern Europe	20.3	2.1	0.2	21.8	16.3	9.0
North America [2]	10.4	0.2	–5.3	8.8	4.2	7.7
Japan	22.6	–5.6	–9.2	–0.9	3.3	5.6
Asia [3]	24.5	–6.0	4.3	8.1	7.6	5.7
Central and South America	3.4	–5.7	–15.5	13.1	3.9	2.1
Other	13.4	–2.7	12.2	4.9	3.2	9.5
Total	15.6	–1.2	–10.0	8.7	3.0	100.0

1. F.o.b., including adjustment.
2. United States and Canada.
3. Dynamic Asian economies.

Source: Deutsche Bundesbank, *Zahlungsbilanzstatistik.*

strongly, taking advantage of the increasing integration of these markets into inter-European trade and of growing production linkages. Despite a steep decline in exports to Mexico, exports to South America also expanded significantly. Overall, German exports benefited from the fact that foreign demand was largely investment driven. Exports of capital goods, which account for about 57 per cent of overall German exports, grew at an above-average rate. In contrast, exports of consumer goods were weak (Tables 3 and 4).

The relative strength of German exports in the face of pressure from increasing labour costs and social charges and a rising exchange rate has partly been achieved by a squeeze of profits in the tradeable goods sector. To prevent a further loss in market shares, German exporters seem to have priced to the market. From January 1995 to May 1996 the export price index for manufactured

Table 3. **Trade by commodity**

Percentage change from corresponding period in previous year

	Exports					Imports				
	1994		1995		Share of total in 1995, per cent	1994		1995		Share of total in 1995, per cent
	I	II	I	II		I	II	I	II	
Energy	9.6	–6.2	–17.7	–10.6	1.0	–3.6	–4.3	–5.2	–9.0	6.5
Basic and producer goods	13.5	15.0	11.8	3.2	23.7	11.5	18.8	16.1	1.6	23.5
of which: Chemical products	15.3	15.1	9.2	0.3	13.5	16.2	17.8	12.0	3.3	9.8
Capital goods	11.1	11.2	6.8	5.7	56.8	9.6	13.4	4.3	3.0	40.5
of which:										
Mechanical engineering products	6.4	10.7	6.4	10.9	15.4	4.7	11.1	4.5	1.4	5.8
Road vehicles	17.9	11.3	11.6	0.6	17.3	7.1	18.5	12.9	8.8	10.6
Electrical engineering products	15.0	13.7	8.5	8.8	13.3	20.1	17.5	6.2	4.2	12.0
Consumer goods	6.7	5.2	1.9	1.5	11.3	8.8	2.5	–4.3	–2.9	16.1
Food and drink	8.1	4.7	–13.0	–1.1	4.3	11.3	9.3	–0.8	–5.5	5.9

Source: Statistisches Bundesamt.

goods increased by less than 0.8 per cent. Similarly, low Deutschemark import prices reduced the scope for price increases by domestic competitors to foreign exporters. As a consequence, there has been a widening gap between the profit mark-ups in the tradeable and non-tradeable goods sectors (Figure 4).[3] The gap was slightly reduced in 1994, but has widened substantially since. In the long run this development could diminish the export base of the German economy by either causing a substitution in favour of the production of non-tradeables or by shifting production abroad.

German direct investment abroad increased in 1995 by 78 per cent to DM 48 billion. Inward direct investment also rose in 1995, but the balance of direct investment deteriorated markedly. Other EU member countries and the United States were the main recipients of German direct investment, experiencing growth rates of more than 100 per cent. Outward direct investment to the central and eastern European countries, whose share in total German foreign investment had increased sharply between 1990 and 1994, grew less rapidly than previously, although the share of the central and eastern European countries in German direct investment reached 10 per cent in 1995, as compared with 3 per cent in 1991.

Table 4. **The current account of the balance of payments**

DM billion

	1991	1992	1993	1994	1995
Goods	+29.9	+41.4	+65.7	+80.0	+98.0
Exports (f.o.b.)[1]	667.6	671.6	632.7	696.0	732.6
Imports (f.o.b.)[1]	637.7	630.2	567.0	616.0	634.6
Services	–28.9	–42.5	–52.1	–61.2	–62.9
of which: Tourism	–34.2	–39.9	–44.9	–49.7	–50.5
Factor income	+29.7	+22.5	+17.8	+8.2	–2.0
of which: Investment income	+32.2	+26.3	+22.6	+12.9	+2.4
Transfers	–62.6	–54.9	–58.3	–61.4	–58.0
of which:					
Net contribution to the EU	–21.3	–24.7	–26.7	–31.0	–29.1
Other public transfers	–26.2	–13.6	–14.2	–12.7	–10.8
Current account	–31.9	–33.5	–26.9	–34.4	–24.9
As per cent of GDP	–1.12	–1.09	–0.85	–1.04	–0.72

1. Special trade, according to the foreign trade statistics, including supplementary trade items; imports excluding freight and maritime transport insurance costs, which are included under Services.

Source: Deutsche Bundesbank, *Zahlungsbilanzstatistik.*

Figure 4. **PROFIT MARK-UPS IN THE TRADEABLE AND NON-TRADEABLE SECTORS**[1]

Index 1991 = 100

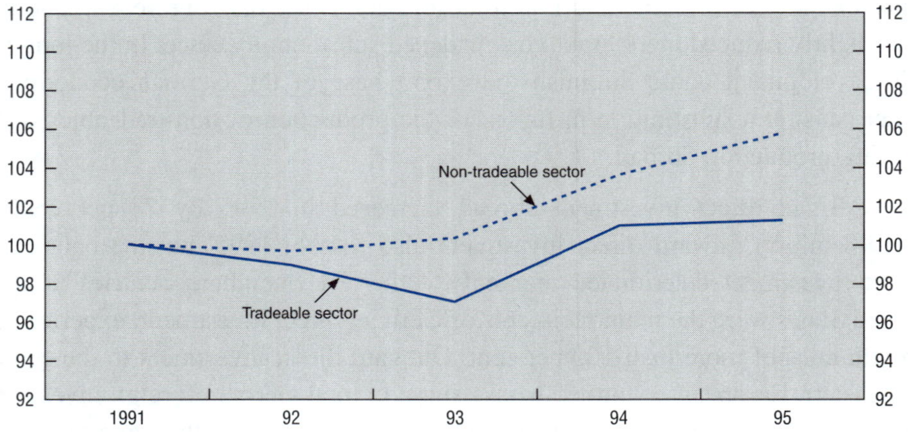

1. Tradeable sector is proxied by the goods producing industries from the national accounts; non-tradeable by the service sector. For each sector the profit mark-up is the sector deflator divided by unit labour costs. The latter is gross compensation of employees in the sector divided by gross value added at constant prices.

Source: Statistisches Bundesamt, *National Income Accounts.*

Rising outward direct investment appears to be normal given the increasing integration of trade within the EU and of world trade in general, and German foreign direct investment is not particularly high by international standards. A recent study has concluded that the bulk of such investment serves the purpose of opening up foreign markets and supporting German exports. However, over the period from 1983 to 1992 shifts in production from Germany abroad can also be observed. In the textile and clothing industry and in the leather industry, for example, German direct investment coincided with a substantial contraction of employment at home. For other branches, like the chemical industry, employment expanded rapidly abroad but stagnated at home.[4] Surveys also indicate that while German direct investment abroad is oriented to a large degree towards marketing and servicing German products,[5] lowering production costs is becoming more important as an investment motive. The geographical proximity of central and eastern European reform countries supports this process.

Investment fails to recover

To a large extent the weak performance of the economy is attributable to the decline in business fixed investment. Orders in manufacturing started to trend downwards in the first half of 1995 and fell sharply in the second, as private non-residential investment declined by 2 per cent at an annualised rate. Since the trough in 1993, business fixed investment has remained relatively weak in comparison with the previous investment cycle. Nine quarters after the trough in investment, only about one seventh of the fall that occurred between the second quarter of 1991 and the fourth quarter of 1993 has been recouped, while investment has again started to contract. By contrast, during the 1980s recovery, most of the fall during the down turn was regained within the same time span, and investment was still on a firm upward trend (Figure 5).

It has been argued that the weakness of business investment in the present upswing reflects a correction of the rapid build-up of the capital stock which had occurred immediately after reunification. In 1991 the ratio of private non-

Figure 5. **PRIVATE INVESTMENT TROUGHS**[1]
Index seasonally adjusted

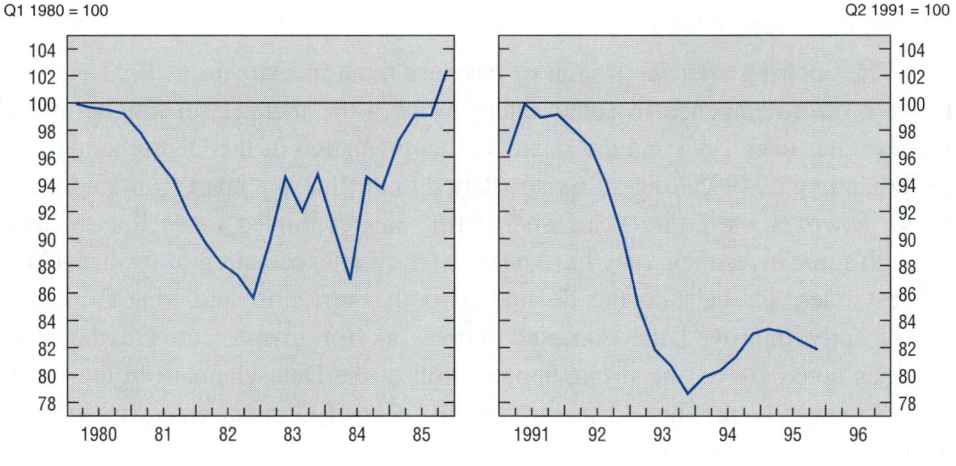

1. Private non-residential investment.
Source: Statistisches Bundesamt.

residential investment to GDP was at its highest level in German post-war history. The extraordinarily high investment rate at that time, together with the fact that bankruptcies of eastern German enterprises have recently been increasing, may indicate that there was a certain degree of "over-investment" which is now being corrected. The impact of unification on the recent weak investment performance should not be overemphasised, however. For newly-founded enterprises, the risk of bankruptcy normally peaks a few years after the foundation. Given that almost all private companies in eastern Germany have either been privatised or founded not earlier than 1991, it is quite normal that the bankruptcy rate for eastern Germany is rising. Also, the ratio of private non-residential investment to GDP had already been reduced prior to the recent slow-down. In 1993 the investment ratio was at about the same level as prior to re-unification, and lower than it was over most of the 1960s and at the beginning of the 1970s.

The weakness in business investment seems to relate to the weak evolution of the returns on capital over recent years. Though the return on capital had started to recover in 1993, by 1994 it was still below its average level of the last 25 years. In the goods-producing sector, even after the upswing in 1994, the return on capital remained substantially lower than the previous trough in the 1993 recession (Figure 6). In view of the fact that the profitability of investment had not been restored to the levels which had formerly prevailed, it is perhaps understandable that investment intentions remained fragile – and collapsed when the prospects of a further recovery had to be revised downwards.

The upswing after the trough of business fixed investment in 1993 is likely to have been dampened to some extent by both the increase in long-term real interest rates over 1994 and the steady real appreciation of the Deutschemark. At the beginning of 1995 long-term rates started to decline and apart from minor setbacks fell over the entire year. Short-term rates continued to decline as well. Though some investment may have been deferred in expectation of further falling interest rates, on balance the decline in both short-term and long-term rates significantly improved the domestic framework for investment. On the other hand, as noted above, the strong appreciation of the Deutschemark in the spring of 1995 severely diminished the competitiveness of German enterprises. Fiscal developments and uncertainty about future economic policy actions also added to the deterioration in the investment climate. With continued financial pressure on the health and the pension funds, it became apparent that further increases in

Figure 6. **RETURN ON INVESTMENT IN WESTERN GERMANY**[1]

Per cent

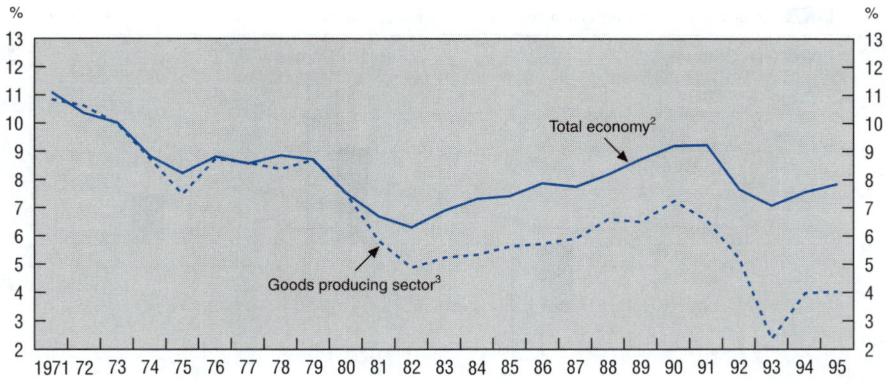

1. For 1995 data are estimated by the Institute of World Economics, Kiel.
2. Gross property and entrepreneurial income/Net stock of fixed assets (at replacement cost).
3. Gross ordinary profits from production activity/Net stock of fixed assets (at replacement cost).

Source: Statistisches Bundesamt; Deutsche Bundesbank. For goods producing sector, *Die Weltwirtschaft*, Heft 1, 1996.

social security contribution rates were to be expected, while the failure to implement the proposed abolition of the trade capital tax and cuts in the trade revenue tax had a negative impact on business confidence.

The worsening of the investment climate is apparent in a survey conducted semi-annually by the German Chamber of Commerce, comprising some 25 000 companies, mainly medium-sized (*Mittelstand*). Between autumn 1994 and early 1995 the share of surveyed companies intending to increase investment exceeded the share of companies which intended to reduce investment, in both western and eastern Germany. But over the following months, investment plans were revised sharply downwards. According to the follow-up surveys in autumn 1995 and at the beginning of 1996 in western Germany, the number of firms planning to reduce investment increasingly outweighs those which plan to invest more. In eastern Germany, the balance has remained in favour of more investment, but has declined substantially (Figure 7). The fragility of the investment climate in Germany is also indicated by the companies' responses about their motives for investing. The survey conducted in autumn 1995 showed that widen-

Figure 7. **INVESTMENT PLANS OF ENTERPRISES**
Diffusion index[1]

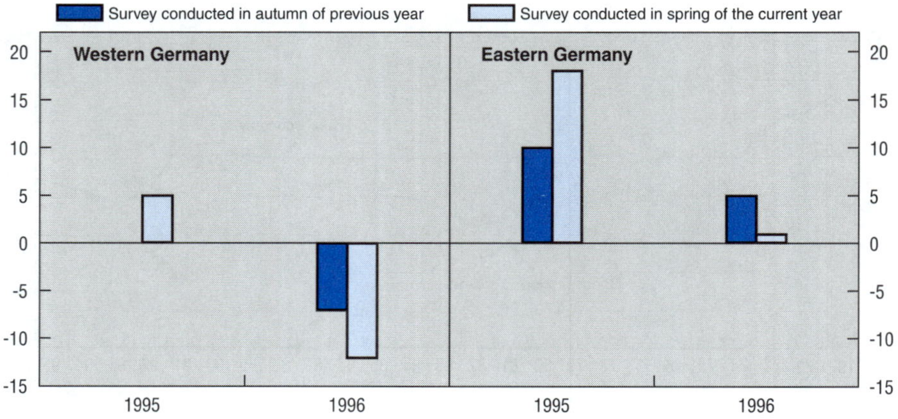

1. Percentage of firms planning to expand investment minus percentage of firms planning to reduce investment.
Source: Deutscher Industrie- und Handelstag, 1996.

ing productive capacity is not a major motive for German enterprises: only 12 per cent of the sampled companies in western Germany and 22 per cent of the companies in eastern Germany stated that their investment serves the purpose of capacity widening. In western Germany the main motive for investing is to reduce production costs and this purpose is also of particular importance in eastern Germany, where it ranks second after replacement investment.[6] In 1995 construction of factories and workshops, which normally accompanies capacity-widening business fixed investment, dropped back to broadly the level which had prevailed ten years before.

The marked slow-down of investment in 1995 was exacerbated by a collapse in construction. In 1994 construction investment had been the fastest growing GDP component, residential construction growing by 13.1 per cent. Over the last year construction growth slowed to 1.2 per cent, again dominated by trends in residential construction in western Germany, but also reflecting the weakness in business gross fixed investment. Weak public investment contributed further to the decline. Overall, construction investment declined at an annual rate of 1.6 per cent from the first to the second semester of 1995 (Figure 8).

In western Germany, the weakness in the residential sector follows eight years of growth, interrupted only by a pause during the recession in 1993. The boom was fuelled by immigration into western Germany of refugees from eastern Europe, an influx of eastern Germans and an increasing number of asylum seekers. Between 1985 and 1994 the number of inhabitants of western Germany increased by some 8 per cent. The growing demand for larger housing space, and the rising share of single-person households put further pressure on the housing market. The government responded to the excess demand by various subsidy programmes which were designed to increase housing supply and partly counter-balance high mortgage rates during the early 1990s. Between 1987 and 1994, when housing investment peaked, 2.5 million flats were completed, increasing the stock of flats by about 9 per cent. Another 500 000 flats were added in 1995. The recent drop in residential construction is thus likely to reflect the fact that the previous excess demand for housing has been substantially reduced, as well as the uncertainty about future income developments, given the slowdown in macro-economic activity. The drop was amplified, however, by the announcement that tax deductions for interest payments on owner occupied housing debt would expire at the end of 1994. This probably acted as an incentive to bring forward purchases and construction into 1994, causing a corresponding drop in construction in 1995. On the other hand, a cut in tax depreciation allowances for the construction of rented housing comes into operation in 1996 and this may have prevented housing investment from dropping even further. This is indicated by the pick-up of long-term loans by private banks for residential purposes that could be observed in the second semester of 1995 (see Chapter II).

In eastern Germany construction has been sustained by public works, mainly financed via transfers, aimed at extending and renovating the infrastructure. Though still registering a rapid growth rate for the year on average, public orders to the main construction sector slowed in 1995, and in the last quarter decreased by 6.5 per cent year-on-year. This reflects the fact that the territorial authorities in eastern Germany are under increasing budgetary pressure, together with the rapid progress already made in building up the infrastructure in eastern Germany. Private residential and business construction, both heavily subsidised by grants and preferential tax treatment, continued to grow strongly in 1995, although

Figure 8. **CONSTRUCTION ACTIVITY**
Per cent change from previous period, 1991 prices

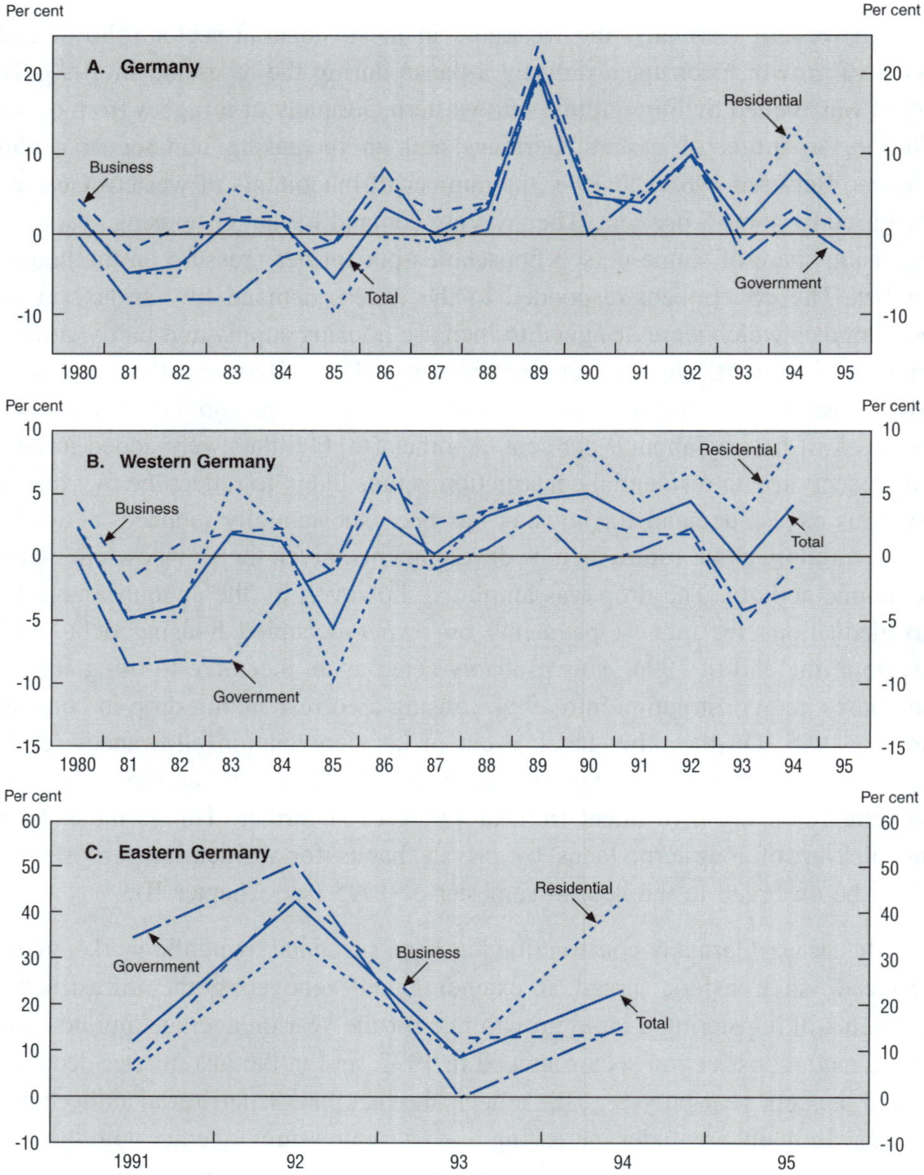

Source: Statistisches Bundesamt.

orders declined over the year, reflecting the downward revision of plans for capacity-widening in eastern Germany and increased uncertainty about the continuation of rapid economic growth. While administrative restrictions on admissible rent increases may be reducing the rate of renovations, the take-over of the bulk of the old debt of the eastern German housing societies, which administer stocks of older dwellings, by the Federal government has increased the potential for renovation activity. In line with overall subsidies to eastern Germany, subsidies benefiting construction in the new *Länder* are likely to be scaled back over the next few years. Given that there is still a considerable gap in the capital endowment between eastern and western Germany, private construction can nevertheless be expected to continue with high growth rates when the overall conjuncture improves.

Rising unemployment

The slowdown in economic activity has led to a further deterioration in the west German labour market and prevented a further improvement in the labour market in eastern Germany. Overall, employment in 1995 continued to decline. This was concentrated on western Germany, where employment fell by 202 000 from the fourth quarter of 1994 to the same quarter of 1995. Though the creation of employment still continued in eastern Germany, it levelled off (Figure 9): in the last quarter of 1995 only 0.5 per cent more persons were employed in the new *Länder* than a year before and in the first quarter of 1996 employment in eastern Germany declined somewhat. The deterioration in the labour market is also apparent in increased unemployment rates. On a seasonally-adjusted basis, the unemployment rate in western Germany stood at 9 per cent in May 1996, up from 8.2 per cent in January 1995. Over the same time span, the unemployment rate increased from 13.7 per cent to 15.5 per cent in eastern Germany. To some degree the sharp increase in unemployment in eastern Germany reflects a drop in the participation of employees in both active labour market measures and training programmes. In April 1996, 515 000 people were participating in such programmes (those on active labour market measures slightly exceeding those in training programmes), which was 70 000 participants fewer than in January 1995. Over the same time period, unemployment increased by more than 150 000, the balance of 80 000 implying that the deterioration has also been due to changing

Figure 9. **EMPLOYMENT AND UNEMPLOYMENT RATES**
Quarterly seasonally adjusted figures

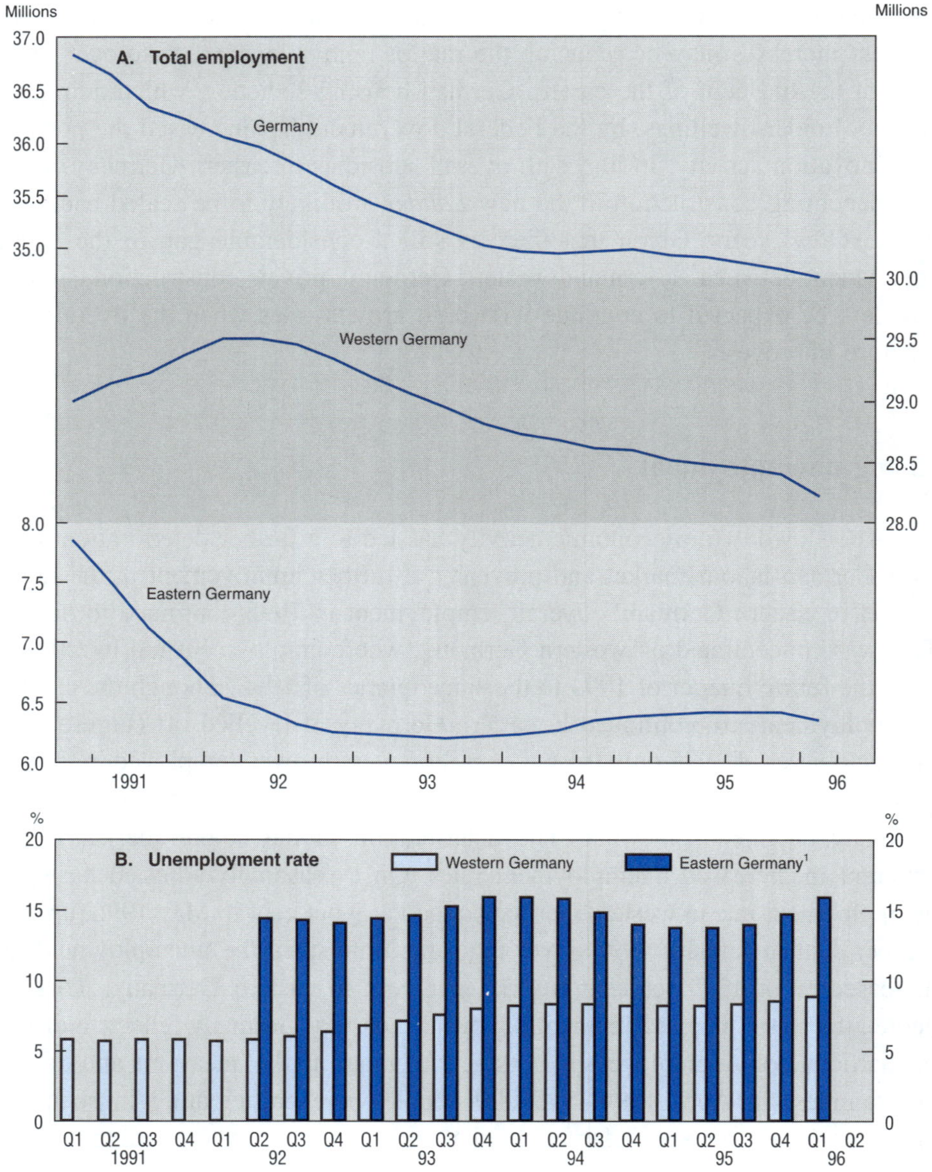

1. Before Q2 1992 data are not available for Eastern Germany.
Source: Deutsche Bundesbank.

economic conditions. Also, in both western and eastern Germany there was a high inflow into early retirement schemes which effectively lowered unemployment.

Short-term economic prospects

Inventory decumulation, declining fixed investment and slowing export growth are estimated to have led to a slight fall in GDP in the first half of 1996, the most positive feature being a moderate expansion of consumption (Table 5). During the second half a modest recovery is projected to get under way, as residential construction stabilises and exports pick up. Gradually-rising world demand should give a stimulus to the economy throughout the projection period, and the German share of world exports should stabilise, in contrast to the substantial fall of recent years. Business fixed investment may be expected to strengthen in response to improving exports, but cost pressures and continuing pressure on profit margins may make for only modest increases. Overall, therefore, GDP growth may not exceed 2½ per cent in 1997.

Employment is projected to decrease by some 1 per cent in 1996, with a stabilisation of the unemployment rate unlikely before 1997. Surveys taken at the start of 1996 indicated that a third of all firms planned to reduce employment levels, while only 7 per cent planned increases. Wage growth is projected to ease over the period, and with labour productivity continuing to improve, inflation is projected to slow to around 1½ per cent. Wage settlements in the current round have moderated to around 2 per cent, and incorporate more flexible working time arrangements, as well as reductions in the overall volume of overtime payments by allowing compensation in the form of fewer working hours in the future. However, because of increased social charges, the growth rate of total compensation will remain high, at around 4 per cent in 1996, the resultant increase in real labour costs continuing the squeeze on profits during 1996.

Against this, rising incomes for those in employment, fuelled in part by the reduction of household taxes at the start of 1996 (some DM 20 billion) should act as a support to demand, as should the deficit of the social security system; during 1996 this will function as an automatic stabiliser although it will require correction in 1997. Monetary policy is also set to remain accommodating. Thus, following its weakening at the start of 1996, consumption can be expected to

Table 5. **Economic projections**

Seasonally adjusted at annual rates, 1991 prices

	1995	1996	1997	1995 S1	1995 S2	1996 S1	1996 S2	1997 S1	1997 S2
Private consumption	1.7	1.3	2.0	2.5	0.4	1.3	2.1	2.0	2.0
Government consumption	2.1	1.4	1.4	3.0	2.3	1.1	1.2	1.4	1.4
Total fixed investment	1.5	–2.4	2.5	0.2	–0.9	–4.3	0.2	3.3	3.4
Construction	1.2	–3.8	1.4	0.2	–1.6	–6.3	–0.9	2.2	2.4
Machinery and equipment	2.0	0.0	4.2	0.3	0.2	–1.0	2.0	5.0	5.0
Stockbuilding [1]	0.0	–0.5	0.1	–0.5	–0.6	–0.7	0.1	0.2	0.1
Total domestic demand	1.7	0.0	2.1	1.6	–0.1	–0.7	1.5	2.3	2.3
Net exports [1]	0.3	0.5	0.3	0.4	0.9	0.5	0.4	0.2	0.3
Exports of goods and services	3.8	5.3	6.9	1.0	7.4	4.0	6.0	7.0	7.5
Imports of goods and services	2.7	3.2	5.9	–0.7	3.8	2.2	4.5	6.3	6.6
GDP at market prices	1.9	0.5	2.4	2.0	0.8	–0.3	1.9	2.5	2.6
Memorandum items:									
GDP deflator	2.2	1.5	1.3	2.4	2.3	1.2	1.4	1.3	1.4
Private consumption deflator	2.0	1.6	1.5	1.8	2.1	1.4	1.4	1.5	1.5
Unemployment (in millions)	3.6	4.0	4.0	3.6	3.7	3.9	4.1	4.1	4.0
Unemployment (per cent of labour force)	9.4	10.3	10.4	9.3	9.5	10.2	10.5	10.5	10.3

1. Contributions to changes in GDP (as a per cent of real GDP in the previous period).

Source: Statistisches Bundesamt; OECD projections.

expand by around 2 per cent a year. There are, nevertheless, downside risks in relation to business and household confidence. In particular, consumption could be weaker than projected if expectations of future employment and income continue to deteriorate. On the other hand, the more favourable wage round, could, if accompanied by indications of future moderation, lead to investment recovering more strongly than projected. Such a positive impact would be re-inforced if visible progress were to be made towards implementing the recently-announced package of structural reforms.

II. Monetary and fiscal policies

Fiscal and monetary policies were under continuous pressure during 1995 from the unexpected slowdown in the economy. For fiscal policy, the need was to minimise the slippage in the budget deficit, while for the monetary authorities the challenge was to identify the appropriate pace and extent to which the policy stance should be eased. Poor economic statistics compounded the difficulties in responding to the evolving situation, but in the event, policy relaxation has been considerable: the repo rate has been brought down from just under 5 to near to 3 per cent while the discount rate is now at an historically low level, against the background of a significant budgetary slippage. The monetary authorities will now have to form judgements about how quickly monetary aggregates can be permitted to expand as and when the projected recovery gathers momentum, and how to respond to the needed fiscal tightening, especially in 1997. Indeed, as concerns budgetary policy the government's objective to promote growth and employment will require both a restructuring of the fiscal system and significant deficit reduction. While the nature of the budget target adopted creates the risk of running a destabilising pro-cyclical fiscal policy if activity should weaken further, it is clear that the key requirement is to ensure that progress towards fiscal consolidation is resumed. This policy constraint calls for the firm implementation of announced policy measures and operates irrespective of the objective to meet the Maastricht fiscal criteria in 1997. This chapter discusses the background to these broad policy issues.

Fiscal policy

The 1995 budget outcome – significant fiscal slippage

The general government deficit amounted to 3.5 per cent of GDP in 1995, marking an improvement of almost 1 per cent of GDP over the extended public sector deficit in 1994, which included the Treuhand and other off-budget activities[7] (Table 6). However, the outcome represented a sharp deterioration compared to plan. The general budget deficit had been expected to decline to around 2.3 per cent of GDP (DM 80 billion), comfortably within the limits of Maastricht.[8] After strenuous efforts to contain the overshoot the Federal budget deficit came in around target (Table 7). Although the deficits of the *Länder* and the local authorities were significantly greater than projected, expenditures by the territorial authorities in general (together with extra-budgetary funds) increased only marginally in 1995, so that despite lower-than-budgeted revenues their combined deficit was smaller than in 1994. By contrast, social insurance expenditures rose by some 6 per cent, only a little below their average annual increase since 1991. The major contribution to the overall budget slippage can thus be traced to the social security system, with both the pension and health funds incurring large deficits: following a combined surplus of DM 4.3 billion in 1994, the deficit in 1995 was around DM 13.6 billion (a reversal of around ½ per cent of GDP).

The outcome for the Federal budget was characterised by significant shortfalls of tax revenues and lower than projected expenditures (Table 7). Tax revenue shortfalls occurred in income tax and corporation tax. Although nominal GDP growth was weaker than assumed (4.2 per cent compared with 5.1 per cent in the tax estimates), this factor only accounted for about a third of the lower revenues. Cyclical factors were nevertheless important in other ways: income tax pre-payments in 1993 proved to be too high, necessitating the payment of reimbursements in 1995, while corporate loss carry-forwards from 1993 were also significant. However, structural factors have also been important and the tax authorities are clearly having difficulty projecting the effects on revenues of changes in tax provisions: the tax system has been altered extensively and the take-up of many benefits is now difficult to project. Higher-than-expected utilisation of tax incentives in the new *Länder* is a case in point. On the spending side, cost overruns occurred with respect to social transfers as unemployment increased. Falling interest rates meant that the costs of servicing the federal debt were less than expected and transfers to the Treuhand successor organisations remained moderate. Nevertheless, in order to stay as close as possible to the budget target, expenditure controls on large items were tightened in October, resulting in savings of around DM 2 billion.

Table 6. **Public sector financial balances**

DM billion

	1990	1991	1992	1993	1994	1995 [1]	1996	1997
General government	**–49.7**	**–94.2**	**–86.7**	**–111.6**	**–82.6**	**–122.7**	**–140.0**	**–125.0**
Per cent of GDP	–2.1	–3.3	–2.9	–3.3	–2.5	–3.5	–4.0	–3.4
of which:								
Territorial authorities	**–94.4**	**–122.7**	**–115.9**	**–137.8**	**–115.3**	**–109.7**	**–136.5**	**–126.1**
Federal government	–48.1	–53.2	–39.3	–66.9	–50.6	–50.5	–64.6	–65.6
State government west [2]	–19.4	–16.5	–15.9	–22.5	–24.2	–30.0	–30.5	–33.0
Local government west	–4.2	–6.0	–9.4	–8.9	–5.0	–12.4	–8.0	–9.0
State government east [2]	–	–12.4	–15.1	–19.9	–19.7	–16.6	–14.5	–17.0
Local government east	–	1.9	–7.5	–4.4	–5.4	–0.8	–5.0	–5.0
German unity fund	–20.0	–30.6	–22.4	–13.5	–3.0	2.3	2.5	2.5
Other funds [3]	–2.8	–5.9	–6.2	–1.7	–7.5	–1.8	–7.0	–7.0
National accounts adjustments [4]	**24.7**	**6.5**	**31.5**	**19.3**	**28.4**	**0.6**	**12.1**	**11.1**
Social security	**20.0**	**22.0**	**–2.3**	**6.9**	**4.3**	**–13.6**	**–20.6**	**–8.0**
Memorandum items:								
Treuhandanstalt [5]	–4.3	–19.9	–29.7	–38.1	–34.4	–	–	–
Public enterprises [6]	–9.9	–15.6	–25.7	–20.5	–20.2	–	–	–
Extended public sector	**–63.9**	**–129.7**	**–142.1**	**–170.2**	**–137.2**	**–122.7**	**–140.0**	**–125.0**
Per cent of GDP	–2.6	–4.5	–4.6	–5.4	–4.1	–3.5	–4.0	–3.4
Cyclically adjusted, per cent of GDP	–3.7	–5.7	–6.0	–4.7	–3.8	–3.2	–3.1	–2.8

1. Provisional. 1995 figures do not include (as a capital transfer item) the takeover by the federal government of debits of the Treuhand (DM 204.6 billion) and of the East German Housing Fund (DM 30 billion). Inclusion of these items would imply a general government deficit in 1995 of the order of 9 to 10 per cent of GDP.
2. After 1990; west without Berlin; east including Berlin.
3. Credit Fund, Economic Recovery Programme Fund, Financial Equalisation Fund, Railway Fund, and Inherited Debt Fund.
4. Including lending operations, privatisation receipts, timing adjustments, and, until 1995, profits paid by the Bundesbank into a debt sinking fund.
5. Wound up at the end of 1994. The successor organisation is financed directly from the federal budget.
6. Until 1995 included Post/Telecom and railway companies in the west and in the east; Post and Telecoms were incorporated in 1995 pending privatisation while subsidies are now paid directly to the railways by both the state and federal governments.

Source: *BMF Finanzbericht;* Deutsche Bundesbank, *Monthly Report;* Ministry of Finance submissions; OECD projections.

Table 7. **The Federal budget**

DM billion

	1993 Outcome	1994 Outcome	1995 Budget	1995 Outcome	1996 Budget
Expenditure	**457.5**	**471.2**	**477.7**	**464.7**	**451.3**
(As a per cent of GDP)	(14.5)	(14.2)	(13.8)	(13.4)	(12.8)[2]
of which:					
Consumption	93.5	90.6	93.4	91.5	93.1
Interest payments	45.8	53.1	54.2	49.7	53.4
Investment	12.5	12.0	12.9	12.3	12.4
Transfers and lending	305.7	315.5	317.2	311.2	292.6
of which:					
To other administrations	81.9	96.4	90.5	89.6	93.7
Other	223.8	219.2	226.7	221.6	198.9
Revenues	**390.5**	**420.6**	**428.2**	**414.1**	**391.2**
(As a per cent of GDP)	(12.4)	(12.7)	(12.4)	(12.0)	(11.1)[2]
of which:					
Taxes	356.0	379.0	382.7	366.1	351.2[1]
Other	34.5	41.6	45.5	48.0	40.0
Financial balance	**–66.9**	**–50.6**	**–49.5**	**–50.5**	**–60.1**
(As a per cent of GDP)	(–2.1)	(–1.5)	(–1.4)	(–1.5)	(–1.7)[2]

1. Includes a reduction of DM 21.2 billion due to the treatment of child benefits from 1996 as reduced tax revenues rather than social expenditures.
2. OECD estimates.

Source: Ministry of Finance submission; *Finanzbericht,* 1995; OECD.

Spending by the *Länder* and the local authorities was inflated in 1995 by a relatively high increase of personnel costs and by rising social assistance expenditures. However, the evolution of the deficit and spending differed between the new and the old *Länder*. The new *Länder* were fully integrated into the fiscal equalisation system[9] in 1995 and this led to lower deficits in eastern Germany. Net transfers to the east increased from 3.8 per cent to 4 per cent of all-German GDP (Table 8) mainly due to an increase in special transfers from the Federal budget to the new *Länder* of around DM 19 billion. Increased outlays and lower net transfer income caused the local communities and *Länder* in western Germany to cut back on public investment.

The deficit in the social security system was attributable to both the health and pension funds, and would have been worse if the new long-term care insurance system had not earned a temporary surplus of about DM 4 billion on a

Table 8. **Public financial transfers to eastern Germany**

DM billion

	1991	1992	1993	1994	1995	1996[1]
1. Gross transfers[2]	**139**	**152**	**168**	**168**	**185**	**181**
Federal government transfers to the eastern Länder and communities[3]	75	88	114	114	136	133
Western Länder and communities[4]	5	5	10	14	10	10
Pension scheme[5]	–	5	9	12	16	15
Transfers of the Federal Labour Office[6]	24	39	39	27	23	20
German Unity Fund borrowing[7]	31	24	15	5	–	–
Transfers from EC[8]	4	5	5	6	7	7
2. Receipts	**33**	**37**	**39**	**43**	**45**	**50**
of which:						
Additional federal tax receipts from the east[8]	31	35	37	41	43	48
Additional federal administrative receipts from the east	2	2	2	2	2	2
Net transfers (1 – 2)	**106**	**115**	**129**	**125**	**140**	**131**
As a percentage of:						
All-German GDP	3.7	3.7	4.1	3.8	4.0	3.7
Western German GDP	4.0	4.1	4.5	4.2	4.5	–
Eastern German GDP	52	44	42	36	37	–

1. Projections.
2. Without the double count of the federal payments to the Federal Labour Office.
3. 1995 including DM 35 billion federal tax losses caused by the revision of the fiscal equalisation measures.
4. 1993 and 1994 including payments to the German unity fund; 1995 including tax losses caused by the revision of the fiscal equalisation measures.
5. Without payments of the federal government.
6. Total deficit east, including federal payments.
7. Without payments of the federal government and Länder.
8. Estimates.

Source: Submission by the Ministry of Finance.

national accounts basis.[10] Following a DM 10 billion surplus in 1993, and a DM 1 billion deficit in 1994, the health insurance funds incurred a deficit of DM 7 billion in 1995. Revenues were depressed by lower payments for the unemployed by the Federal Labour Office, but the development of most concern was the rapid growth of expenditures. After the 1993 health care reform expenditures had stabilised, but in 1995 health expenditures increased by 4.4 per cent (on a national accounts basis, and by 10.8 per cent on a finance basis) led by sick pay and spending on hospitals, spas, and nursing care. Increased employment levels in hospitals, resulting in-part from legislated commitments, contributed significantly to rising expenditures. As for the pension system, a widening of the contribution base led to a reduction in contribution rates at the start of 1995 from

19.2 per cent to 18.6 per cent. In the event, employment did not increase as projected while inflows into early retirement increased. As a result, the deficit of the pension funds increased from DM 1 billion in 1994 to DM 13 billion in 1995.

While the debt of state and local governments continued to rise at a rapid rate, the ratio of public debt to GDP fell somewhat with the winding-up of the borrowing operations of the Treuhandanstalt (Table 9). The combined borrowing requirement of Treuhandanstalt's successor institutions was around DM 1 billion in 1995, compared with a Treuhand debt issue of DM 36 billion in 1994. At the same time, the Treuhandanstalt's outstanding debts, together with those of the Credit Fund (*Kreditabwicklungsfonds*), and a portion of the debt of the eastern

Table 9. **Public debt by government level**[1]

DM billion

	1990	1991	1992	1993	1994	1995
Federal government	542	586	607	685	713	754
Länder West	326	345	365	391	410	439
Länder East	–	4	19	37	51	65
Communities West	114	120	127	134	136	140
Communities East	–	8	12	18	23	26
Unity fund	20	50	74	88	89	87
Credit fund	28	27	92	101	103	–
ERP fund	9	16	24	28	28	34
Railways Fund[2]	–	–	–	–	71	78
Inherited debt fund[3]	–	–	–	–	–	329
Total – territorial authorities[4]	**1 049**	**1 166**	**1 332**	**1 499**	**1 645**	**1 979**[5]
(As a share of GDP)	(43.2)	(40.9)	(43.3)	(47.5)	(49.5)	(57.2)
Treuhandanstalt	14	57	110	169	205	–
Post Office[6]	71	81	97	105	124	–
Railways[2]	48	43	53	66	–	–
Total – public sector	**1 182**	**1 347**	**1 592**	**1 839**	**1 974**	**1 979**
(As a share of GDP)	(48.7)	(47.2)	(51.7)	(58.3)	(59.5)	(57.2)
Maastricht definition	**1 062**	**1 184**	**1 357**	**1 522**	**1 675**	**2 010**
(As a share of GDP)	(43.8)	(41.5)	(44.1)	(48.2)	(50.4)	(58.1)

1. The Ministry of Finance calculation does not correspond to that published by the Bundesbank and which is reported in the *Economic Outlook.* There are differences in valuation methods and in netting intra-government holdings.
2. 1994: Reform of railways.
3. 1995: Debts of Treuhandanstalt, Credit Fund, eastern German public housing sector.
4. Including indebtedness of municipal special-purpose associations and municipal hospitals.
5. Includes debts of two smaller funds not listed in the table.
6. 1995: Reform of the Post Office.

Source: Submission from Ministry of Finance.

German public housing sector, have been taken over by the Inherited Debt Fund (*Erblastentilgungsfonds*), which has become the responsibility of the federal government. With the debts of the railway system also having been taken over by the federal government in 1994, the general government debt ratio has risen, but this is because the budget accounts have become more transparent.[11] In the process, transactions which were previously registered as transfers to off-budget entities, are now shown as transactions with the government sector. As a result of this and other accounting changes, the debt of the territorial authorities – and hence that under the Maastricht definition – was around 58 per cent of GDP in 1995.

The 1996 budget – adjusting to reduced growth prospects

Budget strategy

The Federal budget set a deficit target of DM 60 billion for 1996, an increase of some DM 10 billion in comparison with 1995 (Table 7). On the revenue side, an increase in basic income tax allowances and more generous child allowances, both mandated by the Constitutional Court in 1992 (see Chapter III), are expected to lead to reduced tax revenues of some DM 19 billion. Lower revenues will be partially offset by expenditure restraint, federal nominal expenditures being set to grow by 1.6 per cent after adjusting for the changed treatment of child benefits. Total wage costs, including retirement benefits, are programmed to increase by only 0.3 per cent, wage rate increases being offset by employment reductions, while no increase is scheduled in investment spending. Federal transfers to other public institutions are set to grow by around 4.5 per cent, with transfers to the pension system increasing and payments to the federal labour office being halved to around DM 4 billion. In addition, subsidies have been increased by around DM 8 billion due to the phasing out of the surcharge on electricity consumption used to subsidise electricity producers for buying domestic coal. This is being replaced by a direct cash subsidy. Without this change budget subsidies, including tax expenditures, would have fallen by some 3 per cent to DM 35.2 billion.[12] However, total subsidies granted by all levels of government measured using a broader economic definition remain considerably larger than the official estimates would suggest: in 1993 total subsidies are estimated to have amounted to around DM 200 billion or 7 per cent of GDP.[13]

The drive to reduce the deficit in the social security system is an important feature of the 1996 fiscal strategy. Pension contribution rates were raised from 18.6 to 19.2 per cent and health insurance contribution rates are estimated to have risen by some 0.5 per cent of gross wages. From July, the extension of long-term health care to cover in-patient care will relieve the burden on social assistance which is carried by local government, at the cost of a further rise in contribution rates from 1 per cent to 1.7 per cent of gross wages. Legislation to limit the growth of hospital budgets to no more than net wages in the public sector was passed in late April, but bills to limit the duration of unemployment assistance, and to reduce benefits for asylum seekers, are still blocked by the upper house.

The response to revenue slippage

By the time the budget was passed in October, revised official tax estimates were indicating a likely federal revenue loss of some DM 11 billion (and some DM 29 billion for Territorial authorities). However, reduced debt service expenditures as a result of falling interest rates, better tax enforcement and larger privatisation revenues were considered sufficient to offset this, so that the federal deficit target was maintained. Since that time, further potential revenue losses have emerged as the official estimate of growth has been revised downwards from 2½ per cent to 1½ per cent in January and around ¾ per cent in April. In response to low growth and rising unemployment the government announced a 50 point programme in January which restated the medium term objective of tax and expenditure cuts (see Chapter IV for details). In the meantime the federal government has been taking steps to reduce likely fiscal slippage. Expenditure controls were imposed in March, which are expected to reduce expenditures by some DM 5 billion in 1996 compared with the levels set in the budget. Public investment expenditures are also under review. Budgetary pressures also led the public authorities to take a firm position in wage bargaining with public employees, resulting in low wage increases in both 1996 and 1997.[14]

Little firm information is available at this stage about the 1996 budgets of the *Länder* and local communities or of the number of draft *Länder* budgets currently being revised, but it does appear that it will be very difficult for the original budget objectives to be met. In October 1995, the Financial Planning Council – a co-ordinating body – projected a deficit of DM 25 billion in the old states and DM 15½ billion in the new *Länder*. After allowing for the takeover by the *Länder* of responsibilities for running local railways, it does appear that they are generally seeking to restrain overall expenditure growth to around 3 per cent,[15] with public investment subject to substantial restrictions. With labour and pension costs for *Länder* and local government amounting to around 40 per cent of total expenditures – in contrast to the Federal budget where the proportion is around 10 per cent – the modest public sector wage round was necessary in order to support budget objectives. Nevertheless, further reductions in employment will be necessary.

Table 10. **Appropriation account for general government**

Including social security

	DM billion				
	1993	1994	1995 [1]	1996 [2]	1997 [2]
Receipts					
A. Direct taxes	360.1	362.7	387.0	372.1	374.6
B. Social security contributions	594.1	637.1	667.6	696.7	740.0
C. Other current transfers received	43.0	46.3	46.5	49.4	54.4
D. Indirect taxes	409.1	443.3	446.8	456.2	473.6
E. Property and entrepreneurial income	48.5	53.5	40.5	41.2	41.9
F. Current receipts, total	1 454.8	1 543.3	1 588.4	1 615.5	1 684.5
(per cent of GDP)	(46.1)	(46.5)	(45.9)	(45.7)	(46.0)
Disbursements					
G. Government consumption	631.6	646.2	675.4	695.4	713.7
of which: Wages and salaries	341.5	345.4	358.6	359.3	359.8
H. Property income payable (interest on public debt)	103.9	113.4	130.3	137.8	144.3
I. Subsidies	63.6	70.3	73.5	80.6	80.3
J. Social security outlays	568.3	591.6	624.4	638.1	668.0
K. Other current transfers paid	93.3	108.8	112.0	114.0	115.7
L. Current disbursements, total	1 460.8	1 530.3	1 615.6	1 665.9	1 722.0
(per cent of GDP)	(46.3)	(46.1)	(46.7)	(47.2)	(47.0)
M. Saving (F – L)	–6.0	13.0	–27.2	–50.4	–37.6
N. Gross investment	85.4	86.2	85.4	85.3	86.4
O. Net capital transfers received	–43.8	–33.8	–35.7	–35.5	–36.0
P. Consumption of fixed capital	23.5	24.5	25.6	26.1	26.8
R. Net lending (M – N + O + P)	–111.6	–82.6	–122.7	–140.0	–125.2
Memorandum item:					
Net lending as percentage of nominal GDP	–3.5	–2.5	–3.5	–4.0	–3.4

1. Provisional estimates.
2. OECD projection.
Source: Statistisches Bundesamt; OECD.

Fiscal slippage is, once more, most evident in the social security system, although health expenditures do not appear to be growing as quickly as in the recent past. Slippage is greatest in the pension funds, which are still likely to run a significant deficit of around DM 15 billion due in part to a fall in contribution income as a result of lower than projected employment. At the end of the first quarter it also appears that the deficit of the Federal Labour Office could prove larger than projected, requiring further transfers from the Federal budget rather than the cuts originally intended. While growth of current expenditures by Territorial authorities is likely to remain close to the target growth of 3 per cent, overall social expenditures (including the social security system) could grow strongly by some 6 per cent (after correcting for the changed treatment of child allowance). As a result of this and reduced revenues, the general government deficit is projected to rise to around 4 per cent of GDP although the structural deficit should remain broadly constant at around 3 per cent (Table 10).

Fiscal policy in 1997 – toward the goal of monetary union

The preparations for the 1997 Federal budget are taking place against the background of diminished growth prospects and lower tax revenue estimates, indicating the need for discretionary action if the general government budget deficit is to be lowered. The OECD's baseline estimate suggests that, given the modest projected strength of the economic recovery, under unchanged tax policies and conventional assumptions about the growth of public spending (discussed below) the general government deficit would be unlikely to fall below 3.5 per cent of GDP in 1997. Moreover, this estimate allows for a significant contribution from the mandated increase in pension contributions: according to the pension law, contribution rates would need to be raised in 1997 to cover both projected expenditures and to re-establish a full month's liquid reserves. Despite the announced limit on Federal budget transfers to the labour office, unemployment benefit payments could increase. If the labour office does not fully compensate for lower income and increased benefits by cutting active labour market measures, its deficit would increase and with it pressure on the Federal deficit.

In view of the diminished prospects for 1997, and deteriorating labour market conditions, the government announced a package of measures in April (Table 11) which complements the 50 point programme released in February to promote growth and employment (Chapter IV). The package sets the tone for the

Table 11. **Fiscal programme announced 26 April**

Expenditure cuts			Tax measures [1] (still to be approved)	
Level of government	Value of spending cuts (DM bn)	Implementing measures	Level of government	Value of tax measures (DM bn)
Federal			**Federal, states and local governments**	
Reduced expenditure by ministries	7	Allocations of cuts to be agreed in the summer of 1996. Federal expenditures to decline 2½ per cent.	Delayed adjustment to child and basic income tax allowances until 1998	5½
Low public sector wage round	3	Lower wage round agreed.	Reduction of solidarity tax rate by 1 per cent to 6.5 per cent in 1997 [2]	–3½
Eliminating transfers to the labour office	8	Active labour market measures in the new Länder to be continually reduced to the levels in the West.	Wealth tax abolished and inheritance tax and gift tax modified	–7½
Reduced transfers to pension funds	2½	Measures curbing federal transfers to the pension funds passed into law. Includes spending for recipients of unemployment support. Partly passed into law.	Tax benefits for newly-founded firms	–0.1
			Tax deductions for private household employment	–0.3
Other	1		Abolition of business capital tax and reduction of business profits tax to be compensated by reduction in depreciation allowances	0
Total federal savings [3]	**25**		Reduction of health contribution rates by 0.4 percentage points	–6.5
States and local government			Others	–0.1
Low public sector wage round	20	Lower wage round agreed; estimates of savings later revised to DM 17 bn.	**Total** (excluding adjustments to child allowances)	**18**
Others	1			

Table 11. **Fiscal programme announced 26 April** *(cont.)*

Expenditure cuts			Tax measures [1] (still to be approved)	
Level of government	Value of spending cuts (DM bn)	Implementing measures	Level of government	Value of tax measures (DM bn)
Total savings at level of states and local government [2, 3]	**25**			
Social security				
Pensions	9	Various measures including increase in pension age for women and early retirees, decreased pensions for immigrants, reduction in training time for pension benefits, reduced treatment at spas; partly passed into law.		
Health	7½	Lower sick pay, package of measures to control health costs; pending in parliament.		
Savings	**16½**			

1. Positive sign denotes additional revenues, negative sign denotes revenues foregone. Tax measures have still to be approved by the upper house of Parliament, which has the power to reject all measures.
2. The share of the Länder in VAT revenues is proposed to be cut by 1.2 per cent in 1997 and 1.5 per cent in 1998.
3. Includes higher tax proceeds from the delayed adjustment to child and basic income tax allowances.

Source: OECD.

formulation of the 1997 Federal budget. The programme aims to reduce general government expenditure by DM 70 billion from 1997 onwards, the bulk of this coming into effect in 1997. The modest 1996/1997 public sector wage round secures around DM 17 billion of the DM 23 billion projected from public-sector wage restraint in the overall package (later revised to DM 20 billion), while the *Länder* agreed in June 1996 to lower the target for expenditure growth from 3 to 2 per cent per annum. However, several difficulties remain. Full implementation of the April package will require the passage of legislation in the face of deep-seated opposition from the *Länder* in the upper house of Parliament.[16] Several measures were announced in 1995 as part of the tax package for 1996 only to be delayed by the upper house. Moreover, no agreement was reached about the details of a combined *Länder* austerity programme, leaving each state to follow its own fiscal objectives. Under these circumstances, the credibility effects of fiscal consolidation could take some time to appear, the more so as the package does not effectively tackle the longer-run public spending issues related to government subsidies for non-competitive industries.

If fully implemented, the April package would be sufficient on present projections for the Maastricht deficit criterion to be met in 1997. The OECD's projections are based on legislated or mandated policies and so do not incorporate announced measures which depend on third party agreement. Moreover, the draft 1997 Federal budget has not been taken into consideration in forming the projections. Those which are taken into consideration include *i)* the termination of the business capital and wealth tax at a combined cost of some DM 8 billion,[17] *ii)* increases in pension contribution rates to raise additional revenues of around DM 15 billion, and *iii)* lower public consumption due to the enactment in 1996 of budget limits on the hospital sector. The potential effects of the latter measure need to be netted against the likely net costs of the first full year of social insurance coverage of long term care for in-patients. Under these assumptions – and the macroeconomic conditions described in Chapter I – the OECD projects a general government deficit in 1997 of around 3.5 per cent of GDP with social expenditures continuing to grow at a brisk pace (Tables 6 and 10). The cyclically-adjusted deficit, changes in which can be interpreted as a measure of discretionary fiscal restraint, will fall by about ¼ percentage point of GDP, although numerical estimates must be treated with caution. A great deal of the improvement is due to the effects of increased pension contributions, which it is the policy intention to decrease in 1998.

Medium-term outlook

At the beginning of 1996 the government reaffirmed its long term fiscal goal of reducing the level of public expenditures from 50 per cent of GDP to pre-unification levels of 46 per cent, while at the same time lowering the tax burden and the budget deficit.[18] However, the government has also adopted the additional objective of lowering social security contributions to under 40 per cent of gross wages by the year 2000. The ratio is currently around 41 per cent, but demographic and other pressures are making for further increases, in the absence of action to prevent them. In addition, the priority attached to meeting the Maastricht fiscal criteria has been reaffirmed on numerous occasions.

Medium-term plans also call for a modest reduction of public debt from 60 per cent of GDP in 1996 to around 58.5 per cent in 2000, but in the ensuing years the level should decline more rapidly, to around 52 per cent in 2005.[19] These goals will nevertheless be difficult to meet: the OECD projects that, on the assumptions set out above, public debt (Maastricht basis) will increase to around 62 per cent of GDP in 1997, the primary balance being in slight deficit. Thereafter, the debt ratio would fall only as the fiscal balance net of debt interest (the "primary surplus") exceeds a figure of around 1½ per cent of GDP – a value which depends quite critically on the gap between the interest rate paid on debt and the GDP growth rate. The structure of German public debt is predominantly long-term and under normal conditions carries higher debt service costs than does short-term debt. Several reasons account for this practice. First, there is a clause in the Constitution (Article 115) which limits, under normal circumstances, new debt issues to be no more than the level of public investment. Associating deficit financing with public investment has thus led to the point of view that financing should be long-term. Second, limiting federal debt maturities to three years[20] and above (10 years is customary) leaves greater room for manoeuvre for monetary policy; the Bundesbank has consistently opposed the development of a Treasury bills market. Nevertheless, pressures to reduce budget expenditures and increased financial integration in Europe have led to changes, and this year the Federal government will issue some shorter-term marketable debt.[21]

As discussed in the previous *OECD Economic Survey of Germany,* success in meeting the government's medium term targets will depend on determined policy action over a wide range of spending programmes. Chief among these are: public health expenditure (about 6¼ per cent of GDP); public expenditure on labour market programmes (4 per cent of GDP); subsidies and tax expenditures (4½ per cent of GDP); public pensions expenditure (12 per cent of GDP). Between them these programmes make up around half of public expenditures. However, poor growth and high levels of unemployment have served to throw into relief other important weaknesses of the economy concerning the level and structure of taxation – including social security contributions – and the structure of the transfer system. It is thus appropriate for the government to have added a reduction of contribution rates to its medium term priorities. These more structural aspects of medium-term fiscal policy are discussed in the following chapters.

Monetary policy

Despite the disappointing 1995 wage round, the inflationary background to the setting of monetary policy has eased markedly over the review period and inflation is now in line with the Bundesbank's medium term objective of no more than 2 per cent. Consumer price inflation decelerated by almost a percentage point during 1995 with producer price inflation falling even more steeply, especially in the intermediate goods sector. These developments carried over into 1996 and the IFO index shows that the balance of producer price expectations for the following months is pointing to a further easing (Figure 10). Improved prospects for inflation, together with monetary growth below target, allowed the Bundesbank to ease during 1995. The reduction in policy interest rates was facilitated by the strong exchange rate (especially with respect to the dollar) which has only recently declined from the historical high reached at the beginning of 1995. Monetary growth accelerated sharply in early 1996, to rates well above the target range. However, it is noteworthy that long-term interest rates remain above their historical average, when measured by current inflation. An assessment of current monetary conditions is thus subject to the same problems of interpreting conflicting signals as those which provided the background to the previous *Survey*. This section first reviews recent monetary developments and

Figure 10. **THE INFLATION ENVIRONMENT**
Per cent change over 12 months

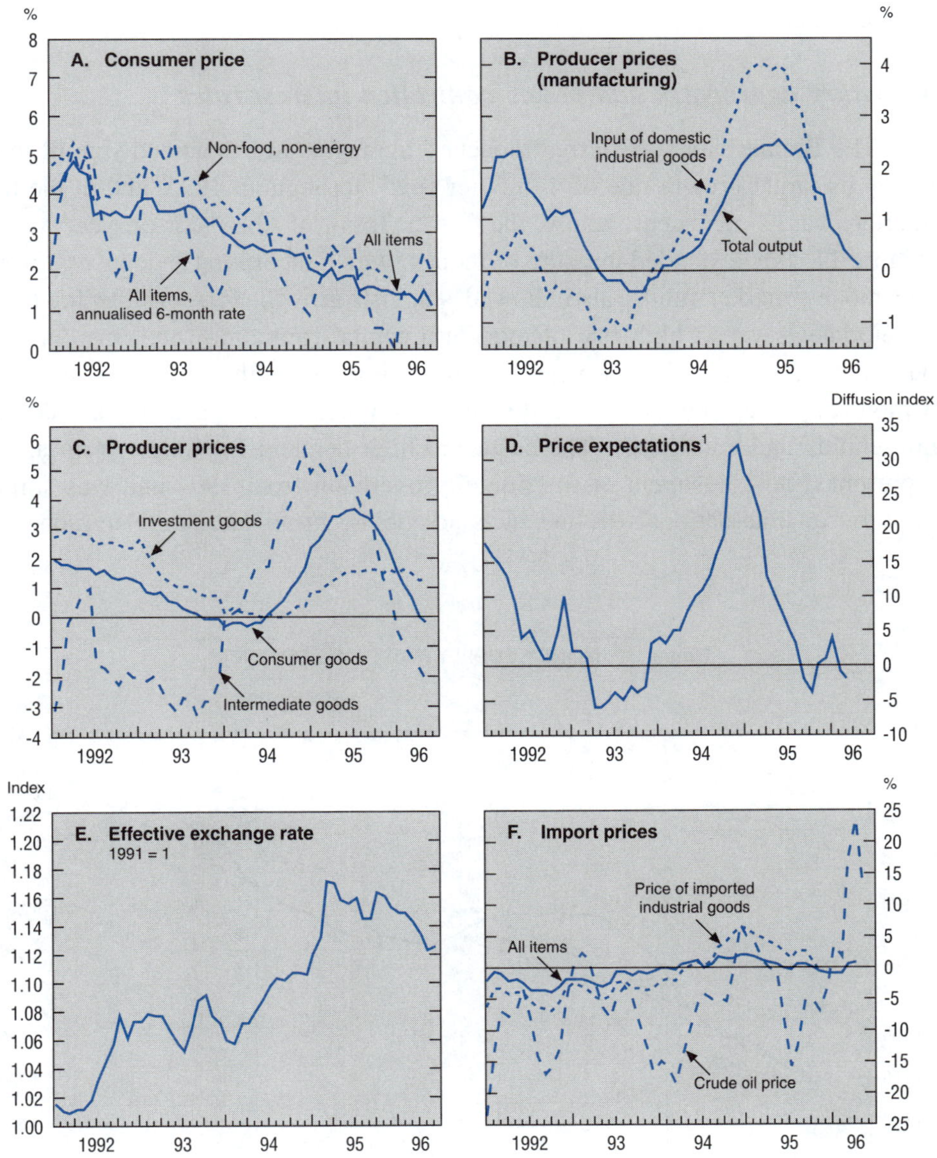

1. Diffusion index. Balance of higher and lower expectations. Seasonally adjusted.
Source: Deutsche Bundesbank, *Monatsberichte*; OECD, *Main Economic Indicators*.

then is followed by a discussion of interest rates; the chapter concludes with an assessment of the challenges facing monetary policy during a period of fiscal consolidation.

Monetary aggregates and policy controlled interest rates

The Bundesbank's preferred monetary aggregate M3 remained significantly below its target growth rate of 4 to 6 per cent[22] throughout 1995, and in the last quarter was 2 per cent below the lower limit of the year-on-year target (Figure 11). The extended measure of money, which incorporates deposits abroad and money market funds, also showed sluggish growth. Responsible for these developments was a high rate of monetary capital formation (*i.e.* time deposits with a term longer than 4 years, savings deposits with a term longer than 3 months, bearer debt securities) together with some slowing of bank credit to households and enterprises. The sustained high demand for longer term assets represented an adjustment of the liquidity overhang from 1994 and was stimulated by an international decline in bond yields. From late summer monetary

Figure 11. **MONEY SUPPLY (M3) DEVELOPMENTS**

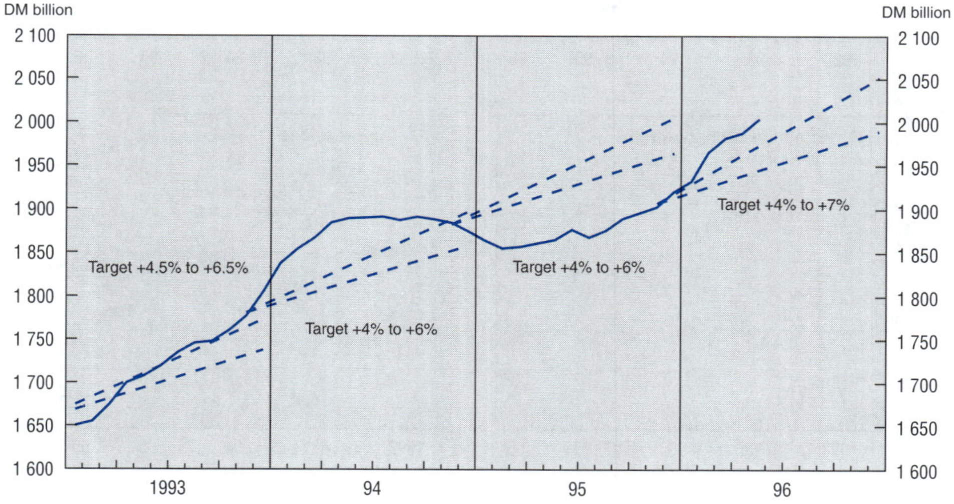

Source: Deutsche Bundesbank.

expansion recovered and the growth of longer-term assets slowed. Money supply growth accelerated sharply at the beginning of 1996, as increased uncertainty about the development of interest rates pushed depositors into shorter-term investments.

Credit growth in 1995 was dominated by the budget, while borrowing activity by industry was weak: credit to households and enterprises was predominantly related to property investment. The growth of credit slowed somewhat in the first semester but recovered, if unevenly, in the second half and into 1996. Expectations of lower interest rates might have contributed to this time profile, with a wait-and-see attitude being characteristic of the first half. However, changes in tax laws and in subsidies for home purchases and for construction have also played an important role. The deductibility of interest on loans for owner-occupied housing expired at the end of 1994 and this had led to a surge of borrowing activity in that year. Lower borrowing during the first half of 1995 might thus represent a normalisation. In 1996 subsidies for apartment construction have been further reduced and this pre-announced policy change might have contributed to increased borrowing in the second half of 1995.

The decision on the part of the Bundesbank to target M3 growth as an intermediate objective rests in part on econometric studies which indicate that excessive M3 growth leads to increased inflation in the medium term. However, in view of the evident short-term volatility of M3 it is also necessary for the authorities to form judgements about how to react to deviations of the money supply from its medium term path. Decisions have to be made about which shocks or deviations are self correcting, and how fast and in what manner policy should respond to deviations which are judged to be more fundamental. Two techniques are in practice possible. One is to use a variety of short-term indicators in order to judge the nature of the deviation of the money supply. The second would be to formulate longer-run targets for money growth, such that only those deviations which were not self correcting would elicit a monetary policy response. The authorities believe that multi-year targets could reduce policy transparency for the public, and through their decisions have implicitly chosen the former option.[23]

Among the factors influencing monetary policy responses have been expectations of inflation, exchange rate movements, market interest rates, capacity utilisation and growth. Mainly in response to weak monetary developments, policy interest rates were cut at the end of March. By the middle of 1995, the short run indicator of monetary growth (six month annualised rate of growth) appeared to be stabilising after having fallen precipitously since late 1994 (Figure 12), but weakened again in the summer. Moreover, the exchange rate remained strong, inflation was declining and indicators of the real economy, which were either absent or inaccurate in the first semester, pointed to a weakening of nominal demand. Monetary policy was thus eased and this stance was maintained until December. At this time monetary growth had accelerated somewhat (Figure 12) but remained below the lower limit of official targets for 1995 – and in level terms money supply was far below its projected path. Inflation, exchange rate and nominal demand indicators also suggested scope for a further easing in monetary policy. Against this background, policy-controlled rates were eased in December and this stance was maintained until April 1996. During this period monetary indicators and those reflecting inflation and output produced conflicting signals. By April monetary growth was far above the new target range (Figure 11), but since this was the result of a low level of monetary capital

Figure 12. **SHORT-TERM INDICATORS OF MONETARY GROWTH**

Percentage changes over 6 months

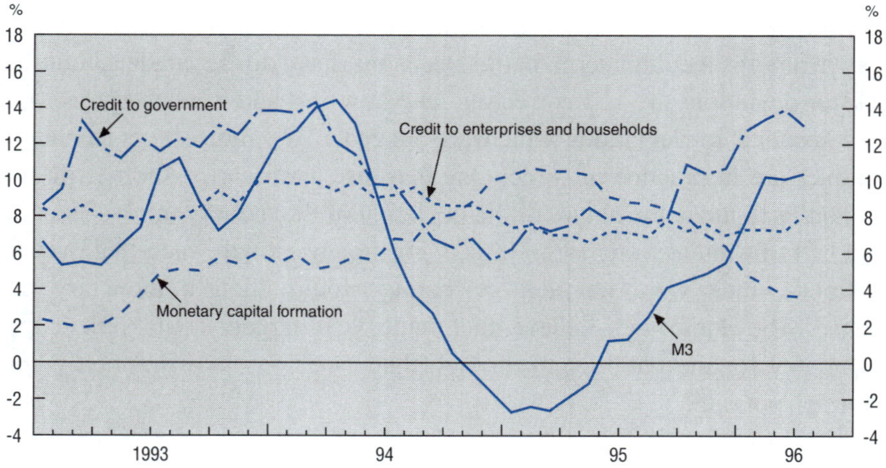

Source: Deutsche Bundesbank.

formation, the surge in M3 was judged to be temporary. The Bundesbank therefore decided to cut the discount and Lombard interest rates once more while maintaining the repurchase rate at 3.30 per cent.

The development of market interest rates

Apart from adverse movements in recent months, cuts in policy-controlled interest rates have been paralleled by declines in long term rates during 1995, so that the yield curve has been steady while shifting downwards (Figure 13). At the same time, econometric studies indicate that US long term rates are an important factor in explaining movements in German capital market interest rates. There has thus been a strong tendency for longer rates to move in line with US rates, in a downward direction until February 1996 and upwards since then. The response has only been partial, but with German inflation 1 to 1½ percentage points below the US rate, the real interest rate premium remains higher than was customary prior to re-unification (Figure 14). One reason put forward by many observers is uncertainty with respect to European Monetary Union. However, implied future

Figure 13. **THE YIELD CURVE**

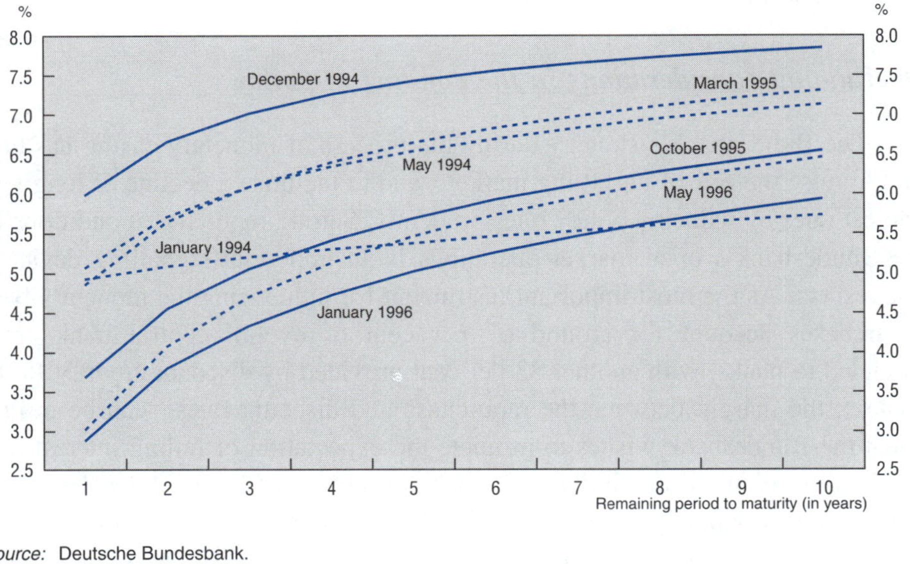

Source: Deutsche Bundesbank.

Figure 14. **INTEREST RATE AND INFLATION DIFFERENTIALS WITH THE UNITED STATES**[1]

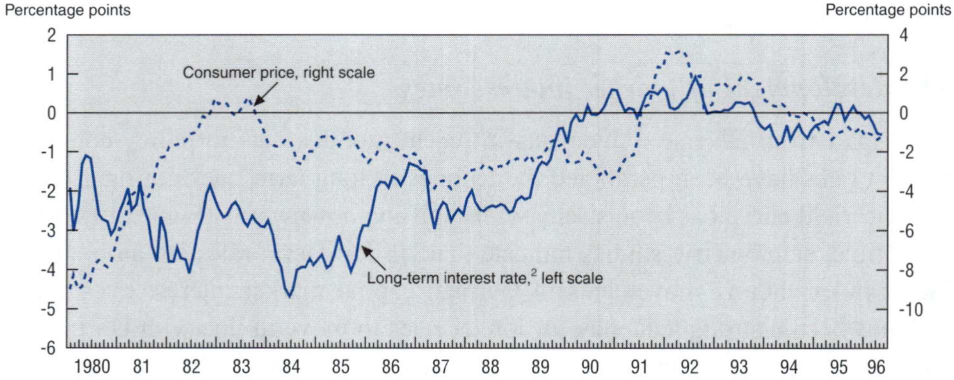

1. Germany-United States.
2. Germany: until 1990 7-15 year German public sector bonds, from 1990 yields on listed federal securities with residual maturities of 9 to 10 years; United States: US Government bond, composite over 10 years.

Source: OECD, *Main Economic Indicators.*

interest rates for the period around 1999, the likely starting date for union, suggest that markets do not now anticipate any great upheavals in the transition.

Operational considerations in the conduct of policy

The Bundesbank's strategy during the process of monetary easing has been to minimise the risk of unsettling markets, and to facilitate a decline of long-term interest rates by reducing policy rates prudently. Setting repurchase conditions for the Bundesbank's open market operations is an important signalling device in this respect. As the most important instrument for influencing the monetary base, repurchases account for around 67 per cent of overall central bank credit extended to banks, with another 33 per cent provided by discount credit.[24] In this context, the margin between the repurchase and discount rates[25] can be utilised when the Bundesbank wishes to promote the expectation of falling interest rates and this has required flexibility in the operation of repurchases. After the relaxation of monetary policy in March 1995 the bank moved from a ''volume'' tender – by which demands for liquidity are met at a pre-set interest rate – to a variable

Figure 15. **INTEREST RATE DEVELOPMENTS**

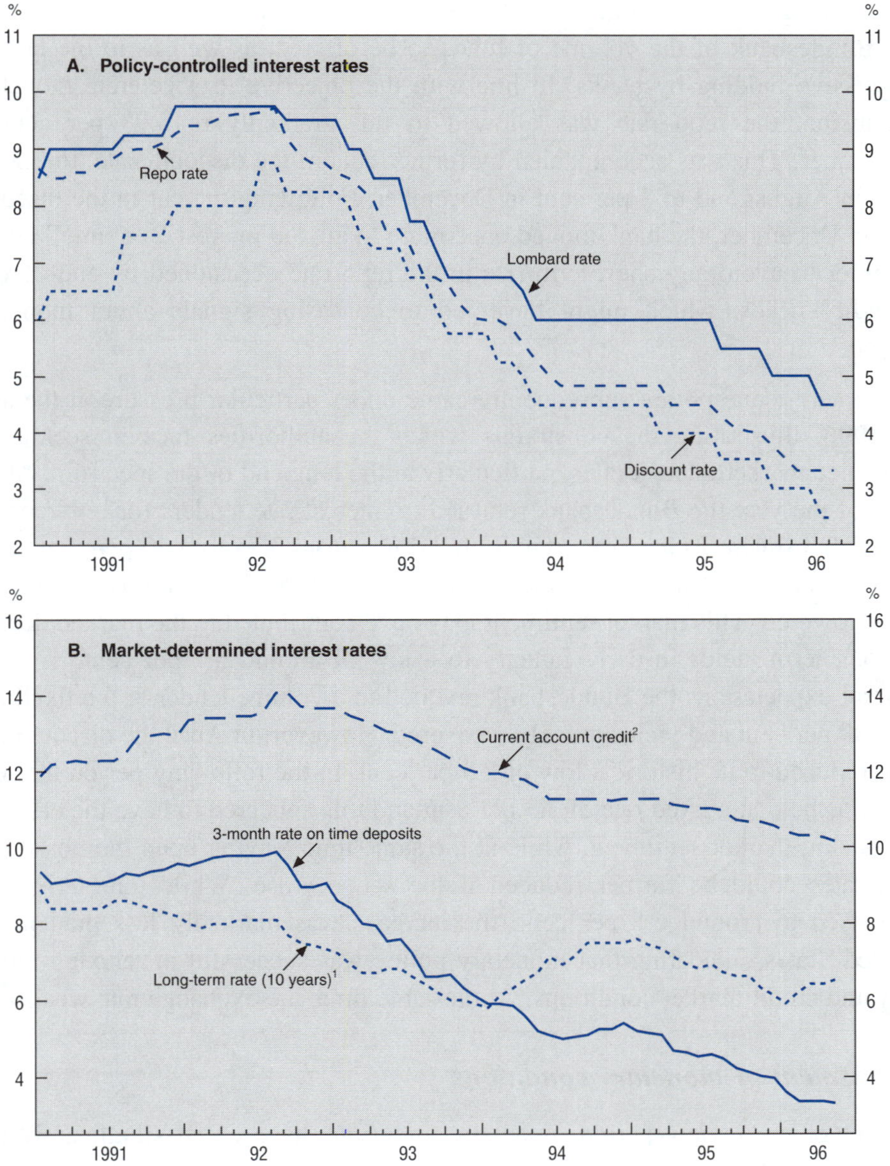

1. Yield on bonds outstanding.
2. Credit of less than DM 1 million.

Source: Deutsche Bundesbank.

interest rate tender, but the repo rate nevertheless remained at 4.50 per cent until August (Figure 15). This development is related in part to the careful selection by the Bundesbank of the volume of funds to be offered, as well as to the lack of aggressive bidding by banks. In line with the objective to accelerate monetary expansion, the repo rate was allowed to fall gradually to 3.98 per cent in December. This was accompanied by further cuts in the discount rate, to 3.5 per cent in August and to 3 per cent in December. Following the cut in the discount rate in December, the bank moved once more to a fixed interest ''volume'' tender in order to avoid any short term rise in the repo rate occasioned by end-of-year liquidity needs, which might have led to confusing signals about monetary policy.

Interest rate policy subsequently came under particular pressure at the start of 1996, illustrating the constraints which the authorities face in seeking to influence market interest rates, particularly at the long end of the spectrum. At the start of the year the Bundesbank returned to interest rate tenders for repurchases. Thereafter, interest rates were rapidly bid down from 3.75 to 3.40 per cent at the start of February, leading to market speculation that the discount rate would have to be lowered. This market sentiment may have contributed to the marked decline of long term yields in early January to a low of around 5.7 per cent. To calm market expectations the Bundesbank reverted to a volume tender at the fixed rate of 3.30 per cent and yields quickly recovered. However, in April the discount rate was reduced to its historical low of 2.5 per cent. In the following period the repo rate was held at a fixed rate of 3.3 per cent and this appeared to have the effect of stabilising market sentiment, while at the same time leaving open the possibility that rates could be further reduced if the scope arose. While long-term rates increased to around 6.5 per cent, the increase was markedly less than in the United States, indicating that monetary policy was successful in relaxing monetary and credit market conditions. At the same time, the exchange rate weakened.

Assessment of monetary conditions

Over the review period monetary conditions have eased significantly and constitute a favourable basis for a recovery. During 1995 money aggregates pointed to a relatively cautious stance of policy while interest rates, which had initially declined more slowly than in previous recoveries, continued to fall (Figure 16). The real exchange rate was also less favourable, contributing to

Figure 16. **RECOVERY EPISODES COMPARED**

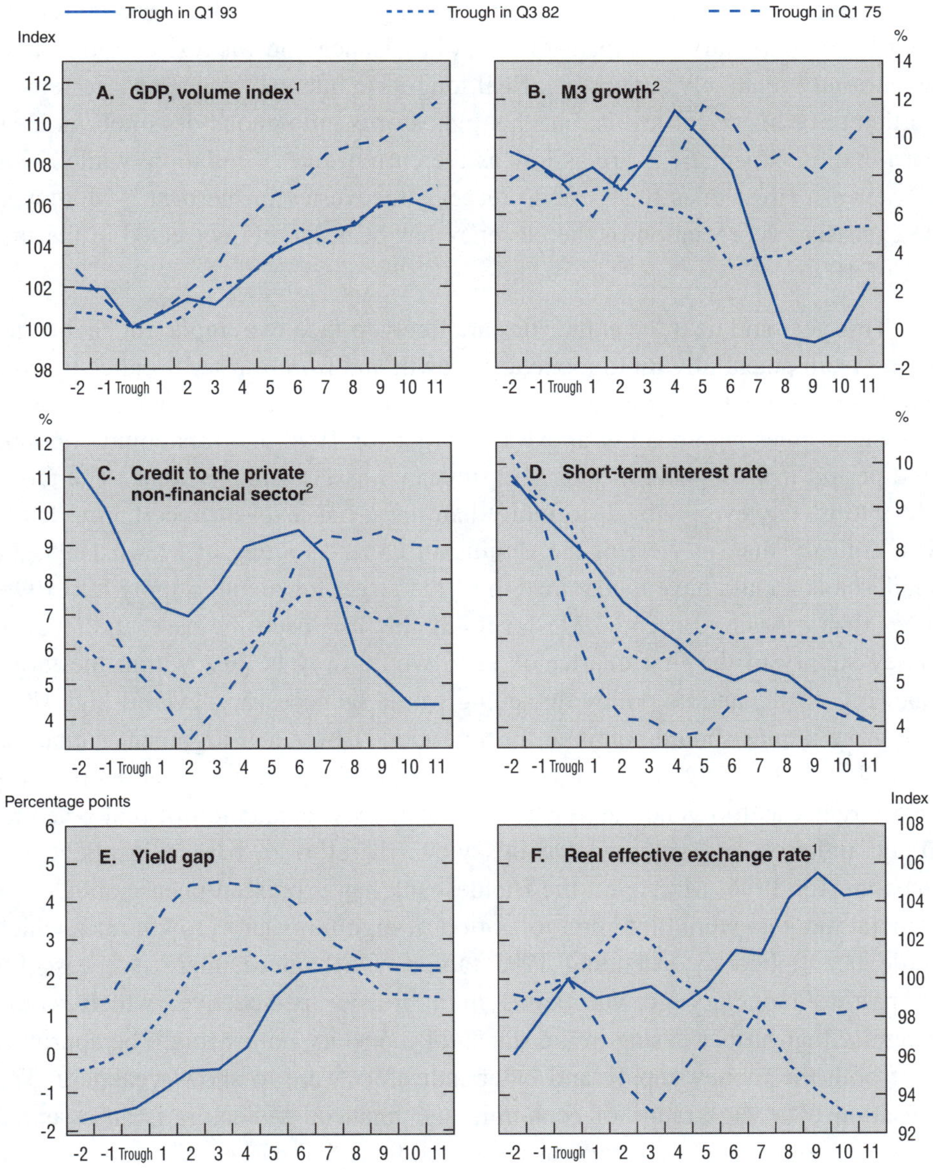

1. Trough = 100.
2. Annual growth rate; for M3, end of period.

Source: Deutsche Bundesbank; OECD.

tighter overall monetary conditions. Monetary impulses have become quite supportive and this is projected to continue throughout 1996. Monetary aggregates point to a comparatively expansionary policy stance and interest rate indicators are currently relatively supportive. Real long-term interest rates appear to remain a little above historical levels, but this indicator is ambiguous: it is not yet clear that inflation expectations are as low as the current rate of inflation, while rising long term interest rates have often preceded recoveries in the past.[26] Moreover, the excessive appreciation of the currency has been largely corrected in the first half of 1996.

This year and next the authorities are likely to face two important challenges arising from potentially rapid monetary growth and from further fiscal consolidation. With respect to the former, at the start of the year monetary aggregates were growing at rates significantly above the target for 1996 and this could continue for a period if investment in long-term financial assets remains weak. The target for 1996 is, however, subject to more than the usual level of uncertainty. It has been argued[27] that, in view of the significant under-shooting of M3 in 1995, the Bundesbank should have maintained the 1995 target for money supply into 1996, rather than rebasing on end 1995 levels. If this had been the case, the level of money supply in the first quarter of 1996 would only be just within the target zone (Figure 11) and no policy tightening would be necessary, even if high short term growth rates should continue for a period. The counter-argument is that the low M3 growth in 1995 had not led to a shortage of liquidity, so that in effect the 1995 target was too generous relative to the *ex post* evaluation of real potential output, inflation and velocity. On this view, therefore, a base adjustment was necessary for 1996. Moreover, the Bundesbank has expressed unease about how financial markets would interpret toleration of high monetary growth rates which would be implied by extending 1995 targets. On balance, there is a case for interpreting monetary growth trends in a broader perspective, which would recognise that further easing in the stance of monetary policy might be appropriate if both the money supply and other indicators were to show weakness. The utilisation of a wide range of economic and financial indicators is an essential complement to annual monetary targeting and financial markets also rely on them in interpreting the stance of monetary policy.

While monetary policy does not respond directly to changes in fiscal stance, there is a case for viewing the stance of monetary policy in the context of plans for further fiscal consolidation – both in Germany and in Europe more generally – as well as the real exchange rate. Incorporating the real appreciation of the Deutschemark (Figure 16, panel F), monetary stance, imperfectly summarised by the monetary conditions index,[28] is tighter than would appear from domestic interest and money trends (Figure 17). Moreover, fiscal policy is scheduled to tighten in the course of the year and especially in 1997. However, as the Figure makes clear, there is no necessary relation between the two measures of policy stance and economic activity. This was especially so in the late 1980s when fiscal consolidation was being actively pursued and monetary conditions were tighter than they are now, but the economy continued to expand. Care is required in drawing conclusions since, without the re-unification shock, the economy was probably moving into a period of slow growth at the start of the 1990s. But since a positive yield spread, such as obtains at present, has not usually been associated with recessionary weakness in the past, the economy should expand even in the face of the planned fiscal restraint. Nevertheless, some negative effects on demand could be expected in the short term. In this context any downward

Figure 17. **MONETARY CONDITIONS, FISCAL STANCE AND OUTPUT GROWTH**

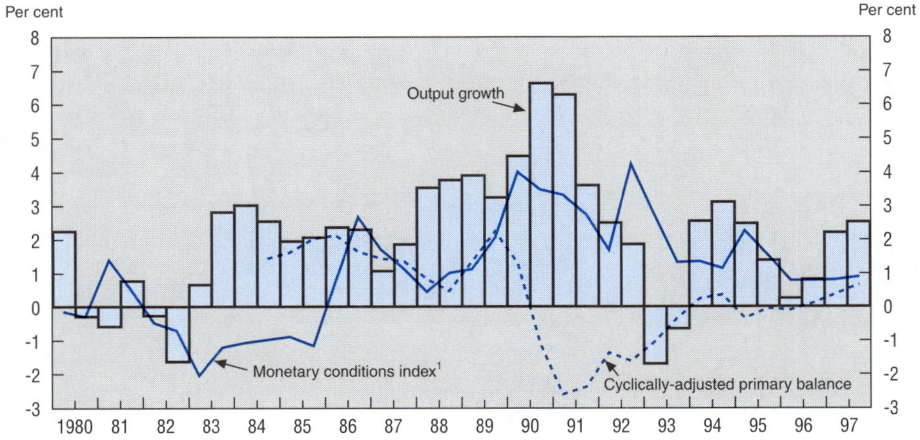

1. Deviations of the index with respect to period average 1975 Q1 to 1995 Q4. The index is the sum of changes in real short-term interest rates and real effective exchange rates weighted by openness. This index equals 100 in Q1 1975.

Source: OECD.

pressure on bond yields might provide scope for lower short rates. A great deal will depend on the structure of fiscal consolidation, and in particular whether it revives the confidence of the private sector and improves incentives: the more this is the case, the less will be pressure on monetary policy to compensate. It is very difficult to make an assessment *a priori,* so that orienting monetary policy directly to announcements about prospective fiscal measures would carry significant risks. Structural policy which would support fiscal consolidation is discussed in the following two chapters.

III. The tax and transfer system

A high tax burden and an increasing number of recipients wholly or partly dependent on public transfers have led to recurrent public debate about Germany's tax and transfer systems. The heavy financial burden of incorporating the population of the new states into the existing welfare system and the poor record of Germany in investment and employment creation during recent years have reinforced these concerns. Two issues are paramount. The first is sustainability: as in other countries there is a fear that a dependency culture is being created, raising doubts about whether the operation of the welfare system is not inadvertently creating new recipients and whether future commitments can be financed. Closely tied to this concern is the ageing of the population, which will increase dependency ratios significantly in the future. The second issue broadly concerns efficiency: the question of whether target groups have been reached effectively, and if so at what cost to the economy and to the incentive structures facing recipients. Key in this respect in the German context is the important role played by wage-based contributions in financing the transfer system: such financing is often thought to be particularly harmful to employment and growth in comparison to broader-based taxes. An important and related theme in this regard is whether the business and wealth tax systems are as suited as they might be to an enterprise-based culture.

The debate is taking place within the framework of a continuing public commitment to the "social market economy", but is hindered by the lack of transparency of the tax and transfer systems. In this light this chapter analyses the operation of the system as a whole and the policy options for dealing with the disincentives and distortions which result from it. It is structured as follows. The first section outlines the motivation for, and institutional features of, the German welfare system. It also presents a broad picture of the financial transfers involved. The second section discusses the structure of the social security contribution regime and the operation of the personal income tax system. Taxes and transfers to the business sector are also briefly considered. The following section discusses the distributional and economic consequences of the system including the impact on target groups, and the resulting incentive structures with respect to both labour demand and supply and the impact on enterprise behaviour. The final section provides an overall assessment.

The German welfare system

Motivation and development

Tradition and law have exercised an important influence on the present structure of the welfare system. The first steps towards establishing such a system date back to the late nineteenth century, when contribution-based retirement and sickness systems were introduced for both miners and state employees. This created a tradition of contribution-based financing, rather than general revenue-based systems, which has lasted to the present; financing and availability of many transfers have been linked closely to individuals' participation in the labour market. Two additional influences have been crucial in the post-war period. The first was the widespread acceptance of the idea of a ''social market economy'' which implicitly guaranteed that the welfare system would be extended in line with the growth of economic resources. Partly as a result, it expanded rapidly in both scope and generosity during the 1960s and into the first half of the 1970s, becoming extremely complex and non-transparent in the process. The other influence, and one which has conditioned the first, has been the incorporation of the concept of a ''social state'' into the federal constitution in 1949. This has led to the concept of ''social subsistence'' as a key determinant in the development of welfare assistance: the state should provide full support for a basic, dignified, standard of living for those who have no resources or access to labour market income and, by implication, for an indefinite period.

The federal nature of the constitution, with its emphasis on subsidiarity, has created a complex institutional structure which has been reinforced by the post-war decisions to set up quasi-independent institutions involving the social partners. Following the principle that communes are responsible for government functions that can be executed best at the local level, social assistance is both administered and financed by the communes subject to administrative guidance by the *Länder* and the federal authorities. The principle of subsidiarity is in turn supported by sharing the revenues of certain taxes between different levels of government according to set allocations. In addition, there is a system of fiscal redistribution (*Länderfinanzausgleich*) both from the federal level to the *Länder,* and between the *Länder* themselves, which emphasises "needs" and the desire to establish a high degree of regional equality.[29] A similar redistribution is made between the *Länder* and their communes. Through their representation in the upper house of parliament (*Bundesrat*) the *Länder* have the right to reject federal legislation concerning their financial interests. Unemployment benefits are administered by the Federal Labour Office, which is supervised by the social partners and by representatives of all three levels of government, but broad policy is determined by the federal parliament.[30] A similar situation applies to both the public health funds and the pension funds which are administered by the social partners. The rationale for the active involvement of the social partners in supervising these institutions is that social security contributions are divided equally between employers and employees.

More recently, the need to raise household income in the new *Länder* has had a marked impact on the transfer system. In 1993, the ratio of transfers to disposable income of private households in eastern Germany amounted to 38.6 per cent as opposed to 25.3 per cent in western Germany,[31] income transfers to east German households being mainly financed via transfers from the west. Social transfers to the new *Länder* totalled DM 74.8 billion (2.6 per cent of GDP).[32] Of this, nearly two-thirds were spent on labour market measures. These comprise programmes financed by the Federal Labour Office (mainly unemployment benefits, early retirement, and work creation projects – see Chapter IV for details) as well as measures directly financed out of the Federal budget such as unemployment assistance and special work-provision measures. Around a quarter of total transfers were payments by the federal government which are not immediately labour market oriented such as federal grants to the pension insurance system, child benefits etc. Finally, just under 10 per cent of the transfers are based on the law of the former German Democratic Republic and are being phased out. These consist mainly of pension provisions.

Whereas the social insurance system was originally intended to deal with acute poverty and temporary spells of unemployment, it has been extended to cover, among other areas, longer spells without work, support of families, retraining, and recently, the provision of long-term care for the elderly. These trends have been common to most OECD countries. However, partly in response to reunification and rising unemployment, transfer payments have once again started to increase in Germany, after a period of consolidation during the 1980s (Figure 18). Since reunification, the share of GDP devoted to social spending has increased by more than 3½ percentage points[33] (Table 12); nearly all programmes have expanded but this has been particularly pronounced for unemployment benefits and old-age pensions. Figure 19 indicates that working-age transfers in western Germany (excluding the effects of reunification) were a little below the international average. However, it would seem that this is largely related to the treatment of sickness benefit: employers in Germany are responsible for this benefit for the first six weeks, in contrast to the countries ranked above Germany in Figure 19. Making allowance for this factor places Germany above average in terms of working-age related transfers.

Figure 18. **PUBLIC SECTOR TRANSFERS, REVENUES AND EXPENDITURES**[1]

Per cent of GDP at market prices

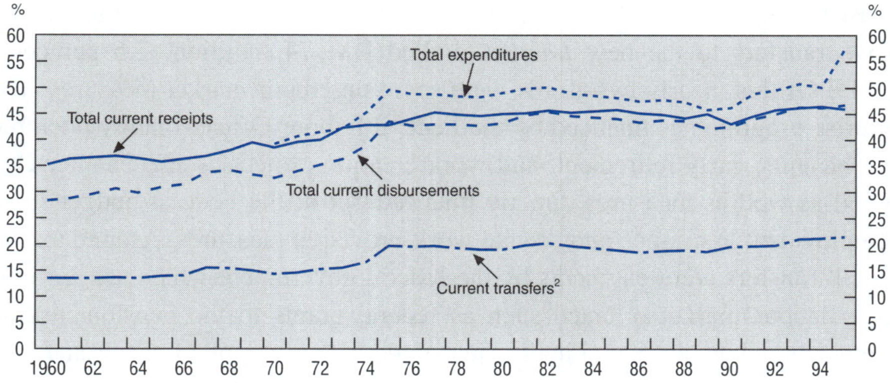

1. From 1991 overall Germany.
2. Includes casualty insurance premiums, social security benefits, social assistance grants, unfunded employee pension and welfare benefits, transfers to private non-profit institutions serving households and transfers to the rest of the world.

Source: OECD, *National Accounts.*

Table 12. **The social budget in Germany**[1]

Social budget[2] by function	1970		1980		1990		1994	
	Per cent of social budget	Per cent of GDP	Per cent of social budget	Per cent of GDP	Per cent of social budget	Per cent of GDP	Per cent of social budget	Per cent of GDP
Total		26.5		32.6		29.5		33.3
Marriage and family	17.2	4.6	14.3	4.7	12.3	3.6	12.0	4.0
Children, youths	8.9	2.4	8.3	2.7	7.7	2.4	8.0	2.7
Spouses	7.5	2.0	5.2	1.7	4.0	1.2	3.4	1.1
Maternity	0.7	0.2	0.8	0.3	0.6	0.2	0.6	0.2
Health	29.3	7.8	32.3	10.5	34.4	10.1	33.7	11.2
Prophylactics, rehabilitation	2.2	0.6	2.1	0.7	2.3	0.7	2.5	0.8
Illness	20.3	5.4	23.6	7.7	24.4	7.5	23.2	7.7
Work-related accident, occupational disease	2.7	0.7	2.5	0.8	2.4	0.7	2.2	0.7
Invalidity	4.1	1.1	4.2	1.4	5.3	1.6	5.9	2.0
Employment	3.1	0.8	5.8	1.9	8.2	2.4	11.3	3.8
Vocational training	1.3	0.3	1.7	0.6	2.2	0.7	2.2	0.7
Mobility	0.9	0.2	1.2	0.4	1.1	0.3	1.8	0.6
Unemployment	1.0	0.3	2.9	0.9	4.9	1.5	7.3	2.4
Old age and survivors	40.5	10.7	39.3	12.8	40.4	11.9	39.2	13.1
Old age	38.1	10.1	36.9	12.0	38.6	11.8	37.7	12.6
Survivors	2.4	0.6	2.5	0.8	1.9	0.6	1.5	0.5
Other	9.9	2.6	8.2	2.7	4.6	1.4	3.8	1.3
Consequences of political events	2.6	0.7	1.7	0.6	0.6	0.2	0.5	0.2
Housing	3.3	0.9	2.2	0.7	1.6	0.5	1.3	0.4
Saving	3.4	0.9	3.9	1.3	2.1	0.6	1.7	0.6
General benefits	0.6	0.2	0.5	0.2	0.4	0.1	0.3	0.1
	Per cent of social budget							
Financing of social budget								
Contributions by the insured	22.1		24.9		28.5		29.4	
Contributions by the employers	35.5		36.9		37.8		35.8	
Taxes	37.2		33.7		29.4		31.2	
Miscellaneous	5.2		4.5		4.3		3.6	

1. Until the first half of 1990 western Germany. Figures for 1990 and 1994 are preliminary, figures for 1994 are partially estimated.
2. Including tax expenditures.
Source: Submission by the Ministry of Labour and Social Affairs.

Figure 19. **WORKING-AGE INCOME TRANSFERS**

Deviation from cross-country average for total spending and components[1]

As percentage of trend GDP, in 1992

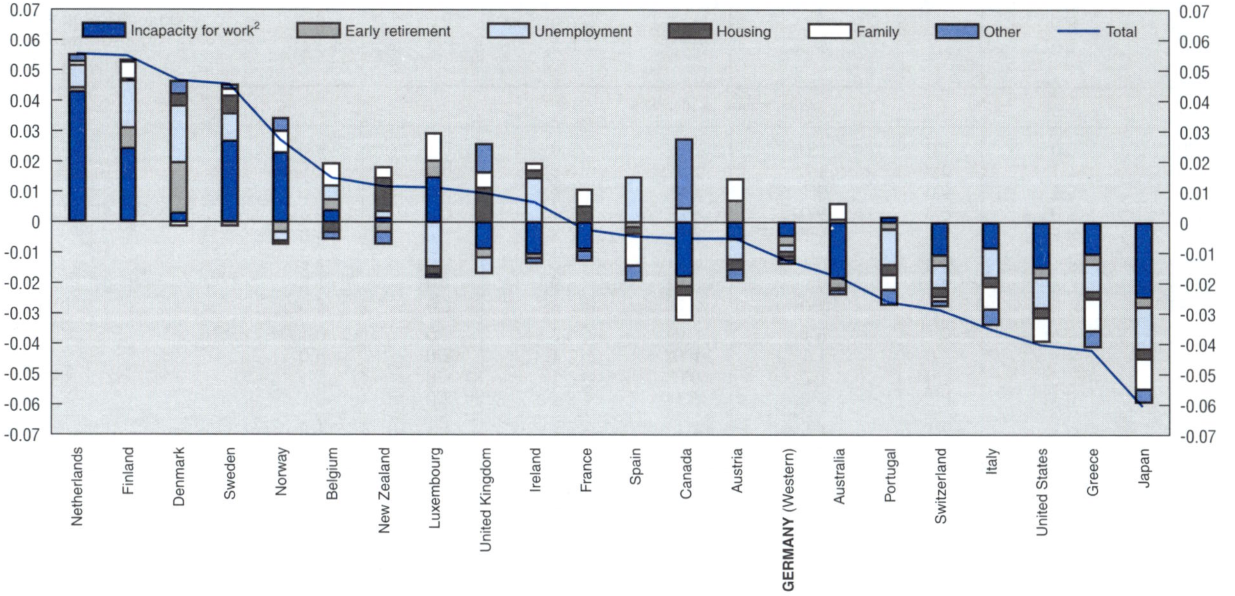

1. Each column is the sum of spending components (as a share of trend GDP) expressed as deviations from the unweighted mean (calculated over all countries). In countries where programmes do not exist (for example, early retirement benefits), spending is zero and the average is calculated over all countries irrespective of whether they have programmes or not.
2. The category "Incapacity for work" includes: invalidity benefit, sickness benefit, maternity benefit and occupational injury and disease benefits. Excludes for Germany sick leave paid by enterprises.

Source: OECD Social expenditure database.

The structure and nature of welfare benefits

Compensation for temporary loss of income: working age income transfers

There are two types of income transfer specifically targeted at the unemployed (see Box 1): unemployment benefits (*Arbeitslosengeld*) which is financed by the unemployment insurance system, and unemployment assistance (*Arbeitslosenhilfe*) which is financed out of general tax revenues and which is available after the eligibility for unemployment benefits has been exhausted. In addition, there are extensive job creation and retraining measures in the new *Länder* with a similar welfare effect. These are described in Chapter IV. The relative importance of unemployment assistance has increased recently, due in part to the larger number of long-term unemployed (Table 13), but unemployment benefits remain by far the most important transfer to the working-age population.

Table 13. **Unemployment benefits and unemployment assistance**[1]

	Total outlays [2] DM million		Real outlays per capita [2] DM per month		Number of recipients[3] Yearly average (thousand)		Proportion of recipients Ratio
	Unemployment benefits	Unemployment assistance	Unemployment benefits	Unemployment assistance	Unemployment benefits	Unemployment assistance	Unemployment benefits by unemployment assistance
1981	13 248	2 850	1 996	1 765	698	170	4.1:1
1982	17 997	5 015	1 940	1 722	926	291	3.2:1
1983	17 091	7 123	1 629	1 419	1 014	485	2.1:1
1984	14 112	8 719	1 551	1 377	859	598	1.4:1
1985	14 066	9 126	1 556	1 366	836	617	1.4:1
1986	14 022	9 160	1 621	1 410	800	601	1.3:1
1987	15 252	9 029	1 688	1 445	834	577	1.4:1
1988	18 039	8 446	1 739	1 458	945	528	1.8:1
1989	17 544	8 203	1 754	1 467	887	496	1.8:1
1990	17 908	7 586	1 838	1 514	798	433	1.8:1
1991	15 908	6 863	1 842	1 464	720	391	1.8:1
1992	31 547	9 106	1 490	1 366	1 678	528	3.2:1
1993	42 588	13 975	1 715	1 398	1 885	759	2.5:1
1994	45 870	17 431	–	–	1 916	950	2.0:1
1995	48 200	20 508	–	–	1 780	982	1.8:1

1. Western Germany until 1991.
2. Includes contributions to the health and pension insurance. Deflated by the consumer price index.
3. Yearly average.

Source: Bundesministerium für Arbeit und Sozialordnung, *Übersicht über das Sozialrecht,* Bonn 1995; Submission by the Ministry of Labour and Social Affairs; OECD.

Box 1. **Selected income replacement schemes**

Compensation for temporary loss of income: working age income transfers

Transfers to the unemployed

- *Unemployment benefits (Arbeitslosengeld)* are financed by the unemployment insurance system. Unemployment benefits are paid at 60 per cent (67 per cent for persons with children) of standardised former net earnings for half a year to 32 months, depending on the contribution period and the recipient's age. The 32 months duration applies to persons older than 53 years. Income from part-time work or self employment is disregarded up to DM 30 per week and above this 50 per cent of the recipient's income from part-time or self employment net of taxes and social security contributions are deducted from unemployment benefits. Additional income is fully deducted from unemployment benefits above the point where the sum of the benefits and the recipient's income exceed 80 per cent of the recipient's former net earnings. Being an insurance payment, unemployment benefits are not means tested against any other income or wealth. After a period of 12 months at work (and paying social security contributions) the unemployed qualify for full employment benefits. Job creation measures financed by the Federal Labour Office and by different levels of government also requalify workers for unemployment benefits since contributions are paid. Retraining schemes requalify workers under some circumstances.
- *Unemployment assistance (Arbeitslosenhilfe)* is financed out of general tax revenues. As a rule, unemployment assistance is granted at a lower replacement rate after unemployment benefits are exhausted. If the contribution period to the unemployment insurance scheme is not sufficient to qualify for benefits, the unemployed may, under special circumstances, qualify for unemployment assistance without a previous spell of unemployment benefits payments. Unemployment assistance is means tested against household income excluding children and is granted for an indefinite duration after unemployment benefits are exhausted. The maximum replacement rate is 57 per cent of standardised previous former earnings for recipients with children, and 53 per cent for persons without children.

Social assistance

- *Support in special circumstances (Hilfe in besonderen Lebenslagen)* is mainly paid for the re-integration of handicapped persons and for exceptional health care needs.
- *Social assistance for income support (Laufende Hilfe)* is usually paid in cash and comprises three components: basic assistance, assistance for housing expenses and one-time assistance which is granted for example for clothing, household

(continued on next page)

(continued)

effects or removals. With a few exceptions, other public transfers are fully deducted from social assistance. The basic assistance, excluding housing benefits, for the head of the household in 1995 was on average DM 525 per month.[1] Assistance for other members of the household, depending on the member's age, is between 50 and 90 per cent of the head-of-household assistance. Certain groups of beneficiaries, such as the elderly or disabled persons and single parents with small children, receive higher basic assistance. In 1995 housing benefits averaged DM 486, and one-time benefits DM 84 per month. Social assistance for income support is means-tested against income and wealth (of the recipients and their spouses).

Transfers linked to household circumstances

Health-related benefits

- *Wage replacement.* For the first six weeks of a sickness spell, the employer pays the average gross wage of the preceding three months *(Lohnfortzahlung).* Subsequently, public health insurance pays 80 per cent of gross wages, but not more than the former net wage for up to 78 weeks *(Krankengeld).* Coverage by public health insurance is mandatory up to an income ceiling. With some exceptions the insured can choose their insurance company. Supplementary private insurance is possible. Contributions are proportional to gross wages up to an income ceiling.
- *Long term care of the elderly (Pflegeversicherung)* is provided to persons who are insured in the compulsory health insurance system and is administered by the health funds. The system is financed on a pay-as-you-go basis. At present the system covers non-stationary care, but from July 1996 onwards has been extended to stationary care as well.

Pension system

- *The public pension system provides old age pensions, pensions to survivors and disability pensions.* Pension insurance is compulsory for employees other than civil servants (Beamte) and self-employed may join voluntarily. The standard legal retirement age is currently 65 years but more than half of the elderly population retires earlier. Employees can retire early if they have a particularly long contribution record (at age 63), if they are handicapped or not capable of gainful employment (at age 60) or if they were unemployed prior to retirement (at age 60). Under special circumstances women can also retire earlier (at age 60). The level of retirement pensions is positively related to both the level of previous gross earnings relative to the average over the whole working life and the length of the contribution period. The retirement age for women is to gradually increase

(continued on next page)

(continued)

to 65 years from 2001 and the age for early retirement will also be raised. Pension indexation was changed from gross wages to net wages with the reform of 1992.

Child allowances and benefits

- *Tax allowances for children (Kinderfreibetrag)* and *child benefits surcharge (Kindergeldzuschlag).* Support for families with children is provided for each child through tax allowances *(Kinderfreibetrag)* and a system of cash benefits *(Kindergeld).*[2] Eligibility for both instruments requires that the child be younger than 17 years of age, or younger than 27 years of age if he/she has not completed education. Prior to 1996 families could accumulate both types of support. The tax allowance aims at exempting from taxation income required for raising children. In 1995 the annual allowance was DM 4 104 per child for a married couple (DM 2 052 for a lone taxpayer). Prior to 1996, families who could not fully benefit from this allowance because their income fell short of the basic tax allowance received a ''child benefits surcharge'' *(Kindergeldzuschlag).* The surcharge was designed so as to secure a transfer of the same value as a fully utilised child allowance at the entrance tax rate.
- *Cash benefits (Kindergeld)* in 1995 ranged for each child from DM 70 to DM 240 per month depending on the number of children and family income.
- Following the ruling of the Federal Constitutional Court on the *tax exemption of subsistence income,* the 1996 tax code aims at securing a higher level of tax free subsistence income allocated to raising children, while at the same time eliminating the peaks in marginal tax rates characteristic of the previous system. The tax allowance per child was raised to DM 6 264 per year and the old system of cash benefits and child benefit surcharges was replaced by income tax credits for children which cannot be accumulated with the taxpayer's child allowance. Instead, tax allowances for children and child benefits now constitute alternative instruments of support. The tax authorities examine what instrument is more beneficial for the taxpayer, and assess income taxes accordingly. Monthly benefits per child amount to DM 200 for the first two children, DM 300 for the third and DM 350 for each further child. The benefits are not means-tested.
- *Child-minding benefits (Erziehungsgeld)* supplement the system of child allowances and benefits. They are targeted at parents who stay at home for the first months after the birth of their child. Child-minding parents with no employment are eligible for a monthly transfer of at most DM 600 per child up to the first two years after their child's birth. Depending on the number of children, benefits are means tested against family income and from the seventh month onwards benefits are reduced with the withdrawal rate depending on the level of income.

(continued on next page)

(continued)

Housing benefits

- Housing benefits *(Wohngeld)* are paid as a percentage of rents or the costs of other occupied housing. The grant depends on family income, the size of the family and the type of flat or house.

---

1. DM amounts refer to western Germany. The level of the basic assistance for the head of the household is determined by the *Länder* in accordance with federal law and varies across regions.
2. Taxpayers who are eligible for child allowances or child benefits can claim a further tax allowance for children attending school *(Ausbildungsfreibetrag)*. It ranges from DM 1 800 per annum for children under 18 years of age living away from their families to DM 4 200 for children over 18 years who live separate from the family. The allowances are means-tested against the income of the children above a certain threshold. Taxpayers who are single and are eligible for child allowances or child benefits also qualify for a ''household tax allowance'' *(Haushaltfreibetrag)* of DM 5 616.

Since 1994 unemployment benefits have been paid at a rate of 60 per cent (67 per cent for persons with children) of standardised former net earnings for six to 32 months depending on the contribution period and the recipient's age. During the late 1980s the system became more generous, the ratio between the contribution period and the benefits period decreasing.[34] As an insurance payment, unemployment benefit is not means-tested against any other income or wealth. Unemployment assistance is means tested against household income excluding children and is granted for an indefinite duration after the expiration of unemployment benefits; the maximum replacement rate is 57 per cent of standardised previous former earnings for recipients with children, and 53 per cent for persons without children.

Effective replacement rates of former net earnings for unemployed who do not receive other social transfers or income from other sources are lower than the formal replacement rates suggest, since these are based on standardised former net earnings and disregard special earnings, in particular overtime premia and a thirteenth month salary. Moreover, only standard tax allowances are taken into consideration in calculating earnings and these may fall short of actual personal allowances. However, if the unemployed receive means-tested social transfers in addition to unemployment transfers, effective replacement rates may be considerably higher. The combined impact of income from various sources on net replacement rates is considered below.

The unemployed qualify for full unemployment benefits after a period of twelve months at work (and paying social security contributions). Job creation measures financed by the Federal Labour Office and by different levels of government also requalify workers for unemployment benefits since contributions are paid. Retraining schemes requalify workers under some conditions. Both unemployment benefits and unemployment assistance are granted subject to the recipient being available for suitable work: if such a job offer is refused, benefits may be frozen, reduced, or even withdrawn. The number of cases so sanctioned is, however, not large: for unemployment benefits it is around 1 000 new cases per month (800 for unemployment assistance) but very few have benefits withdrawn. The grounds for refusing a job offer are specified by law *(Zumutbarkeit)*, but more important has been a rather liberal interpretation on the part of the courts. A key feature of the regulation is that a job need not be accepted by an unemployed person if, *inter alia,* the wage is beneath the level set by collective agreements, if it diminishes the chances of returning to similar employment as before, and if it pays less than the benefits currently being received. During the first four to six months of unemployment a job need not be accepted if it does not correspond to the vocational qualification of the unemployed, but this requirement is relaxed over the subsequent months. Unemployed persons older than 58 years who want to retire as early as possible are entitled to unemployment benefits even if they are not ready to accept a job. Taken together these provisions could discourage re-entry into working life, especially for unskilled industrial workers.[35]

Social assistance

Social assistance is available to everyone – including non-nationals – with insufficient resources to achieve a social subsistence level of income. It comprises two programmes: support in special circumstances (*Hilfe in besonderen Lebenslagen*) mainly for the reintegration of handicapped persons and for exceptional health-care needs, and support in case of temporary or permanent loss of income (*Laufende Hilfe*), with the latter accounting for about 35 per cent of outlays. Individuals have a legal claim to receive social assistance, whether they work or not, and for an indefinite period. However, income support is means-tested and refusal to accept suitable work can result in a reduction of assistance to minimum levels. Overall, about one-third of recipients are classified as available for employment (around 400 000 people) and therefore subject to such a control. Among the German recipients of income support more than a half were of working age (Table 14). Of these, around one-third in western Germany and two-thirds in the new *Länder* received assistance on account of unemployment. Child care problems often justify social assistance without an obligation to seek work. Although there is a hard core of long-term recipients, around 60 per cent of people receiving income support did so for a year or less.

Social assistance payments have grown faster than nominal GDP for quite some time, increasing from around ½ per cent of GDP in 1970 to 1½ per cent in 1994. Between 1970 and 1993 the number of recipients of assistance in special circumstances almost doubled but the overall increase in outlays was mainly due to a strong rise in benefits per recipient. More than 95 per cent of this type of assistance is health-related, so that the rise in outlays is mainly attributable to the general rise in the cost of health care and long-term care. Since 1995 these provisions are being partially replaced by the newly established insurance scheme to cover the elderly requiring care. Underlying the growth of income assistance has been a fivefold increase in the number of recipients, although during the 1970s the growth in expenditures was also strongly influenced by an increase in average benefits. The increase in the number of recipients has been reinforced in recent years by developments in the new *Länder*.

Since 1985 the share of income assistance paid to non-nationals has increased from 13 per cent to around 30 per cent. This sharp increase mainly reflects the inflow of asylum seekers into Germany, which is encouraged by the country's liberal asylum law. No work permits are granted to this group during the first three months. The rise in the number of recipients under 7 years of age (*i.e.* support of children) mainly reflects an increase in the number of single mothers. For single parents, the fixed costs of working which arise from child-minding are particularly high, posing a special hurdle for the transition into full-time employment.

The authorities have tried to minimise the disincentive effects on employment which could arise from too generous social assistance. In its current form, the principle is that the level of assistance for a family with three dependents must not exceed the local average of net incomes for low wage and salary groups

Table 14. **Social assistance: outlays and number of recipients**[1]

	Outlays, per cent of GDP				Recipients, in thousands			Recipients of income support, outside of institutions[4]					
	Overall	Income support		Support for special circumstances	Overall[2]	Income support[3]	Support for special circumstances[3]	Foreigners	Nationals By age, per cent of recipients of income support				
		Overall	*of which:* Outside institutions						Less than 7 years old	7 to 18 years old	18 to 25 years old	25 to 60 years old	60 years old and over
1970	0.49	0.17	0.11	0.32	1 491	749	965						
1975	0.82	0.29	0.19	0.52	2 049	1 190	1 147						
1980	0.90	0.29	0.20	0.61	2 144	1 322	1 125						
1985	1.14	0.44	0.32	0.70	2 814	2 063	1 108	13.2	12.4	21.7	11.9	39.8	14.3
1990	1.31	0.53	0.41	0.78	3 754	2 890	1 510	27.3	14.7	19.1	9.2	41.7	15.4
1993	1.55	0.57	0.43	0.98	5 018	3 995	1 916	30.4	17.8	19.2	8.7	42.1	12.1
1994[5]	1.57	0.54											

1. Until 1990 West Germany, after 1990 all Germany.
2. Inflow over the year, without multiple counting.
3. Inflow over the year, recipients receiving different types of assistance are counted for each type.
4. Stock at the end of the year.
5. The figures for 1994 are influenced by the fact that since the end of 1993 asylum-seekers are in general no longer eligible for social assistance, but receive income support under another public programme.

Source: Statistisches Bundesamt; OECD.

(*Lohnabstandsgebot*). However, the current criteria have been strongly criticised as leading to too high a reference wage:[36] the reference family is typical of only some 3 per cent of recipients while the law is unclear about what should be the wedge between the reference wage and the level of social assistance. Responding to such criticisms, the government proposed to set the wedge at 15 per cent from 1999, while retaining the concept of the reference family (see Chapter IV). After negotiations in Parliament the former proposal was abandoned.

Social assistance for income support is means-tested against income and wealth (of the recipient and their spouse) and the withdrawal of benefits as income increases results in high marginal rates of implicit taxation of 90 to 100 per cent (Figure 20). Even after social assistance ceases, the marginal effective tax rate is approximately 43 per cent. This comprises income tax of around 22 per cent and social insurance contributions which come into force at this level of income. Although such high rates of implicit tax risk creating an unemployment trap,[37] a full assessment must consider the tax system more generally and examine the level of assistance in comparison to likely alternative earnings.

Figure 20. **EFFECTIVE MARGINAL TAX RATES AS SOCIAL ASSISTANCE IS WITHDRAWN (WESTERN GERMANY)**

Single person[1]

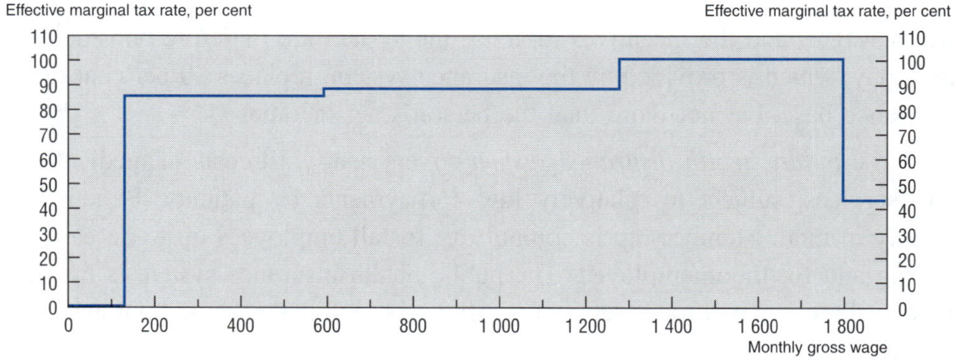

1. Based on the 1996 income tax schedule. For the long-term care insurance the contribution rate as of July 1996 is assumed. For the withdrawal of social assistance the following assumptions regarding net earnings are made: earnings are disregarded up to DM 130; social assistance is withdrawn at a rate of 85% between DM 131 and DM 1 010, and at a rate of 100% between DM 1 011 and DM 1 358 where eligibility for social assistance ceases.

Source: Submission from the Ministry of Finance; Deutsche Bundesbank, *Monatsberichte*, February 1996; OECD.

Transfers linked to household circumstances

- Child-minding benefits

Child-minding benefits (*Erziehungsgeld*) supplement the system of child tax allowances and benefits (see below). They are targeted at parents who stay at home for the first months after the birth of their child and are designed to enhance family and early childhood welfare. Child-minding parents who are not employed full-time are eligible for a monthly transfer of at most DM 600 per child up to the first two years after their child's birth. Depending on the number of children, benefits are means-tested against family income and from the seventh month onwards benefits are reduced with the withdrawal rate depending on the level of income. At some levels of income the withdrawal schedule of child minding benefits leads to an increase in effective marginal tax rates by about 30 percentage points. Since provision of child-minding benefits per child is transitory, work disincentives may be small given a single episode of benefits. The outcome may be different, however, with repeat spells for several children extending over several years.

- Health-related benefits

Sickness benefits. Employers are obliged to pay wages for six weeks in the case of sickness and after that the health insurance system pays replacement wages (*Krankengeld*) for up to 78 weeks. As discussed in Chapter IV, sickness benefits constitute a significant labour cost, in part because they are based on all regular earnings over the preceding three months, including overtime and additional wages, and the incentives to abuse the system are therefore considerable. Sick pay, which is provided by the insurance system, replaces 80 per cent of the insurance base, but not more than the person's net income.

The *public health insurance system* covers nearly all costs of medical care and services, subject to relatively low co-payments by patients. Benefits are mainly in kind. Membership is compulsory for all employees up to an earnings ceiling and for the unemployed. The public health insurance system is financed by contributions, with rates set on a yearly basis such that expected outlays equal expected revenues and the maintenance of a statutory liquidity reserve. There is no direct transfer from the government budget. As in other countries, the structure of health insurance implies an element of redistribution. This occurs in three ways. First, non-working dependents are covered by an employees' contribution. Since the contribution rate is unaffected, there is an element of income redistribution in favour of larger families.[38] Second, because contributions are proportional to gross wages (up to a ceiling) and independent of the use of medical services, there is a redistribution in favour of low incomes. Third, there is a redistribution of incomes in favour of pensioners whose health costs are much higher, but for whom the same contribution rates apply.[39] With minor exceptions the West German health care system was generalised to eastern Germany in January 1991. Insurers in eastern Germany are required to finance spending out of their own revenues in eastern Germany, there being no equalising transfers between the insurance systems in the new and the old *Länder*. However, because contributions for the unemployed are paid by the labour office, there is an indirect transfer from the federal government budget to the east German health insurance funds. Over the past two and a half decades several reforms have aimed at containing costs in the health care system. The most recent, in 1993, attempted to foster competition among the insurers by removing restrictions from 1996 on the right of the insured to choose their insurance company. Nevertheless, outlays have been under strong upward pressure because hospital costs, in particular, have been difficult to contain.

Care for the elderly. Over the years an increasing number of older people requiring long-term nursing care have been supported either by social assistance or by the health insurance system (for care provided in hospitals). In view of the increasing financial burden posed by the elderly, a fourth pillar of the transfer system was added in 1995. In the initial stage 1.2 million people have received benefits mainly related to care at home, and in mid-1996 the system has been extended to cover stationary (*i.e.* residential) care. The intention of this second phase is to encourage the development of special institutions to provide long-term nursing care, thereby relieving the relatively expensive hospital system of this burden which it is ill-suited to provide. However, difficulties have arisen in part because of the complex federal fiscal system. In return for financial relief of the social assistance system it was intended that *Länder* and local governments would invest in facilities to provide long-term care. This has not yet happened, the local authorities maintaining that other decisions by the federal authorities have increased the financial burden on them, leaving no additional resources available for this purpose.[40]

The fourth pillar is controversial since it does pose moral hazard issues. In the past, a great deal of long-term care for the elderly was financed or provided by the families concerned. The provision of benefits to support the elderly requiring care reduces personal incentives to save in order to meet these expenses and weakens incentives to economise on demand. There is therefore a danger that the system could be abused and will prove expensive in the longer run. The new insurance system is financed on a pay-as-you-go basis, with both per capita benefits and contributions being legally fixed.

- The public pension system

The provision of retirement pensions in Germany is dominated by the public system which provides around 85 per cent of pensions; private life insurance provides around 10 per cent and company based systems around 5 per cent.[41] Old age insurance by the public system is compulsory for employees other than civil servants (*Beamte*) whose pensions are financed out of the government budget, but voluntary for the self-employed. The number of new pension payments by all branches of the public pension system increased from about 1 million (gross) in 1992 to about 1.8 million in 1995. About half of the inflow was on account of old-age pensions, one-third survivors' pensions and the remainder disability pensions. The stock of pensioners increased by 2.8 per cent in 1994 alone. The level of old-age pensions is positively related to both the level of lifetime gross earnings relative to the average and the length of the contribution period. Pensions are adjusted in line with the development of net wages. The system is financed on a pay-as-you-go basis by contributions and by a transfer out of the Federal budget which rises with average gross income and the contribution rate. The contribution of the federal government currently covers about a fifth of the outlays of the pension insurance for workers and salaried employees.

In contrast to the public system, private pension schemes are funded, contributions to supplementary private pension insurance being provided by employers on a voluntary basis. Employees' contributions to private pension schemes, together with premia for life insurance, are tax-deductible up to a ceiling, while returns remain largely untaxed. Employers' contributions to private schemes are taxable above a limit, with the notable exception of company reserve systems; as a result, pension capital is predominantly held within the firm in the form of accounting reserves (*Pensionsrückstellungen*).[42] About a half of private sector employees are covered by an employer's scheme but entitlements are relatively minor and sometimes constitute a barrier to labour mobility. In 1993 the combined capital of such funds amounted to only 15 per cent of GDP. A number of legal, institutional and tax impediments appear to have limited the development of private provision of pensions, including restrictions on the extent to which pension funds may invest in equities.[43] However, the major impediment is probably the size of the public unfunded system which provides little room or incentive for private provision.

At the time of the currency union in 1990, public pensions in eastern Germany were converted to Deutschemarks at a conversion ratio of 1:1. The adaptation of the eastern German pension system to the west German standard proceeded in two major steps. In the first stage, the ratio of pensions to net earnings was raised to 70 per cent of earnings for those with 45 years or more of employment, as in western Germany. In mid-1990, after the currency conversion, the average pension level increased by 30 per cent. The second major step occurred in January 1992 when the western German pension system was legally extended to eastern Germany in accordance with the Pension Transition Law (*Rentenüberleitungsgesetz*). In cases where the new pension fell short of the pension previously paid, supplementary pensions (*Auffüllbeträge*) were introduced for the period up to 1996, after which they will be decreased as pensions rise. Up to 1996 the level of eastern German pensions has been adjusted twice a year in accordance with the development of net wages in the new *Länder* and this now takes place once a year. With wages rapidly converging to levels in the old states, pensions are consequently also following this trend closely; since reunification, pensions in the new states have risen by 127 per cent

While the standard legal retirement age is currently 65 years, more than half of the eligible population retires earlier. Employees can retire early if they have a particularly long contribution record (at age 63), if they are handicapped or not capable of gainful employment (at age 60), or if they were unemployed prior to retirement (at age 60). Women can retire at the age of 60 if they fulfil certain eligibility criteria. In the last few years a severe burden has been placed on the pension system by a rising tide of early retirements occasioned by unemployment. In western Germany such early retirement rose by 66 per cent in 1993, 25 per cent in 1994, and 13 per cent in 1995 (Figure 21). The increase was even more pronounced in eastern Germany: in 1993 and 1994 it increased by several hundred per cent and in 1995 by more than 80 per cent. Overall, in 1995 almost

Figure 21. **INFLOW INTO OLD AGE PENSIONS**[1]
Workers and salaried employees
Number of new pension payments

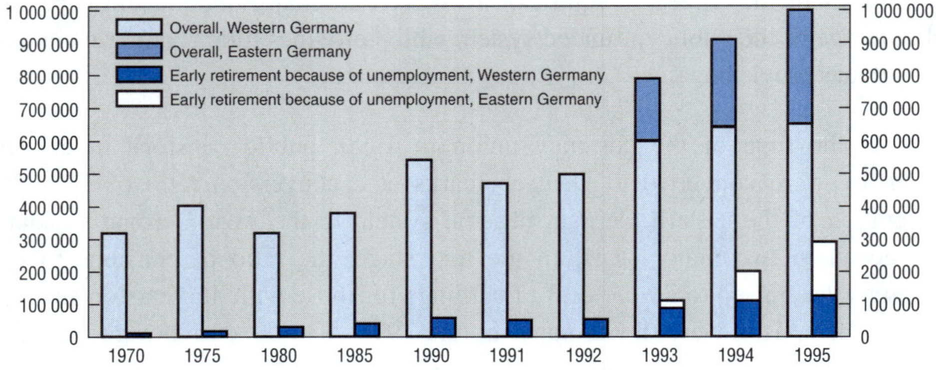

1. Excludes inflows into the pension scheme by younger persons on account of disability and survivors pensions.
Source: Deutscher Bundestag, Rentenversicherungsbericht 1995.

300 000 persons took early retirement on account of unemployment. This development reflects an increasing utilisation of early retirement schemes by firms to reduce their workforces (see Chapter IV for details).

The old-age retirement system was last reformed in 1992 to cope with the financial burdens which will arise from unfavourable demographic developments in the next century. Under this reform, retirement ages for women and for early retirees are gradually to increase to 65 years from 2001, and pension adjustments were changed from gross wages to net wages, thereby avoiding increased costs which could arise when contribution rates are increased. It is apparent, however, that further policy changes are necessary if the system is to be sustainable in the long run (see Box 2). To curb the inflow into early retirement, the minimum age for receiving a full pension on account of unemployment will be raised gradually between 1997 and 1999 from 60 to 63 years. Early retirement between 60 and 63 would still be possible but only at pensions reduced by 0.3 percentage points per month. In addition, the age of retirement will be raised for other early retirement schemes.

Box 2. **The sustainability of the pension system**

Into the next century, a sharply increasing share of the population aged above the current retirement age will place stress on the German pension system.

The elderly dependence ratio, as defined by the number of persons aged 65 and older divided by the number of persons aged between 15 and 64, was 21.7 per cent in 1990, and is projected to increase further to 23.8 per cent in 2000. Thereafter, projections show sharp increases in the dependency ratio which is projected to peak at 56 per cent in 2035. It then declines with the outflow of the baby boom generation.

Based on the projected evolution of the age structure, the OECD has constructed illustrative scenarios to highlight the fiscal dimension of the problem. Four scenarios are considered:

- The baseline scenario assumes that policies remain unchanged.
- The price indexation scenario assumes that pension payments are adjusted only for price increases. Germany is currently the only major country in which pensions are adjusted in line with net wages; in all other G7 countries, pensions are linked to price movements.
- In the late retirement scenario, retirement age is gradually increased to seventy years, beginning in 2006. This proposal corresponds to suggestions to increase further the retirement age made, for example, by the German Council of Economic Advisors.
- The targeting scenario limits the provision of public pensions to poorer people with higher income groups relying on private pension schemes. As an illustration, the scenario assumes that from 2010 onwards the proportion of recipients gradually falls to 30 per cent of the retirees who continue to receive the average pension of the baseline scenario.

Under the no change in policy assumption, old age pension outlays as a percentage of GDP would increase steadily from 11.1 per cent of GDP in 1995 to 12.3 per cent in 2020 (Figure 22). The increase is dampened by the gradual increase in the retirement age legislated as part of the 1992 reform. Spending is predicted to reach its peak by 2035 at almost 19 per cent of GDP, and to decline to 15½ per cent in 2070. This path is unsustainable: under current conditions, it would produce deficits of 7½ per cent of GDP in 2040 and about 5 per cent in 2070, and an explosion in public debt.

Alternatively, pension contribution rates would have to be increased sharply. Even though the indexation of pensions since 1992 to wages net of contributions dampens the growth of pensions as contribution rates rise, in the absence of other measures it does not alleviate the need for further increases in the longer term: one study projects a rise in rates from 19.2 per cent in 1996 to 28.5 per cent in 2030. Spending could be lowered to some extent if pensions were adjusted for changes in the price level instead of net wages.

(continued on next page)

(continued)

Figure 22. **PENSION EXPENDITURE SCENARIOS**
Per cent of real GDP (1994 prices)

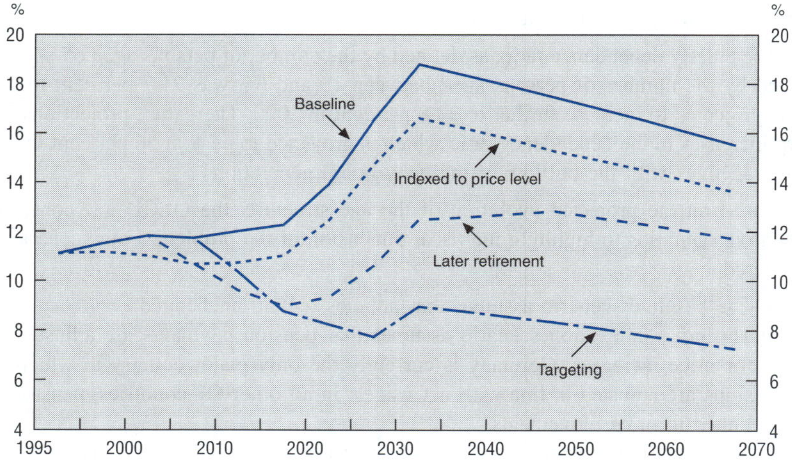

Source: OECD.

Under the late retirement option, spending would drop rapidly over a period of about fifteen years. Raising the retirement age would have the two-fold advantage of decreasing the number of pensioners and raising contribution revenue. Not surprisingly, the targeting scenario would lead to the most pronounced decrease in spending, but it would have to be introduced sufficiently gradually to allow people enough time to make private arrangements.

The tax and contribution regime: structure and progressivity

An important consequence of the broadening scope of the welfare system and its complex institutional structure has been a blurring of the division between the social insurance system and social assistance, and between contributions and taxes: about a third of the social budget is financed by general tax revenues (Table 12). The financial and social pressure arising from reunification have also contributed to this development, as has rising unemployment. Taking taxes and contributions together, the increase in the tax wedge on labour incomes was 3.5 percentage points between 1990 and 1994 (Figure 23). The increase is higher when the 7.5 per cent solidarity surcharge, reintroduced at the beginning of 1995, and higher social insurance contribution rates in 1996, are taken into account.

Social security contributions have become an increasingly important source of revenue accounting for almost 40 per cent of general government receipts from tax and contribution sources in 1994 (Table 15). However, in view of the fact that the transfer system is not self-financing, attention also needs to be devoted to the tax system. Two taxes are of overwhelming importance: the tax on wages and salaries which provides for about 26 per cent of revenues, and value added tax which accounts for 18 per cent of revenues. Tax receipts from corporate business profits, have tended to decline and are comparatively unimportant, contributing about 3 per cent to overall revenues, although in 1994 they were still depressed by the after-effects of the 1993 recession. The relatively low share of revenues from corporate profits is attributable to the fact that unincorporated companies constitute a relatively large proportion of German enterprises. The share of taxes on property has also declined, amounting now to about 3 per cent. Tax revenues are often earmarked to particular levels of government: 85 per cent of the taxes on wages and salaries and of the assessed income tax is shared equally between the Federal government and the *Länder* with the remaining 15 per cent accruing to local government. The corporation tax is shared equally between the Federal government and the *Länder* while the division of the value-added tax is currently 50.5 per cent and 49.5 per cent respectively.[44] The communes have the right to levy a tax on business capital (*Gewerbekapitalsteuer*) and business-turnover (*Gewerbeertragsteuer*), and retain about 85 per cent of the receipts; the remainder is shared equally between state and federal government. They also levy a tax on land which is fully retained by them.

Indirect taxes

The standard rate for value added tax (15 per cent) is the lowest in the European Union (together with Luxembourg and Spain). There are currently two rates (15 per cent and 7 per cent) while rents, an important consumer expenditure, are exempt. The value-added tax and duties do not especially disadvantage poorer groups as often claimed. In western Germany the average indirect tax rate

Figure 23. **THE TAX/CONTRIBUTION WEDGE ON LABOUR COSTS**[1]

Percentage of annual gross labour costs

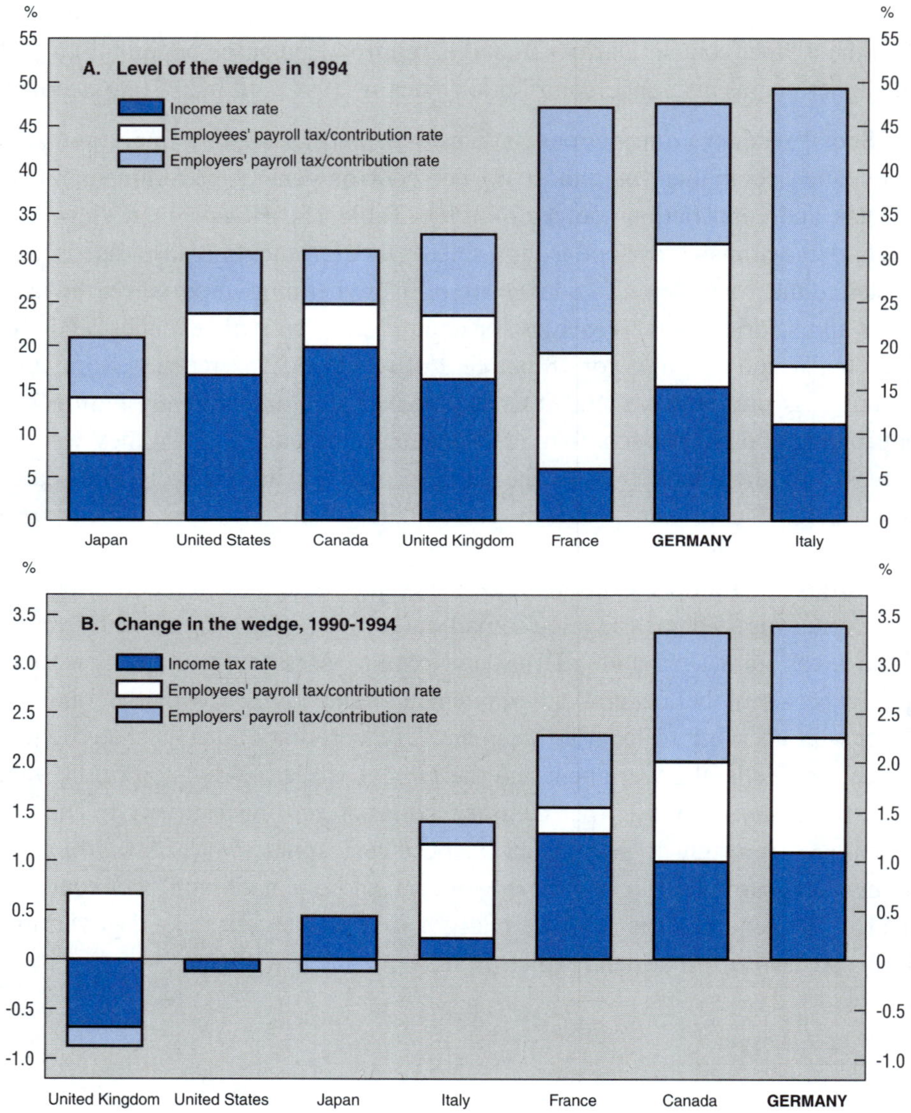

1. The wedge is calculated as the sum of income tax, and employees' and employers' payroll taxes and social security contributions paid on gross labour costs for the average production worker. Gross labour costs are the gross earnings plus employers' payroll taxes and contributions.

Source: The tax/Benefit Position of the Average Production Worker, OECD, Paris, 1995.

Table 15. **Principal sources of general government revenue**[1]

	1970	1980	1990	1994
Percentage of GDP				
Social security contributions	10.0	13.1	13.7	15.4
Taxes	22.9	25.1	22.9	23.9
Total revenue	32.9	38.2	36.7	39.3
Percentage of total revenue				
Social security contributions	30.3	34.3	37.5	39.1
Taxes on personal income	26.7	29.6	27.6	26.5
Taxes on wages and salaries	15.8	19.9	20.0	20.4
Assessed income tax	7.2	6.5	4.1	2.0
Withholding tax on dividends	0.9	0.7	1.2	1.4
Enterprise tax	2.5	2.5	2.3	1.8
Other	0.3	0.0	0.0	0.9
Taxes on corporate income	5.7	5.5	4.8	2.9
Corporation tax	3.9	3.8	3.4	1.5
Enterprise tax	1.6	1.7	1.4	1.1
Other	0.1	0.0	0.0	0.3
Taxes on payroll	0.6	0.2	0.0	0.0
Taxes on property	4.9	3.3	3.4	2.8
Value added taxes	17.1	16.6	16.6	18.1
Taxes on specific goods and services	12.9	9.3	9.2	9.5
Miscellaneous taxes	1.8	1.2	1.0	1.1
Total revenue	100.0	100.0	100.0	100.0

1. Western Germany until 1990 and all Germany from 1991 onwards. Excluding other sources of revenue such as entrepreneurial earnings and transfers.

Source: OECD, *Revenue Statistics.*

for lower income households was around 8 per cent of disposable income in 1994, increasing to 8.7 per cent for middle income groups, but declining to 7.6 per cent for higher income levels.[45] In eastern Germany a different structure of consumption results in a more compressed but similar profile.

Social security contributions

All employees with monthly incomes exceeding DM 590 (DM 500 in eastern Germany) are obliged to pay social insurance contributions, although individuals with high incomes may opt out of the compulsory health insurance system. The unemployed have their contributions paid by the Federal Labour Office, while pensioners also make contributions to some schemes. The social insurance system comprises five branches, covering health, work injury, unemployment, pensions and long-term care for the elderly. Apart from work injury insurance, which is financed by employers alone, contribution rates are the same for employees and employers.[46] Contributions are proportional to gross wages for monthly earnings exceeding DM 590 (DM 500 in eastern Germany) up to a relatively high ceiling, but thereafter they are constant. Employee social insurance contributions are withheld from earnings and are paid by the employer to the employee's health insurance fund, which in turn is responsible for distributing the contributions to the other branches of the social security system. Studies indicate that the system is particularly costly for smaller firms to administer.[47]

Contribution rates have been rising steadily and for 1996 amount to around 41 per cent of gross wages, excluding work injury insurance (Figure 24). The combined contribution rate for pension insurance is 19.2 per cent, and for unemployment insurance 6.5 per cent. There is no uniform contribution rate for health insurance since there are various insurance companies between which employees can choose, but the estimated average contribution rate is some 13.5 per cent of gross wages; for insurance covering nursing care of the elderly the contribution

Figure 24. **SOCIAL SECURITY CONTRIBUTION RATES**[1]

Per cent of gross wages[2]

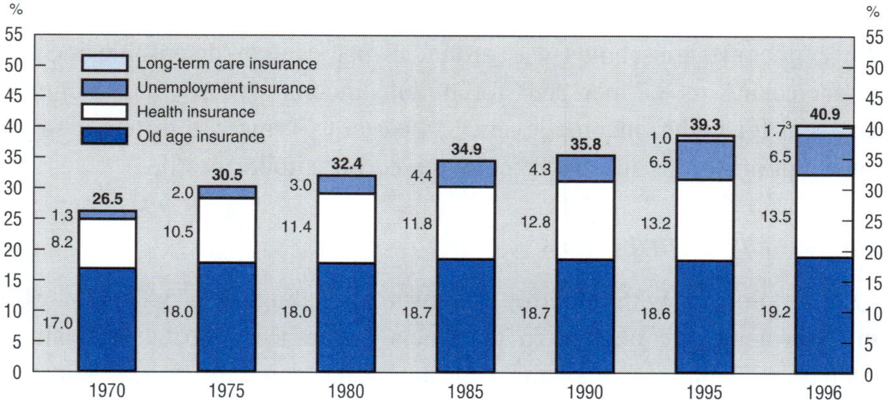

1. In Western Germany.
2. Up to the earnings ceiling.
3. From the 1st of July.

Source: Submission from the Ministry of Finance.

rate is 1.7 per cent of gross wages from mid-1996. The income ceiling for health and nursing care insurance above which contributions are constant is three-quarters of the income ceiling for pension and unemployment insurance.

The personal income tax

The income tax system comprises both a wage tax and an assessed income tax (covering self-employment and investment income), the share of which has been steadily declining (from 22.1 per cent of taxes on personal income and profits in 1983 to 7.3 per cent in 1994). It has recently declined further as deductions related to expenditures in the east have gained in importance. Certain types of income are not subject to taxation, notably capital gains from sales of real estate and other assets not related to business activity, except where they arise from "short-term speculation";[48] public or private old-age pensions;[49] and overtime premia for working hours on Sundays, holidays and at night. Taxation is assessed on a personal basis, but married couples can pool their income (*Ehegattensplitting*), thereby reducing household taxation. This income splitting system is part of the family support system. Unemployment benefits and other forms of social assistance are, for practical purposes, tax-free.[50]

The two most striking features of the personal income-tax system are its complexity and its progressivity. There are a wide variety of tax exemptions reflecting a multitude of policy goals and a relatively large share of tax revenue is derived from those taxpayers who are subject to the higher marginal rates (Table 16). Moreover, tax rates are also high by international comparison (Table 17). Excluding the effects of the solidarity tax surcharge from which low earners are exempted, the marginal income tax rate rises gradually from around 26 per cent to 53 per cent, at which point the average tax rate is around 35 per cent (Figure 25). Entrepreneurial income is, however, taxed differently, with a top marginal tax rate of 47 per cent (see below). The income tax schedule comprises different zones. In the first zone income remains untaxed ("basic tax allowance"), while in the "progressive zone", marginal tax rates increase continuously to a maximum value after which they remain constant.[51]

In successive tax reforms over the last two decades the system has been changed repeatedly. Key in this respect was a ruling of the Constitutional Court in 1992, determining that income should be untaxed up to the subsistence level as defined for the purposes of social assistance. From 1990 to 1992 the basic

Table 16. **Who pays income tax?**[1]

Proportion of tax-payers Per cent	Income subject to tax above DM	Per cent		
		Cumulated share of income tax receipts	Cumulated share of pretax income	Cumulated share of taxable income
Top:				
5	133 500	37.3	21.0	25.2
10	107 000	48.6	31.8	36.1
15	92 000	57.4	40.9	45.2
20	81 500	64.5	48.8	53.0
25	73 000	70.5	55.8	59.8
30	65 500	75.7	62.1	65.8
35	59 500	80.3	67.9	71.3
40	54 100	84.2	73.1	76.1
45	49 000	87.7	77.8	80.5
50	44 250	90.9	82.1	84.6

1. 1995 estimates.
Source: Submission by the Ministry of Finance.

allowance amounted to DM 5 616 for a single person (DM 11 232 for a married couple), after which a constant marginal tax rate of 19 per cent applied up to DM 8 153 (DM 16 306) for a married couple, and thereafter the marginal tax rate increased linearly to its maximum value of 53 per cent. In response to the Court ruling,[52] from 1996 the basic allowance has been raised to around DM 12 095 (DM 24 191), and the initial marginal tax rate was increased from 19 per cent to 25.9 per cent. At a taxable income of DM 55 728 (DM 111 456) the new schedule kinks upwards and becomes identical with the 1992 schedule. It is estimated that the adjustment to the subsistence allowance in 1996 will result in lower tax revenues of around DM 15 billion – 0.5 per cent of GDP.

Tax allowances are particularly important in the German system. In addition to outlays necessary to acquire, secure or maintain taxable income (*Werbungskosten*), there are a range of ''special expenses'' (*Sonderausgaben*). Social security contributions and premia for life insurance contracts are deductible, but there is an upper limit which is doubled for married couples. Expenses which represent ''extraordinary burdens'' to the taxpayer are also deductible. An important example, which is intended to promote labour-force participation, is child-minding expenses incurred by working single parents for children younger than 16 years of age. Child maintenance has been given a high priority and, as elsewhere, has led to a marked increase in the complexity of the tax system. Support for families

Table 17. **An international comparison of tax rates**

Tax as a percentage of income

	Germany	Australia	Belgium	Canada	Denmark	Finland	France	Italy	Netherlands	Norway	Sweden	United Kingdom	United States
A. Two-earner couple, no children[1]													
% of APW income (principal/secondary earner)													
66/66	**32.8**	15.7	27.4	22.2	42.4	28.4	22.9	20.8	42.0	25.5	25.0	19.0	24.4
100/33	**32.8**	19.3	29.1	22.5	42.7	31.1	22.9	20.9	43.6	26.8	26.8	19.2	24.4
100/66	**35.1**	20.0	32.3	24.2	44.8	32.4	24.2	23.2	44.6	27.5	26.8	22.0	25.6
100/100	**36.4**	22.8	35.5	25.5	47.7	35.0	25.4	24.8	46.4	28.8	28.0	24.0	26.9
B. Two-earner couple, 2 children[1]													
% of APW income (principal/secondary earner)													
66/66	**30.5**	15.7	25.0	20.6	42.4	23.3	21.8	20.4	42.3	23.6	25.0	19.0	21.6
100/33	**30.5**	19.3	26.7	21.2	42.7	25.4	21.8	20.4	43.1	24.9	26.8	19.2	21.6
100/66	**33.0**	20.0	30.3	24.2	44.8	27.8	23.1	22.8	44.9	26.0	26.8	22.0	23.3
100/100	**34.5**	22.8	33.9	25.7	47.7	31.2	24.2	24.5	46.6	27.5	28.0	24.0	24.4
C. Single persons[1]													
% of APW income													
66	**31.9**	15.7	27.1	22.2	42.4	28.4	24.2	20.8	41.0	25.5	25.0	21.3	23.8
100	**36.4**	22.8	35.3	25.5	47.0	35.0	27.2	24.8	46.4	28.8	28.0	25.6	25.9
133	**39.3**	27.5	39.8	29.9	51.6	39.2	29.7	26.7	46.1	33.1	31.5	27.7	29.0
D. Social security contributions[2]													
Paid by employee	**19.4**	1.4	13.1	5.4	6.9	8.6	18.6	10.0	33.5	7.8	2.0	8.4	7.7
Paid by employer	**19.4**	n.a.	34.8	6.6	n.a.	3.8	33.5[3]	46.1	7.9	12.8	30.1	10.2	7.7
E. Consumption tax rates[4]	**19.8**	7.4	16.8	12.5	31.7	26.5	19.3	15.1	17.9	33.5	24.1	16.7	5.5

1. In 1992.
2. In 1994.
3. Estimated by the OECD.
4. In 1993. Data for France and Norway refer to 1991. Data for Canada refer to 1992.

Source: *The OECD Jobs Study;* ''Taxation, Employment and Unemployment'', Paris, 1995; *The Tax/Benefit Position of Production Workers,* OECD, Paris, 1995; OECD *National Accounts.*

Figure 25. **MARGINAL AND AVERAGE INCOME TAX RATES**[1]

Excluding the 7.5 per cent solidarity surcharge

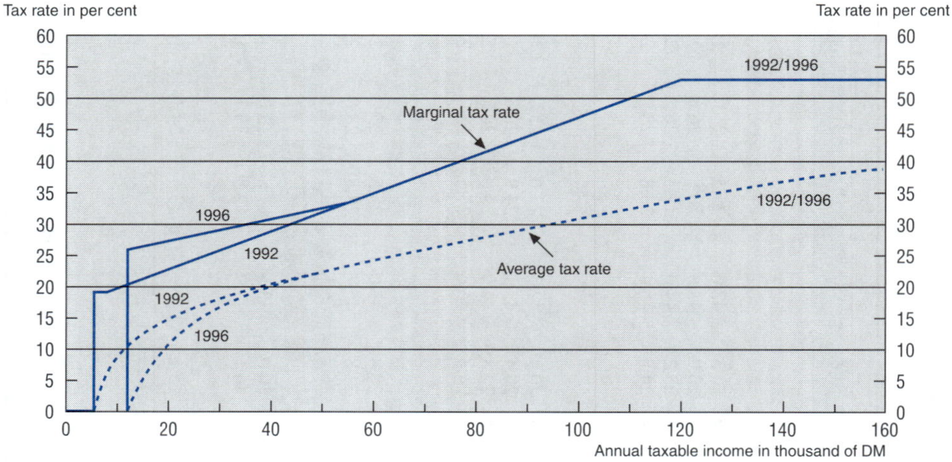

1. In 1992 and 1996. Tax rates for non-enterpreneurial income only.
Source: Submission from the Ministry of Finance; OECD.

with children is provided for through child allowances (*Kinderfreibetrag*) as well as the system of cash benefits noted above.[53] Prior to 1996 families could accumulate both types of support and families who could not fully benefit from the tax allowance, because their income fell short of the basic tax allowance, received a ''child benefits surcharge'' (*Kindergeldzuschlag*). The surcharge was designed so as to secure a transfer of the same value as a fully utilised child allowance at the entrance tax rate. In combination with the cash benefits system, the tax system produced peaks in effective marginal tax rates at various segments on the income scale. In particular, at the point where benefits were finally reduced to minimum base levels, effective marginal tax rates could exceed 100 per cent.

Following the ruling of the Constitutional Court on the tax exemption of subsistence income, the 1996 tax code aims at securing a higher level of tax free subsistence income allocated to raising children, while at the same time eliminating the peaks in marginal tax rates characteristic of the previous system. The tax allowance for children was raised and the old system of cash benefits and child benefit surcharges was replaced by income tax credits for children which cannot be accumulated with the taxpayer's child allowance. Instead, child tax allowances and benefits now constitute alternative instruments of support, whichever is more beneficial for the taxpayer. The benefits are not means-tested. While the new system is an improvement, administrative complexity and the associated costs have increased. These are now borne to an increased extent by companies (with employment greater than 50) which are now responsible for paying cash allowances at the same time as wages.

Taxes and transfers to the business sector

Taxation of business income and capital

Entrepreneurial income is taxed according to either the corporate tax law or the income tax code, depending on whether or not the enterprise is incorporated. Until 1994 the income tax code did not differentiate between entrepreneurial income and income from other sources. In 1994 the top income tax rate for self-employment income was reduced to 47 per cent while for other income sources it remained at 53 per cent.

Corporate tax rates have been successively lowered from 56 and 36 per cent for retained and distributed profits at the end of the 1980s, respectively, to flat rates of 45 and 30 per cent. The corporate tax system is integrated with the income tax in that there is full imputation for dividends paid to resident tax payers: shareholders receive a tax credit for the profits tax paid by a company so that gross dividends are taxed at the personal income tax rate.[54] The current corporate tax rate is still high by international standards, but tax deductions and imputation for distributed profits as well as depreciation allowances which are relatively favourable by international comparison lower the effective taxation of profits. Losses may be carried backwards for two years and forward indefinitely to be deducted from the first available taxable income.

One of the most controversial sources of revenue is the locally-levied business tax (*Gewerbesteuer*), The basic tax rate is 5 per cent for the local business tax on profits (*Gewerbeertragsteuer*) – graduated rates apply for small unincorporated businesses – and 0.2 per cent for the local business tax on capital (*Gewerbekapitalsteuer*). Local governments are permitted to levy a multiple of the basic tax. The basic idea of the local business tax is that capital and profits serve as proxies for the utilisation by businesses of the services provided by the communities. The tax is deductible for personal and corporate income taxes. Although these business taxes account for only 5 per cent of total tax revenues of general government, they are particularly important for communes, accounting for almost 40 per cent of their tax revenues. The capital tax is at present only levied in the old *Länder:* at the time of reunification it was considered inappropriate to levy a tax on business capital in the new states since newly established and restructuring enterprises were probably in no condition to comply. The arrangement does, however, distort competition. The European Commission extended an exemption until 1997 at which time either the tax has to be introduced into the new *Länder,* or abolished throughout Germany.

Industrial subsidies: selective distributional policy

As is the case for the tax and transfer system as a whole, unification has had a major impact on industrial subsidies in Germany. Subsidies in eastern Germany were originally motivated by the goal of speeding up the replacement of obsolete real capital of enterprises inherited from the GDR and to build a modern infrastructure to make the eastern German economy competitive. However, an equally, if not more important, objective has been to reduce the transition costs to particular workers and regions. Following reunification, subsidies, including tax expenditures, as measured by the five leading research institutes in Germany, increased from 5.4 per cent of GDP in 1989 to 7.1 per cent in 1993.[55] According to the institutes' measure, the share of eastern Germany in overall subsidies has increased from 34.7 per cent in 1991 to 43.3 per cent in 1993.[56] At the same time, after growing for some years, since 1991 subsidies in western Germany have started to decline.[57]

Besides aid given to eastern German companies by the Treuhandanstalt and its successor organisation, industrial subsidies in the new *Länder* are mainly targeted at aiding investment and fostering the foundation of new enterprises, as well as supporting research and development. There is also liquidity and marketing aid, and aid for improving the quality of management. Though all the measures of the federal and regional governments and public banks combined add up to several hundred programmes, the principal instruments of providing financial aid are investment tax credits, accelerated depreciation allowances for investment, investment cash grants, low interest loans, and loans which are designed to substitute for a lack of risk bearing capital.

The IFO institute has provided a break-down of subsidies for enterprises in the new *Länder* into sector-specific aid and general subsidies which in principal are granted to all sectors. Cumulated over 1991 to 1994, non-sector specific investment tax incentives are estimated to have led to revenue losses of DM 31.7 billion. Excluding the Treuhand, transfers to enterprises in the new *Länder* amounted to DM 79 billion over the same period, of which 28 per cent was general and the remainder sector specific. There is a high concentration of sector specific aid on sectors which are also especially subsidised in western Germany, mainly agriculture and transport. Without aid for agriculture and railways, the cumulated sector specific financial transfers to enterprises would be reduced from DM 57.1 billion to DM 4.4 billion. It may be concluded, therefore, that in eastern Germany, apart from the two sectors mentioned, financial aid is predominantly general. These programmes are mainly designed to support small and medium-sized companies (*Mittelstand*). Transfers by the Treuhand over the same period, which have often resembled social transfers in objective, amounted to DM 80 billion.

As stressed in previous *Surveys* there is a danger that subsidies could lead to a ''subsidy mentality'' of the recipients and distort competition, and that they may be difficult to remove. In its 1995 economic report the government announced a stepwise reduction of aid to eastern Germany. In 1995 and 1996 the overall allowance for the most important investment grant which is jointly funded by the federal government, the *Länder* and the European Union has been reduced.[58] The restructuring of tax incentives in the 1996 tax reform law also implies a reduction in tax expenditures.

The efficiency of the tax and transfer systems

This section considers the likely impact on the economy of the extensive and complex system of transfers to and taxation of households and businesses. A summary measure of the interaction between taxes and transfers – the net replacement rate – is first presented and the potential effects of the system as a whole on labour supply and on labour demand are then considered. The impact of the tax/transfer system on income distribution is then outlined. This is followed by a brief discussion of the impact of business taxation on corporate finance and organisation, drawing on the analysis contained in the 1995 *OECD Economic Survey of Germany*.

The incentive effects of the tax/transfer system

The generosity of the system: net replacement ratios

As part of the follow-up to the *Jobs Study,* the OECD has commissioned an analysis of net replacement rates based on the sample of households included in the German Socio-economic panel. A description of the techniques of micro-simulation, as well as more information about the study, which is based on the 1995 tax system, are given in Annex I. The net replacement rate is defined as net household income, both benefits and other income, when the head of household or his/her spouse is not working, divided by the estimated household income net of taxes and social security contributions when in work.[59] With respect to in-work income, two alternative scenarios are considered. The low-wage scenario assumes that the gross wage earned in employment equals the lowest decile of the wage distribution of the employed. This scenario is intended to reflect a situation where non-working persons find employment at relatively low entry wages. The second scenario assumes that gross wages when working are equal to the median earnings of employed households. This scenario is intended to allow for both higher entry wages and the fact that earnings may increase over time.

The results indicate that net replacement ratios are on average around 70-85 per cent for the unemployed and around 50-60 per cent for the heterogeneous group termed ''non-employed''. However, for some segments replacement rates are close to and may even exceed 100 per cent. For the non-employed, net replacement rates rise with family size, possibly reflecting to some degree the ''needs-based'' design of the social welfare system where benefits become more generous as the number of dependants increase (Figures 26 and 27). For the non-employed, replacement rates vary considerably with respect to both the level of family income when out of work and family composition (Figure 26). Families in the lowest out-of-work income quintile represent just over a third of the households and on average have net replacement rates of only about 20 and 30 per cent. Around three-fifths of the households in the low wage scenario (half in the median wage scenario) nevertheless enjoy replacement ratios above 60 per cent, while for a half (a third) it is above 70 per cent.

Figure 26. **NET REPLACEMENT RATES IN WESTERN GERMANY**[1]

Non-employed

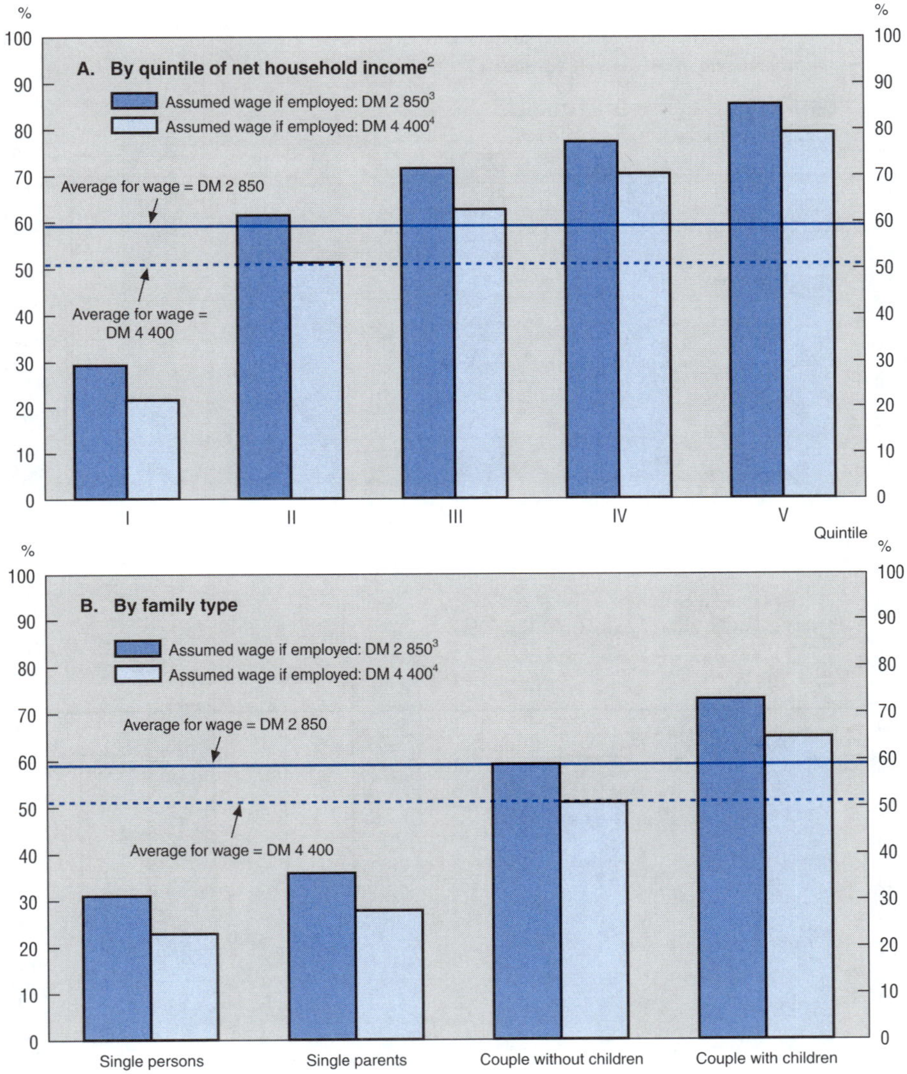

1. In 1995. Non-employed refers to a head of household or spouse who does not receive any unemployment related benefit or a pension. Mothers with young children are excluded.
2. The quintiles are ordered from the low to the high.
3. Lowest decile of the earnings distribution of the employed.
4. Median of the earnings distribution of the employed.

Source: OECD.

Figure 27. **NET REPLACEMENT RATES IN WESTERN GERMANY**[1]

Recipients of unemployment benefits and unemployment assistance

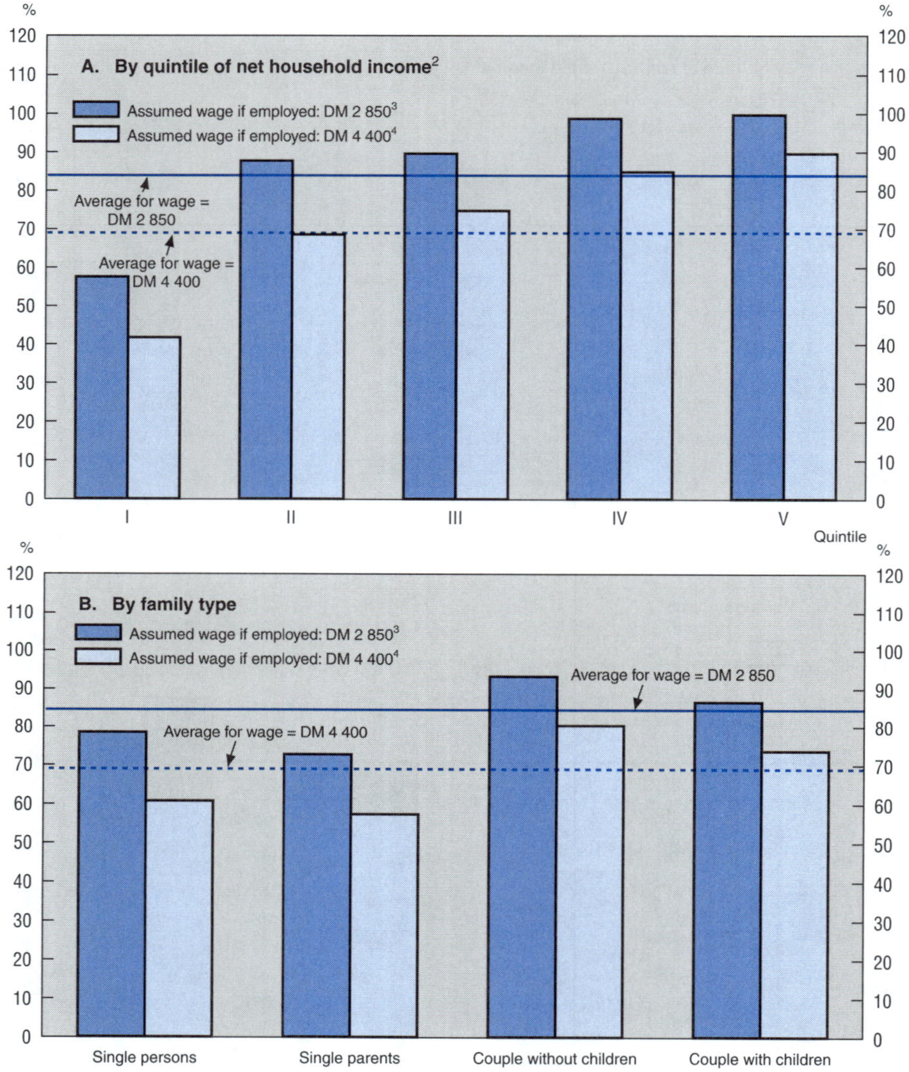

1. In 1995. Social assistance is also received by some households.
2. The quintiles are ordered from the low to the high.
3. Lowest decile of the earnings distribution of the employed.
4. Median of the earnings distribution of the employed.

Source: OECD.

For families with a head of household or spouse receiving unemployment-related benefits including social assistance, the average replacement rate is 84 per cent under the low wage assumption, and 69 per cent under the median wage assumption (Figure 27). Around three-fifths of recipients of unemployment benefits and unemployment assistance represented by the sample have replacement ratios exceeding 80 per cent in the low wage scenario. In the median wage scenario a third of the unemployed have replacement ratios of 80 per cent or more. About a fifth of the families in the low wage scenario, and 6 per cent of the families in the median wage scenario face replacement ratios exceeding 100 per cent of potential income when working.

Other studies have specified quite specific groups of welfare recipients and have attempted to define replacement rates in terms of benefits relative to the wages which might be available for them in full time employment. The results are broadly similar to those outlined above, though the instances of unemployment traps in which the net replacement ratio exceeds 100 per cent, are more pronounced. For example, one study of social assistance recipients showed that even under the reformed 1996 tax code, the derived net replacement ratio lay between 75 and 118 per cent when employment could be found in the hotel and restaurant trade, 63 per cent to 103 per cent in the retail sector, and 61 to 100 per cent in the metal industry.[60] Unemployment traps were more pronounced with increased family size.

The potential impact on labour supply

As discussed in Chapter IV below, the combination of generous criteria determining the suitability of a job offer together with a long period of unemployment benefits and unemployment assistance until now linked to previous earnings, may allow an extended period of job search. Higher levels of unemployment would result. In addition, under conditions of major structural change in which unskilled industrial workers are particularly affected (see Chapter IV), reservation wages could remain too high to induce pressure for adjustments in relative wages. More generally, there is a risk that high tax wedges resulting from the operation of the tax/transfer system could discourage work participation, and reduce hours of work and work intensity for those already employed.[61] These are important empirical issues on which theoretical models are often ambiguous, but a number of empirical studies, which are briefly summarised in Annex II, do indeed point to wage taxes and replacement rates having a negative influence on labour market activity:

- Empirical investigations, while not unambiguous, suggest that the transition from unemployment to employment in Germany is responsive both to the income replacement rate and the duration of benefits. For example, the propensity to find employment increases before unemployment benefits are set to decline or become exhausted, while the lengthening of the eligibility period for unemployment benefits in the 1980s led to a statistically significant negative impact on exit rates from unemployment.
- Evidence on the responsiveness of hours worked with respect to net wages is sparse, but available studies indicate that high marginal tax rates may indeed discourage people from working longer hours. In this respect, however, male labour supply is relatively unresponsive compared to female labour supply.
- In the latter respect, also, there is strong evidence that tax splitting (*i.e.* equally dividing the combined family income for tax purposes, even where the wife does not work) reduces female labour force participation in comparison to a system where incomes are taxed individually. While the ability to reduce the marginal tax rate faced by the higher-income earner should lead to a positive labour-supply response, this may be more than offset by the deterrent effect on potential new entrants to the workforce.

As for social security charges *per se,* there is no *a priori* reason why the level of social security contributions should affect wage costs and employment: if social security contributions are perceived as insurance then wage claims could adjust so as to keep gross wages more or less constant. However, in Germany as elsewhere in Europe, this is not likely to be the case: as noted above the insurance element has been considerably weakened over the years. Contributions thus increasingly resemble normal income taxes so that the rapid rise in contribution rates since 1990 has added to the tax wedge. Even if taxes and contributions are eventually borne by labour – which over the long term is probably the case – the short-term impact will probably be a rise in business costs, with negative employment consequences.

In this case, substituting contributions (which act, in effect, under the above conditions, as a wage tax) by more generally based revenues such as a value-added tax – environmental taxes have also been proposed – could increase employment by improving competitiveness. Labour demand could also rise. But whether this would be permanent would depend on whether unions would react to higher taxes by demanding wage increases and whether the government would come under pressure to compensate retirees and receivers of social transfers for the increase in prices; the results may thus be rather ambivalent in the longer run.

How is income distribution affected?

At 12.4 per cent, western Germany had the smallest proportion of low income families before taxes and transfers among OECD countries (Table 18). After taxes and transfers, the low-income ratio is only a little below the western European norm, a finding supported by expenditure based measures of relative household purchasing power (Table 19). Hence, while the tax/benefit system is important in reducing income inequality, the decline is less pronounced than in other western European countries. On the other hand, Germany has the highest dispersion of income amongst low-income families before taxes and transfers, while after these are taken into account low-income families have the most equal income distribution after Luxembourg (measured by the low-income gap) and Austria (measured by the Gini coefficient) (Table 18). This finding reflects the operation of the "needs-based" social assistance system which is designed to lift very low incomes above a predetermined minimum standard. In the process, there is a significant redistribution from wage earners to pensioners, the unemployed and non-active families with young children. The tax/benefit system thus results in a substantial life cycle redistribution from families in peak earnings to both retirees and younger members of the population. However, the unique situation arising from unification may play a role in this.

Transfers from west to east, both social and non-social, have been used extensively to raise income levels in the new *Länder* towards those in the west, as well as to support groups disadvantaged by the transition process. Such transfers have underpinned the rapid growth of wages at levels far above the growth of productivity. Households are generally much more dependent on transfers than in the west: 54 per cent of all households (including pensioners) had a non-working head in 1991, in contrast to 45 per cent in the west and had fewer sources of

Table 18. **Measures of income distribution**

Population below 50 per cent of median income

	Before taxes and transfers				After taxes and transfers				Percentage change			
	Low income rate (LIR)	Low income gap (ALG)	Gini (poor) (GP)	SEN Index * 100	Low income rate (LIR)	Low income gap (ALG)	Gini (poor) (GP)	SEN Index * 100	Change in LIR	Change in ALG	Change in GINI (poor)	Change in SEN index
Australia	17.6	57.0	0.4361	13.33	15.7	30.7	0.1952	6.94	–10.80	–46.14	–55.24	–47.94
Austria	–	–	–	–	6.2	24.0	0.1187	2.05	–	–	–	–
Belgium	22.7	26.6	0.1619	8.74	5.4	25.0	0.1748	2.06	–76.21	–6.02	7.97	–76.43
Canada	19.0	46.5	0.3141	12.03	15.4	33.2	0.1890	7.05	–18.95	–28.60	–39.83	–41.40
Denmark	20.2	53.9	0.4034	14.63	5.7	38.5	0.2714	3.14	–71.82	–28.70	–32.72	–78.56
France	20.6	37.1	0.2466	10.84	8.9	33.3	0.2185	4.26	–56.80	–10.24	–11.39	–60.70
Germany (West)	**12.4**	**59.5**	**0.4837**	**9.80**	**8.5**	**23.2**	**0.1340**	**2.84**	**–31.45**	**–61.01**	**–72.30**	**–71.02**
Ireland	26.3	57.1	0.4227	19.79	15.7	24.9	0.1730	5.94	–40.30	–56.39	–59.07	–69.98
Italy	–	–	–	–	10.1	27.3	0.1616	3.94	–	–	–	–
Luxembourg	–	–	–	–	4.5	22.4	0.1513	1.54	–	–	–	–
Netherlands	18.9	45.8	0.2965	11.70	4.7	28.8	0.1971	2.01	–75.13	–37.12	–33.52	–82.82
Norway	–	–	–	–	7.8	35.5	0.2292	3.93	–	–	–	–
Sweden	18.4	54.4	0.3865	13.25	12.1	41.0	0.2485	6.74	–34.24	–24.63	–35.71	–49.13
United Kingdom	24.0	57.1	0.4526	18.37	12.4	27.6	0.1907	5.13	–48.33	–51.66	–57.87	–72.07
United States	19.4	49.3	0.3484	12.99	18.7	39.5	0.2326	10.02	–3.61	–19.88	–33.24	–22.86
Average [1]	20.7	48.5	0.3469	13.57	11.5	32.3	0.2091	5.30	–44.62	–33.48	–39.73	–60.72

Key:

Low income rate: Share of persons living in families with income below 50 per cent of median income (per cent).

Low income gap: Average difference in income (over the low-income population) relative to the low-income line, as a ratio of the low-income line.

Gini coefficient: Average deviation (within the low-income population) from equal income distribution.

SEN index: LIR * (ALG + (1 – ALG) * GP). The values of the index lie between 0 and 1, with no low-income families where SEN = 0, and rising income inequality as the index approaches 1.

1. Excluding Germany and covering only countries reporting distributions before taxes and transfers.

Source: Förster, M.F., ''Measurement of Low Incomes and Poverty in a Perspective of International Comparisons'', *OECD Labour Market and Social Policy Occasional Papers,* No. 14 (1994); Danish Ministry of Foreign Affairs.

Table 19. **Expenditure-based measures of relative purchasing power**[1]

	Average expenditure per equivalent adult ECUs [2]	Expenditure Per cent		
		Less than 40 per cent of average	Less than 50 per cent of average	Less than 60 per cent of average
Belgium	12 007	1.7	6.6	14.1
Denmark [3]	11 324	1.4	4.2	13.3
France [4]	13 966	7.5	14.9	24.5
Germany (West)	**13 771**	**5.3**	**12.0**	**21.2**
Greece	10 593	13.0	20.8	29.8
Ireland [3]	10 202	7.9	16.4	26.9
Italy	12 210	12.5	22.0	32.2
Luxembourg [3]	18 920	3.7	9.2	17.2
Netherlands	12 984	1.9	6.2	13.9
Portugal [4]	8 546	17.3	26.5	35.2
Spain	10 341	9.3	17.5	27.1
United Kingdom	14 018	7.4	17.0	28.0

1. Relative purchasing power is defined as an annual expenditure below 40, 50 and 60 per cent of the national arithmetic average, respectively. Figures relate to 1988 unless otherwise stated. The first person in a household is given a weight 1; further persons over 14 years of age are given a weight 0.3.
2. Converted by 1988 PPP-based weights. Due to differences between the treatment of publicly-subsidised services, direct comparison of average expenditure between the countries is difficult.
3. Figures relate to 1987.
4. Figures relate to 1989.

Source: Eurostat, *Poverty Statistics in the late-1980s: Research based on micro-data,* Brussels (1994).

additional income.[62] The distributional consequences are most noticeable for two groups: pensioners and the unemployed. Since the west German pension system was transferred to the new states in 1992 the relative position of pensioners has improved considerably, the percentage of aged persons receiving more than average adjusted income surging from 43 per cent to nearly 60 per cent (Table 20). Increases were most pronounced for women whose average pension is now 25 per cent above the level in the west.[63] For the unemployed, two effects appear to be operating. On the one hand, unemployment benefits are relatively more generous than in the west (Table 21). On the other hand, due to the rapid growth of wages and pensions in the new states, the relative incomes of the unemployed households have deteriorated (Table 20). Overall, while income inequality, as measured by the Gini coefficient on net adjusted income

Table 20. **The distribution of the unemployed and the elderly by income brackets in eastern Germany**

Income bracket: Per cent of average equivalence income	Less than 50 per cent	50 to 75 per cent	75 to 100 per cent	100 to 125 per cent	125 to 150 per cent	More than 150 per cent	All
	Percentage of unemployed persons						
1991	10.2	27.7	36.3	14.6	7.4	3.7	100
1992	12.7	33.0	30.6	14.1	6.7	2.6	100
1993	13.6	34.3	25.9	18.0	5.5	2.7	100
1994	18.9	35.5	24.2	11.6	6.1	3.4	100
	Percentage of persons aged 65 or older						
1991	0.0	20.1	47.4	24.4	(5.9)	0.0	100
1992	(1.6)	14.2	41.6	27.6	12.7	2.3	100
1993	(3.0)	14.0	38.6	29.0	11.3	4.1	100
1994	(3.6)	8.4	29.8	38.0	14.0	6.2	100

( ) Unreliable statistical information.
Source: Müller, K., ''Einkommensmobilität und Einkommensverteilung in Ostdeutschland'', *Wirtschaftsbulletin Ostdeutschland,* No. 4, 1995.

(Table 22), has increased since unification, it is still much lower than in western Germany despite the proportionately much higher level of unemployment.

Impact on entrepreneurial behaviour

As noted in the 1995 *OECD Economic Survey of Germany,* the combination of income and corporation taxes may not be particularly distortive with respect to the choice of corporate finance, but the income and wealth tax systems may affect corporate organisation and structure, and inhibit the development of newly-established enterprises. Dividends from shares in incorporated enterprises are taxed up to a top personal income tax rate of 53 per cent, whereas income from unincorporated enterprises is taxed up to a (preferential) top income tax rate of 47 per cent. At the top levels of marginal tax, the system implies little distortion with respect to choice of financing, but with marginal rates below these levels there is an inducement to borrowing. Moreover, the system may inhibit the development of joint-stock companies by favouring income from direct proprietorship. This bias is increased because wealth continues to be taxed at both the corporate and shareholder level, implying double taxation for proprietors bring-

Table 21. **Relative income position of recipients of unemployment benefits**

Net income in eastern Germany as a ratio of income in western Germany

	One person working	
	Before unemployment	When unemployed
Single man		
Unskilled worker	77	86
Skilled worker	75	81
Lower management	75	78
Medium management	65	65
Couple without children		
Unskilled worker	82	87
Skilled worker	78	82
Lower management	76	81
Medium management	63	66
Couple with two children		
Unskilled worker	80	96
Skilled worker	82	90
Lower management	81	85
Medium management	67	74

	Working couple with two children	
	Before unemployment	When unemployed
Female supplementary earner unemployed		
Unskilled worker	82	81
Skilled worker	80	76
Lower management	79	75
Medium management	66	65
Main earner unemployed		
Unskilled worker	82	82
Skilled worker	80	80
Lower management	79	81
Medium management	66	66
Couple unemployed		
Unskilled worker	82	84
Skilled worker	80	82
Lower management	79	82
Medium management	66	69

Source: Rheinisch-Westfälisches Institut für Wirtschaftsforschung Essen, *Das Zusammenwirken von Steuern und Sozialtransfers in den jungen Bundesländern – eine empirische Analyse anhand von Fallbeispielen und Problemdarstellung,* Essen 1994.

Table 22. **The distribution of personal income in eastern and western Germany**

	Eastern Germany					Western Germany			
	1990	1991	1992	1993	1994	1990	1991	1992	1993
	Gross earnings								
Gini coefficient	0.198	0.228	0.216	0.226	–	0.285	0.280	0.273	–
	Net personal equivalence income[1]								
Gini coefficient	0.185	0.198	0.200	0.216	0.221	0.267	0.263	0.264	0.274
Quintile shares in per cent									
1st quintile	11.8	11.3	11.1	10.6	10.2	9.4	9.5	9.5	9.2
2nd quintile	15.8	16.1	15.9	15.5	15.5	14.0	14.0	14.1	13.8
3rd quintile	19.2	18.9	19.1	18.8	18.9	17.7	17.8	17.7	17.7
4th quintile	22.9	22.3	22.5	22.7	23.0	22.5	22.8	22.8	22.8
5th quintile	30.2	31.2	31.3	32.4	32.4	36.4	35.9	35.9	36.5
Lower income ratio									
50 per cent line[2]	3.4	4.4	5.9	7.3	–	10.9	10.7	10.1	11.5

1. Net personal income is derived by dividing net household income by household size. This is calculated using the demographic equivalents used for calculating social benefits.
2. Share of incomes below 50 per cent of average net equivalence income.

Source: Hauser, R., ''Problems of the German Welfare State after Unification'', *Oxford Review of Economic Policy,* Vol. 11; Müller, K., ''Einkommensmobilität und Einkommensverteilung in Ostdeutschland'', *Wirtschaftsbulletin Ostdeutschland,* No. 4, 1995; Müller, K. *et al.,* ''Zur Entwicklung der Einkommensverteilung und der Einkommenszufriedenheit in den neuen und alten Bundesländern 1990 bis 1993'', in Glatzer, W., and H. Noll, *Getrennt vereint – Lebensverhältnisse in Deutschland seit der Wiedervereinigung,* Frankfurt/New York, 1995.

ing their companies to the stock market. Furthermore, the basis for taxable (net) wealth is higher for incorporated businesses, because it is derived from the stock-market value of assets.

Wealth tax and inheritance duties are also controversial, although not important for overall tax revenues (Table 15). To keep both taxes administratively simple, different assets have been valued according to a fixed, partially *ad hoc* schedule. The Constitutional Court ruled this invalid in 1995 and the government must introduce a new system by 1997. For assets to be valued on a similar basis and at current values would require an enormous administrative load, and one which may not be justifiable in terms of revenues. With respect to the inheritance tax, a key issue in Germany concerns the potential transfer of numerous small/medium sized firms (*Mittelstand*) in the immediate and near future to family members. Although there is a relatively high tax exemption in the present system, there is no provision similar to those existing in other countries encouraging ownership transfer within a family.

In addition there is a locally-levied tax on business capital comprising equity and a proportion of long-term borrowing. A major criticism of this tax is that it is levied regardless of profitability and that it is a particular burden on small/medium enterprises.[64] On the other hand, exemptions are generous, many enterprises not paying the tax at all. German companies are not unique in having to pay fixed, locally-based taxes and international comparisons indicate that such taxes are often higher in other countries.[65] However, it is true that in other countries the tax base is more often related to real estate, or to other proxies for demand for local services, than to business capital as such. The tax is also undoubtedly a problem for newly-established enterprises.

Assessment

The German tax/transfer system has generously supported household incomes of the population through a mixture of work related and non-work related transfers. Support has to a great extent been directed to the younger and older ends of the population distribution and has been financed through high social insurance contributions from the employed and a highly progressive income tax system. As such, the system has elements of both vertical redistribution and redistribution over the life cycle. The welfare system has contributed to the elimination, for all practical purposes, of absolute poverty and to a comparatively equitable income distribution, although relatively high wages for the unskilled have probably made an even greater contribution. The welfare system has proven flexible enough to adapt to evolving social conditions and to changing demands. Foremost among the latter has been the need to facilitate the integration of the new *Länder* where wide sections of the population have needed to be supported during the transition. The system has undoubtedly been a contributory factor in good industrial relations, both directly by supporting living standards for those out of work, and indirectly through the decentralised structure which has served to integrate numerous groups into administration and policy-making.

On the other hand, the original social solidarity principle on which the welfare system was based led to individual contributions becoming less related to future benefits and contributions have been used in place of other revenues to finance more general social programmes. Moreover, the system has become increasingly removed from the principles which initially underlay the concept of a social market economy: promoting the efficiency and growth potential of the economy has become less and less a guidance to the development of the system. Several potential flaws stand out in this respect:

- Net replacement ratios are often very high, increasing the risk that people will not search actively for jobs as well as underpinning high wage levels by raising the reservation wage. Important in this respect has been the rigid relationship of unemployment benefits and assistance to past earnings. The effect may have been to weaken the forces which would lead to the reintegration of the unemployed. Amplifying these effects is the indefinite nature of social assistance and unemployment support, as well as a rather generous interpretation of what constitutes acceptable work.
- Certain groups are caught in a welfare trap with very high rates of marginal effective tax. This is a consequence of the orientation of the system towards those out of work, while marginal workers are disadvantaged by high marginal tax rates including social security contributions.
- Tax wedges arising from the income tax system and social security contributions are high, leading to efficiency losses. Particularly important are high effective marginal rates of tax for large segments of the population which could discourage work effort and entrepreneurial activity.
- Differential taxation of the income of incorporated and unincorporated enterprises, as well as the capital and wealth of their owners appear to discourage the development of stock market listings and may inhibit the expansion of certain enterprises.

Demographic developments will place the pension system under strain in the next century and reforms are needed now in order to cope with this challenge. One area requiring attention is the development of funded private pensions which are currently held back not only by an inadequate legal/tax framework, but also by the generosity of the public pay-as-you-go system. The financing difficulties of the public pension system have been made worse by failure to act until too late to control the growth of early retirees. Indeed, in the new *Länder* – as well as in the old – early retirement has been promoted as a means of dealing with the unemployment problem. Adding to the problem is the growth of invalidity pensions, where rights are being defined partly by the situation on the labour market in addition to the level of incapacity for work. Many of the problems related to the tax/transfer system are clearly intimately connected to the wider issue of job creation. Indeed, in response to the employment implications of the tax and benefit systems, the government has introduced an extensive programme of reforms, which is described in the next Chapter.

IV. Implementing the OECD Jobs Strategy

Introduction

The German labour market has been characterised by a trend rise in the level of unemployment since the early 1970s. Unemployment has increased markedly with cyclical downturns and supply-side shocks, but in recovery periods has failed to drop back to previous cyclical lows. Reunification temporarily decreased the rate of unemployment in western Germany, but for the country as a whole unemployment soared as employment in the new *Länder* collapsed. Moreover, with 1.5 million on job creation schemes, retraining or in early retirement in 1995, the employment situation is considerably worse than it first appears. Early retirement has been used extensively to lay off surplus labour and the employment/population ratio for older adults is very low in comparison with the OECD average (Figure 28). Thus, although the recent problems faced by Germany are to some extent unique, the economy in general has not been able to utilise increasing labour resources effectively. Present projections do not point to a significant improvement in the labour market even if the recovery resumes as projected, as companies are expected to continue to restructure and labour market institutions remain focused on job preservation rather than on job creation.

Faced with what appear to be significant structural weaknesses, an economic policy seeking to make significant inroads into high unemployment, and to increase labour utilisation more generally, would need to embrace a broad range of structural measures aimed at increasing the flexibility of labour and product markets. Macroeconomic policies have a supportive role to play in creating the conditions for sustained non-inflationary growth. As far as monetary policy is concerned, the achievement of virtual price stability implies a relatively favourable background. Fiscal consolidation is still incomplete but it is evident that fiscal retrenchment and measures to improve the performance of labour and

Figure 28. **LABOUR MARKET INDICATORS**

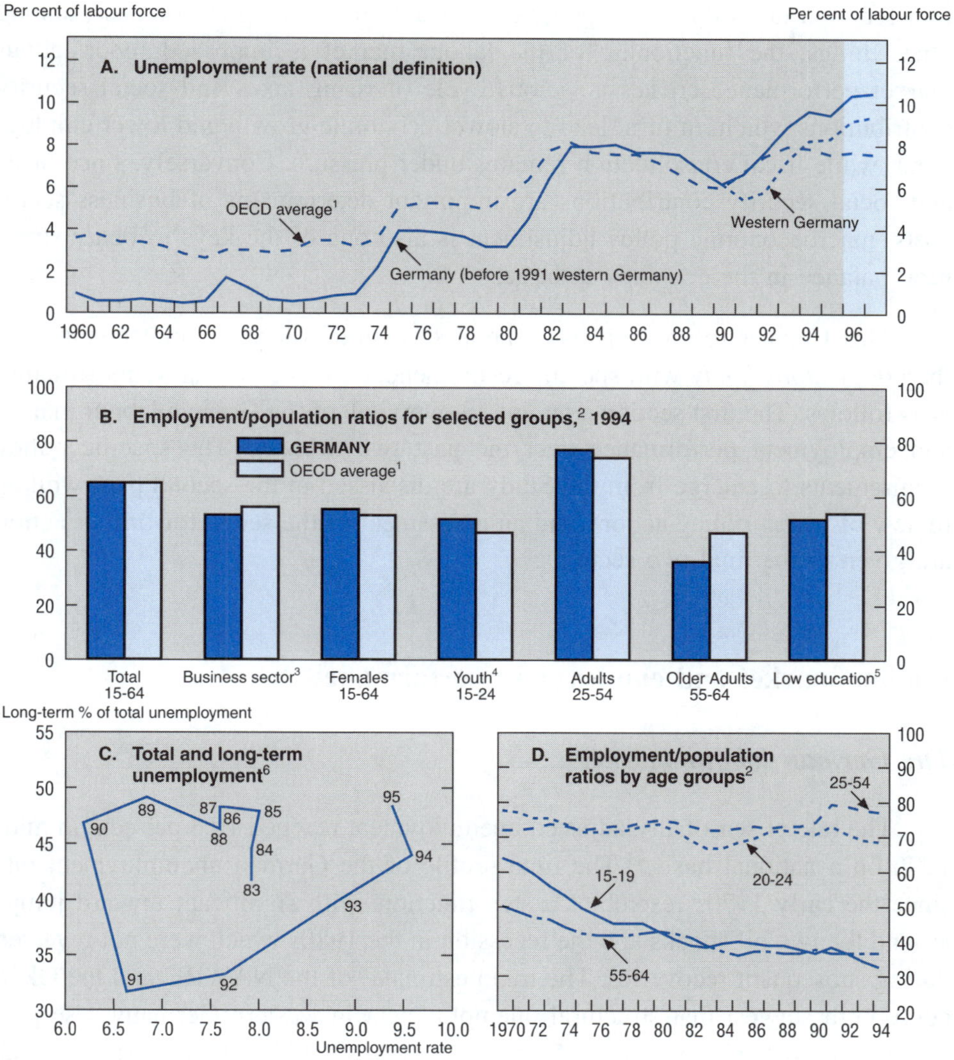

1. For countries for which data are available.
2. Defined as the percentage of each population group that is employed.
3. Business sector employment divided by working-age population. Excluding the Netherlands.
4. The minimum age for youth differs across country (either 14,15 or 16).
5. In 1992. Completed less than upper secondary education.
6. Long-term unemployment is defined as individuals looking for work for one year or more. It is derived from the labour force survey and leads to a higher estimate of the population of long-term unemployment than estimates derived from registered unemployment: 45 per cent and 33 per cent respectively.

Source: OECD, *Employment Outlook* and *Economic Outlook*.

product markets are essential complements. For example, the present system of transfers and taxes does not appear to be viable in the long term unless, among other things, the functioning of the labour market is improved: poor labour market performance creates a vicious cycle of rising taxes and social security contributions which, in turn, lead to slower economic growth and lower employment, while fiscal consolidation remains under pressure. Conversely, since taxes and social security contributions are important determinants of business sector costs, macroeconomic policy adjustment is also one of the keys to better structural balance in the economy at large.

This Chapter follows up the general structural policy recommendations of the *OECD Jobs Study* with specific recommendations for Germany. Its structure is as follows. The first section contains an overview of the German labour market and employment performance over the past two decades. The specific policy requirements to emerge from the Study are discussed in the second part, while a review of recent policy actions and an assessment of the scope for further action are given in the final two sections.

Labour market and employment performance

The German labour market

The rate of seasonally-adjusted unemployment reached 10.3 per cent in mid-1996 on a national basis.[66] The time profile of the German unemployment rate since the early 1970s resembles a step function, with significant upward jumps around the two oil shocks and the recession in the 1980s which were not reversed during subsequent recoveries. The trend estimates of the NAWRU and the Okun curve both suggest that structural unemployment in western Germany rose persistently up to 1987, to between 5 and 7 per cent, stabilising temporarily thereafter before rising once more in the wake of the reunification boom (Figure 29). Associated with this development was a steady decline in the employment rate from the early 1960s to the beginning of the 1980s (Figure 30). From the early-1980s to the start of the reunification boom, employment increased by around 1.5 million and labour force participation rose; the employment rate recovered by some 3 percentage points but in the 1990s the trend decline resumed.

Figure 29. **TREND INDICATORS OF STRUCTURAL UNEMPLOYMENT**[1]

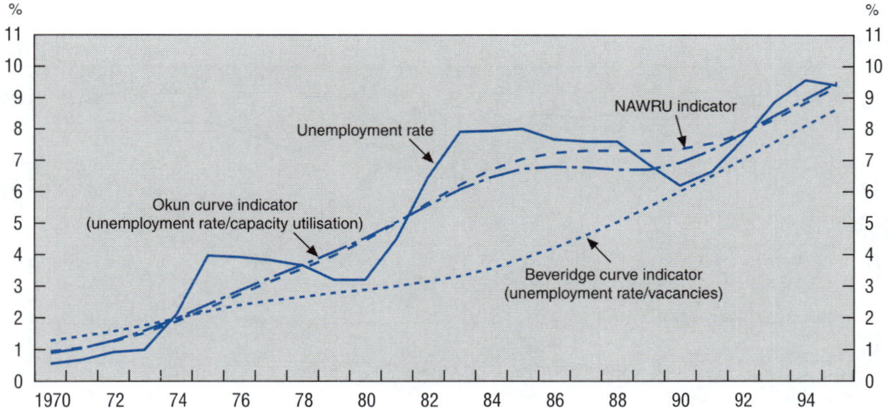

1. From 1991 overall Germany. The trends of the three indicators are based on yearly estimates of unemployment rates which would have (a) resulted in a normal vacancy rate, (b) stabilised wage inflation or (c) led to a normal rate of capacity utilisation. These estimates have subsequently been smoothed using a Hodrick-Prescott filter.

Source: OECD.

At the same time as unemployment increased in steps following a pattern of persistence, three underlying trends related to industrial and occupational changes have been evident.[67] In the first place, the decline in employment occurred in manufacturing and agriculture, and this was only partially offset by growth in the service sector (Figure 30); the rate of growth of service employment has been relatively modest in comparison with other major countries – even though Germany started from a lower level – and manufacturing has remained especially important in western Germany (Figure 31).[68] Secondly, employment growth has also been skill-intensive: skilled employment has increased in all sectors, including those in overall decline (Figure 32). Moreover, the supply of skills has also changed correspondingly: the proportion of high skilled labour increased from 5 to around 9 per cent of the working age population while the proportion of low skill workers fell from 39 to 26 per cent. Finally, demographic developments have also been important. Since the early 1980s, the work force in western Germany has increased markedly as a result of a temporary increase in the number of young people joining the work force and immigration of around 2 million ethnic Germans, many of whom were young and well educated.

Figure 30. **EMPLOYMENT AND THE LABOUR FORCE**

Per cent of working age population[1]

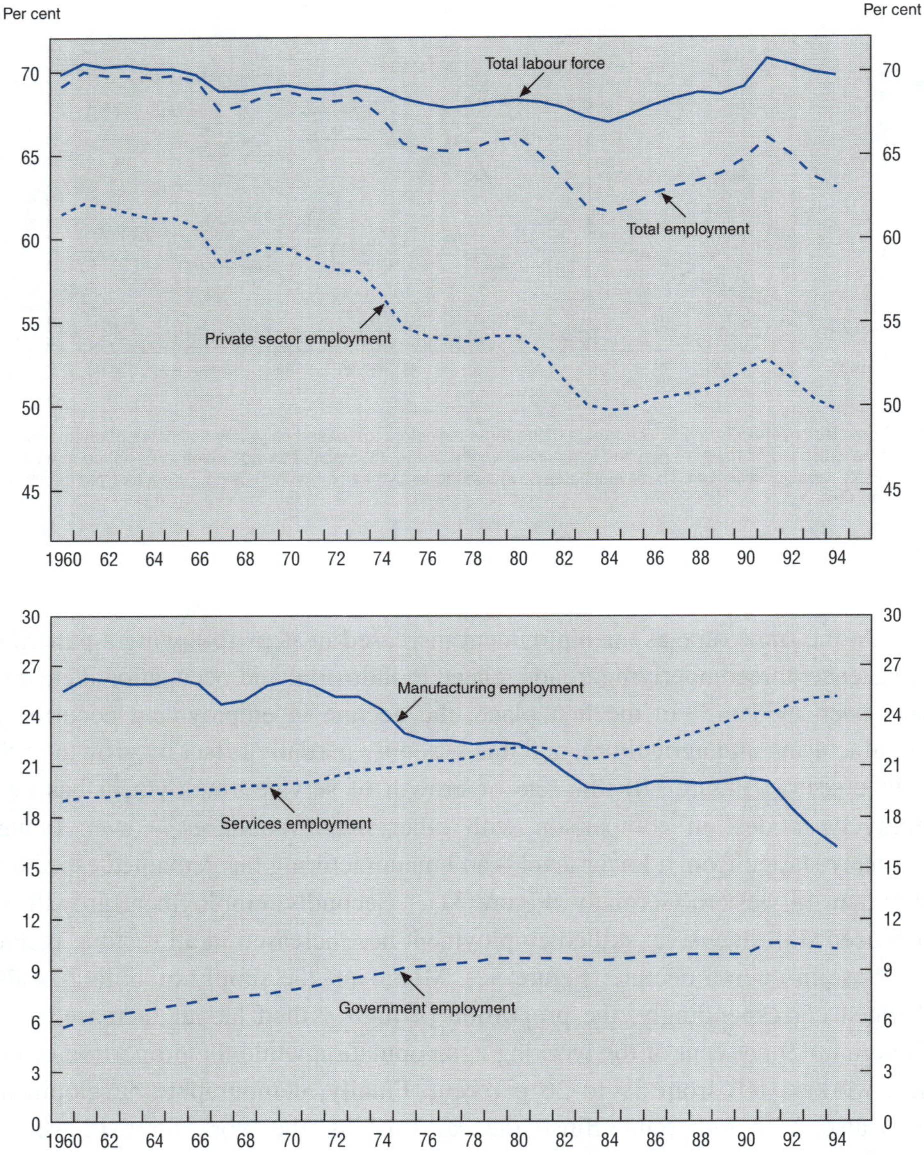

1. Population from 15 to 64 years. From 1991, data refer to Germany.

Source: Statistisches Bundesamt and OECD, *Labour Force Statistics.*

Figure 31. **THE GROWTH OF EMPLOYMENT IN INDUSTRY AND SERVICES**

Average annual growth 1981 to 1994

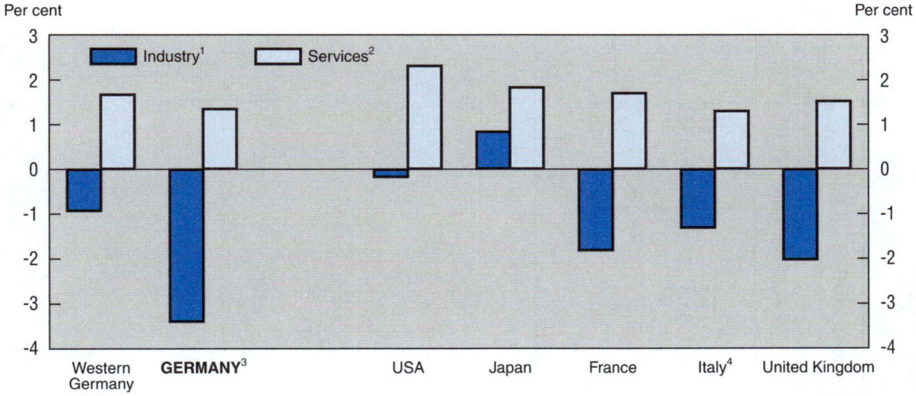

1. Civilian employment. Includes ISIC 2 to 5.
2. Civilian employment. Includes ISIC 6 to 9.
3. Average annual growth rate 1991 to 1994.
4. 1994 based on the first three quarters.

Source: OECD, *Labour Force Statistics.*

Figure 32. **EMPLOYMENT GROWTH HAS BEEN SKILL-INTENSIVE**

Percentage change in employment in western Germany, 1973-1989

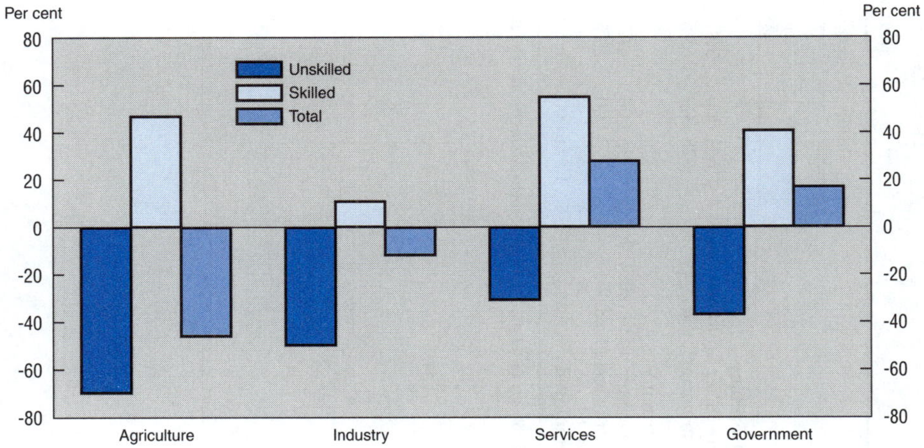

Source: Klodt, H. and J. Stehn, *Standort Deutschland: Strukturelle Herausforderungen im neuen Europa*, Tübingen, 1995.

Table 23. **Characteristics of the long-term unemployed**

Registered unemployed, end September 1995

	Gender (per cent of group total)			Age (per cent of group total)					Health problems (in per cent)	Without qualifications
	Total	Men	Women	40 to 44 years	45 to 49 years	50 to 54 years	55 to 59 years	60 to 64 years		
Western Germany										
Unemployed for up to one year	1 661 000	56.1	43.9	9.6	8.0	7.8	12.4	2.3	21.4	44.8
Long-term unemployed	828 000	55.5	44.5	9.0	9.9	14.6	33.3	6.3	36.2	50.0
Eastern Germany										
Unemployed for up to one year	735 000	41.5	58.5	12.5	9.5	11.7	12.2	0.7	14.8	19.3
Long-term unemployed	297 000	23.3	76.7	12.0	10.4	16.3	23.6	1.5	18.4	25.3
Total unemployed	3 521 000									

Source: Gröbner, G. *et al.,* ''Langzeitarbeitslosenprogramm'', *Bundesarbeitsblatt,* No. 4, 1995.

These developments are reflected in both the level and pattern of unemployment. A notable feature of German labour market performance is the high proportion of long-term unemployed in total unemployment: around a third in 1995 on the basis of registered unemployment. In western Germany 60 per cent of the long-term unemployed were older than 45 years of age and 50 per cent were over the age of 50 (Table 23). They also had a higher incidence of health problems and were less qualified than other unemployed; these characteristics are

Table 24. **The role of small- and medium-sized firms in employment**

Increasing importance of SMEs in employment...

A. Structure of employment in industry, 1960-1992

	Size of establishment by employment Per cent of employment			
	1-19	20-99	100-499	500 and more
1960	4.0	15.0	28.0	53.0
1970	3.9	14.6	28.0	53.4
1980	0.8	17.3	29.5	52.4
1985	0.8	17.2	29.6	52.4
1990	0.7	17.2	30.3	51.9
1992	0.8	17.7	31.0	50.4
	New States			
1991	0.6	11.0	28.2	60.2
1992	1.2	19.8	33.4	45.6

Source: Statistisches Bundesamt.

... and declining employement in large establishments

B. Changes in the level of employment

	Size of establishment by employment (Old States) Thousands				
	1-99	100-199	200-499	> 500	Total
1960-1970	112.3	93.0	144.1	485.5	834.9
1970-1980	–241.1	–78.0	–139.4	–705.3	–1 163.8
1980-1985	–132.6	–66.8	–124.7	–353.7	–677.8
1985-1990	73.0	63.6	123.2	204.4	464.2
1990-1992	14.4	8.6	–1.1	–200.8	–178.9

Source: Dicke, H., ''Wege zu mehr Beschäftigung – die Rolle kleiner und mittlerer Unternehmen'', *Die Weltwirtschaft,* No. 4, 1995.

even more pronounced when compared with the population at large. For nearly two-thirds of the long-term unemployed, the current unemployment spell is their first and they have a long work history in industry characterised by few changes between employers.[69] By contrast, Germany has been very successful in maintaining low rates of youth unemployment and the youth employment/population ratio is significantly above the OECD average (Figure 28, panel B).

At the same time as industrial employment has declined, there has been a clear restructuring toward smaller enterprises. Since 1985 employment growth in establishments with fewer than 500 employees has been significantly stronger than in larger plants, which have actually suffered shrinking employment since the late 1980s (Table 24). Smaller establishments have been particularly dynamic and this is even more evident from the preliminary information regarding the service sector.[70] However, the share of employment in industry accounted for by firms with less than 100 employees has been very stable at around 18 per cent, because of a declining share in the smallest establishments.

The special case of the new Länder

Eastern Germany accounts for almost one third of total German unemployment compared with around one-fifth of the workforce. The discrepancy is even greater if account is taken of early retirement and job creation schemes (Table 25).[71] A unique feature is that the female unemployment rate is about twice as high as the male rate. Long-term unemployment is nearly the same as in the west, accounting for around a third of the unemployed in 1994, but its concentration among older workers is not so pronounced. However, these similarities are more apparent than real, since extensive active labour market programmes have sometimes served, in effect, to reclassify the unemployed into a shorter duration category. Although GDP has been growing since 1992 at an annual rate of between 6 and 9 per cent, unemployment has declined by only 1 percentage point; regular, unsubsidised, employment has picked up modestly, but the effect on total employment has been offset by a reduction in active labour market measures.

A notable feature of the transition of the east German economy has been a massive decline in manufacturing employment from 3.5 million in 1989 to 1.2 million in 1993. The reduction is even greater if those employed in active labour market measures in manufacturing companies are excluded. For those

Table 25. **Labour market developments in eastern Germany, 1989-95**

Thousands

	1989 I	1991 I	1993 I	1995 I
Working age population	10 721	10 527[1]	10 505[2]	10 540[3]
Labour force participation rate (per cent)	92	81[1]	77[2]	76[3]
Total employment	9 836	7 462	6 183	6 411
Including commuters to western Germany	. .	7 908	6 738	6 961
Employment in manufacturing	3 509	2 171	1 120	1 032
Total persons in labour market measures		1 917	1 565	984
Job creation (ABM)[5]	. .	147	237	213
Job creation (Article 249H)[5]	. .	. .	14	109
Short-time work (full-time equivalents)	. .	1 078	89	36
Full-time training	. .	170	368	255
Early retirement	. .	521	857	370
Total "regular" employment	9 836	6 236	5 843	6 051
Total unemployment		843	1 100	1 003
Unemployment rate (per cent)		9.5	15.1	14.3
"With hidden unemployment"[4] (per cent)			29.0	26.0

1. Second half-year 1991.
2. Second half-year 1993.
3. Second half-year 1994.
4. Excluding self-employed in the definition of the labour force.
5. ABM refers to general work creation measures which are also available in western Germany. A special programme was also developed for eastern Germany covering, *inter alia,* social services, environmental improvements and youth assistance (Article 249H of the employment promotion law).

Source: *Employment Observatory East Germany,* European Commission 1995, No. 16/17, and further sources cited therein.

remaining in manufacturing, employment is now likely to be in small to medium-sized firms (Table 24). At the same time, there has been a significant growth in construction which now accounts for about 17 per cent of GDP. As noted in Chapter I, this sector is currently under severe pressure to downsize.

Policy requirements

A strategy for a sustained reduction of unemployment has to comprise a broad range of measures aimed at improving short and long-term labour market flexibility. Short-term flexibility is called for to prevent workers from falling into unemployment – and to avoid their remaining in unemployment. To a large degree this has to be provided by ensuring that both the aggregate wage level and relative wages correspond to productivity levels at full employment. Just as importantly, labour market institutions need to be flexible enough to allow people to re-enter employment once unemployed. High standards in the education system, adequate training of the work force and activation of the unemployed to prevent loss of human capital are basic elements in the *OECD Jobs Strategy* to foster economic growth and secure rising living standards. An overall strategy to foster flexibility thus calls not just for a reassessment of the wage formation process and the incentives built into the tax and transfer systems, but also of the process of human capital acquisition and product-market competition which should ensure an efficient allocation of resources in the economy at large.

The above elements of a comprehensive strategy are particularly relevant in view of the scope and nature of the unemployment problem confronting Germany. The German labour market has needed to absorb a large number of immigrants as well as to facilitate inter-sectoral shifts in production and a changing skill composition of employment. Even allowing for the special situation caused by re-unification, success has been modest judged by the level and persistence of unemployment, and by the low level of labour utilisation occasioned by early retirement. The long duration of benefits has encouraged older, unskilled, industrial workers to undertake prolonged job search and to maintain a high reservation wage since replacement rates are linked not to current employment opportunities but to past earnings. In combination with early retirement, this has led to a large part of the unemployed becoming ''outsiders'' from the viewpoint of wage negotiations: the German labour market has thus become dualistic and wage negotiations more concerned with job preservation than with employment growth. Restrictive employment regulations relating to hiring and dismissals reinforce this tendency. High wage demands, together with non-wage costs arising from the transfer system, have reduced labour demand and hindered the inter-sectoral restructuring of the economy. In particular, the development of the service sector may have been retarded, although the regulatory framework is also important in this area. The situation in eastern Germany is more extreme. Public transfers are underpinning a process of rapid real wage convergence between east and west at levels incompatible with full employment. The net result is that, while the economy is growing strongly, it is still not self-sustaining, and the increase in employment remains inadequate to make large inroads into unemployment. A synopsis of the recommendations made below, which address these issues, can be found in Box 3.

Box 3. **The OECD Jobs Strategy: synopsis of recommendations for Germany**

The *OECD Jobs Study* sets out a strategy based on nine recommendations for improving the ability of OECD economies to cope with structural change, through enhancing the ability to adjust and to adapt, and increasing the capacity to innovate and be creative. The nine distinct policy areas covered included the macreconomic policy framework and the creation and diffusion of technological know-how. With respect to labour and product-market flexibility it identified the need for initiatives in the following areas: working-time flexibility, the entrepreneurial climate, wage and labour cost flexibility, employment security provisions, active labour market policies, labour force skills and competencies, and unemployment and related benefits systems.

The government's new 50-point strategy for growth and employment will, together with the proposals to revise the employment promotion law (AFG) substantially, if fully implemented, go part of the way to redress the causes of weak labour market performance. Nevertheless, the German benefits system would still remain generous with strong disincentives for active job search, in particular for low-skilled and for older workers with an employment history in industry.

Following from the detailed review of labour market and employment performance, and the assessment of policy requirements, this chapter identifies the need for Germany to move ahead in the following areas:

Increase wage and labour cost flexibility

- *Greater wage differentiation with respect to skills, regions, sectors and firms should be encouraged.* Existing possibilities for plant-level bargaining need to be exploited more frequently by collective contracts. The trend of the wage bargaining system towards framework agreements that leave greater scope and flexibility for plant-level bargaining needs to be supported and not hindered by inappropriate laws. At the same time, unemployed individuals need more scope for pricing themselves back into jobs. Opening clauses in wage contracts need to be encouraged and the social security system reformed to stimulate re-entry into work. *The tendency toward more differentiated wage developments in eastern Germany needs to be supported,* with an increasing number of firms setting wages and conditions outside industry agreements. The government as a major employer could give the lead in setting wage convergence more in line with economic fundamentals.
- *The employment of older workers needs to be facilitated.* Increased wage flexibility should help by lowering the relative wages of older workers, but for this to

(continued on next page)

(continued)

happen the financial incentives for early retirement need to be reduced significantly.

Reform unemployment and related benefit systems

- *Overly generous benefits, including a long duration of benefit payments, should be reduced* in order to lower reservation wages and reduce the obstacles to employment of low-skilled workers. The criteria for not accepting job offers needs to be further restricted and penalties for refusal strengthened. Job-search controls and benefit sanctions need tightening: benefit recipients should be controlled more often than quarterly. Incentives could be given to recipients to accept lower-paid jobs by providing some employment-conditional transfer to them.
- *Social security contribution rates need to be lowered especially for low earners.* Preferably this could be financed through expenditure cuts. If the financing of benefits were to be shifted partly to a wider tax base, pronounced improvements in employment could not be expected over the longer term. Incentives for the social partners to take into account the employment consequences of their actions should not be reduced.
- *The personal tax system needs to be drastically simplified and marginal tax rates lowered in order to improve work incentives.*
- *The generosity of sickness benefits should be reduced.* Present arrangements are exceptionally generous and contain incentives which lead to widespread abuse. Legal provisions which hinder the ability of employers to control absences need to be relaxed. Incentives to avoid abuse need to be strengthened: the government as a major employer should take the lead by, for example, reducing replacement rates for initial periods of sickness or introducing a waiting period.

Increase working-time flexibility

- *Regulations which underpin some inappropriate aspects of collective agreements need to be reformed.* Flexible working practices are underdeveloped, and although regulatory provisions are often less stringent than those established by collective agreements, they sometimes underpin them. In particular, the possibility for renewing fixed-term contracts needs to be liberalised.
- *Part-time work needs to be facilitated.* Current proposals to make part-time jobs and casual jobs liable for social security contributions could be premature unless accompanied by wider reforms of the benefits system, possibly including a reduction of rates for the lower-paid.
- *The agreement to end early retirement in its present form is welcome* even though the grandfather clauses are extremely generous and fiscal pressures will remain

(continued on next page)

(continued)

for some time. The subsidisation of part-time employment for older workers linked to new hirings does not address the need to improve labour utilisation.

Reform employment security provisions

- *Dismissal protection, both collective and individual, needs to be reformed.* The object is to encourage new hirings by reducing the uncertainty and costs of dismissal. Courts need to be issued with a clearer set of criteria for making judgements about unfair dismissal and to interpret social responsibility provisions in mass layoffs.

Expand and enhance active labour market policies

- *Active labour market policies need to become more cost-effective.* They currently act more as an extension of unemployment transfers and should be excluded from the requalifying period for unemployment benefits. Programmes need to be more closely targeted on at-risk groups: the special programmes for the long-term unemployed which have been relatively successful need to be expanded at the cost of other programmes. The current practice to base employment subsidies on wages below market rates should be continued and if necessary, strengthened.

Improve labour force skills and competencies

- *Decisions have to be made about how to preserve or restore the attractiveness of the dual system* and its relationship to higher education needs to be clarified. The dual system of vocational education and training has proved effective but circumstances are changing and a large and growing number of young people are moving on to higher education.
- *Higher education needs to be aimed at shorter and more occupationally-oriented studies.*

Enhance the creation and diffusion of technological know-how

- *Taxation and legal changes need to be made in order to foster the development of venture capital markets, and regulatory barriers to new activities should be reduced.* However, new subsidies, either direct or indirect, in the form of taxation expenditures need to be avoided.

(continued on next page)

(continued)

Nurture an entrepreneurial climate

- *The establishment of new enterprises needs to be facilitated.* The proposal to defer tax payments in the early years of an enterprise is useful and should be enacted. In view of the high level of bankruptcies in eastern Germany, efforts still need to be made to increase the knowledge of the new owners of many of these enterprises. An overall reduction of the tax burden is nevertheless the most effective long-term measure to promote entrepreneurship.

Increase product market competition

- *Major deregulation efforts are still needed* since regulation remains an important impediment to economic growth and increased employment. Planning approvals still need to be simplified. Shop-closing hours should be liberalised further.
- *Competition in the network sectors (electricity, gas, telecommunication) needs to be encouraged* and exclusive concessions more tightly controlled. Regulatory and competition arrangements need to be closely coordinated.
- *Services provided by communities need to be more closely market-tested and competition between public and private suppliers placed on an equal basis.* In this respect harmonisation of the VAT regime is overdue. The preferential treatment of non-profit making organisations in supplying social services should be examined.
- *Privatisation opportunities need to be pursued.* While substantial progress has been achieved at the federal level, activity needs to be stepped up at lower levels of government.
- *Further reductions of direct and indirect industrial subsidies are necessary.* Support measures in the new *Länder* providing equity and funds for firms in difficulty need to be closely controlled in order to prevent a distortion of competition.

Enhancing the ability to adjust and adapt

Empirical studies point to two key features of the German labour market which have contributed to the high persistence of unemployment in the wake of both demand and supply shocks: *i)* wages adjust to unemployment in the short term, but the effect is short-lived; and *ii)* labour demand adjusts to wages at an extraordinarily slow pace, adjustment in the short run occurring through changes in hours of work.[72] Underlying these aggregate relationships are a variety of institutions which determine the behaviour of the social partners. Many of these are not directly under the control of policy makers, but they are often underpinned by legal provisions and institutions which the following sections set out to identify.

The wage formation system

Increases in real labour costs were high relative to productivity gains throughout most of the 1970s, resulting in downward pressure on profits and disincentives for hiring and for investment. From 1982, however, real wage growth in the business sector persistently lagged productivity growth and the share of profits in business-sector value-added rose, thereby partially correcting the excesses of the 1970's (Figure 33); the rate of return on investment recovered. Wage moderation was accompanied by a rise in private sector employment up to the 1990s. However, since reunification real wages have risen faster than productivity in the new *Länder*. In the old states wages surged in 1995 (see Chapter I), while employment has declined and unemployment has increased. This recent experience raises a question mark about the flexibility of real labour costs in the face of rising unemployment – and whether, in the absence of reforms, the present level of unemployment would remain at high levels for some time.

Aggregate wage formation is characterised by strong short-term flexibility, as evidenced by a high semi-elasticity of nominal wages with respect to unemployment. However, a feature of the wage adjustment process which is of particular importance is that wages appear to be negatively influenced by both the level and change of unemployment, indicating a substantial degree of hysteresis: after an initial impact the unemployed have only a weak influence over the wage formation process, so that unemployment tends to persist. Indeed, econometric estimates suggest that the impact of long-term unemployment on wage developments is only one third of the influence of unemployment of shorter duration, suggesting a marked insider/outsider effect at the aggregate level.[73] The most recent instance seems to be the increase in wages in Spring 1995 which followed signs of an emerging economic recovery, but occurred before unemployment had started to fall.

Of equal importance to the intertemporal flexibility of wages is their structure and dispersion, and in this area important weaknesses are also apparent. Despite rising unemployment of unskilled workers and major changes in the pattern of labour demand, the wage structure appears to have been relatively

Figure 33. **REAL WAGE, PRODUCTIVITY AND LABOUR SHARES IN THE BUSINESS SECTOR**[1]

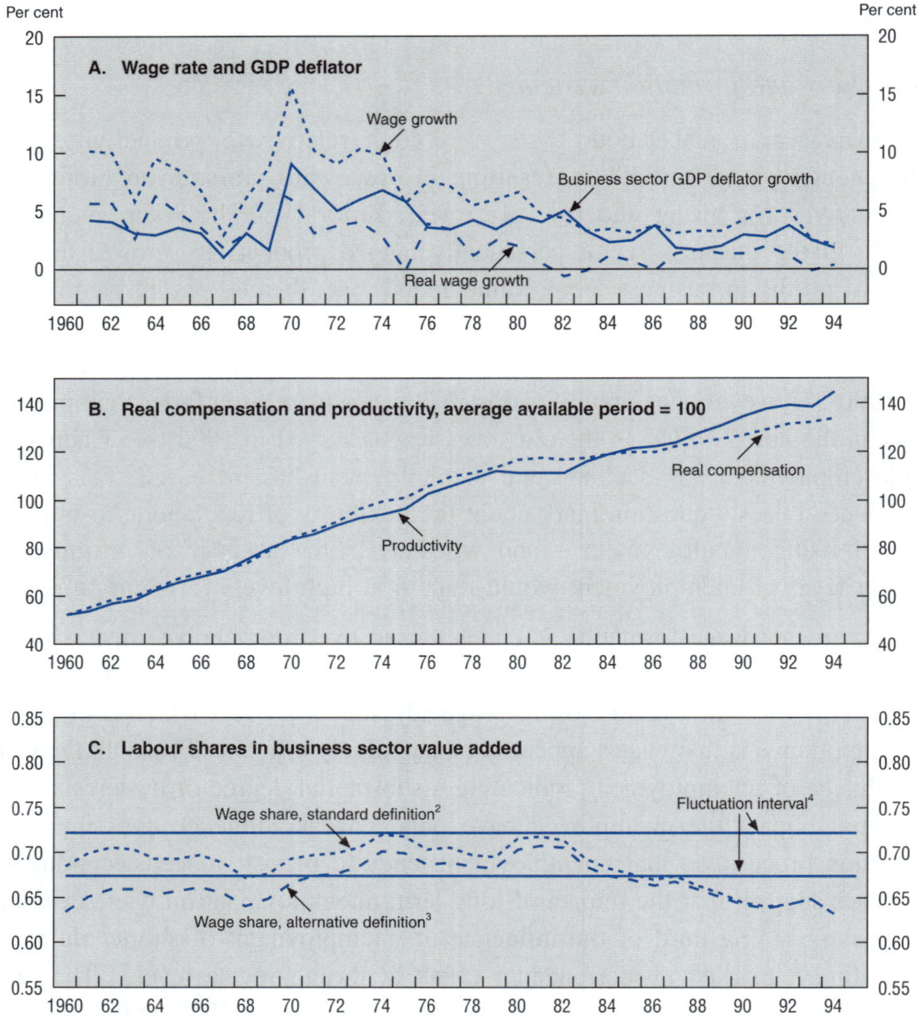

1. Western Germany.
2. Calculated by imputing a wage compensation to self-employed equal to average compensation for wage earners.
3. Calculated by imputing a wage compensation to self-employed rising from 70 per cent of average compensation in 1960 to 100 per cent in 1993.
4. Horizontal lines show fluctuation interval over the period up to and including 1980. They have been calculated as the mean wage share based on the first method, +/- twice is standard deviation.

Source: OECD.

unaffected. Germany (together with France) is exceptional among the major seven economies in that there was no tendency over the 1980s for the earnings distribution to widen; indeed the opposite occurred (Figure 34). Reflecting this development, the growth in real wages of low-paid workers over the 1980s was the highest in the OECD (around 2.5 per cent annual average),[74] raising the question why the employment record was not in fact even worse. In addition, inter-sectoral/regional wage relativities also appear to be sticky. A marked dispersion in regional unemployment rates in the context of a rather narrow regional dispersion of wage increases suggests a high degree of inter-sectoral wage rigidity, in addition to low geographical mobility of labour (Figure 35): the regional distribution of unemployment has tended to reflect the sectoral problems caused by structural change – modern services and high-tech manufacturing being characteristic of low-unemployment states as Baden-Würtenberg, while high unemployment rates are found in traditional heavy-industry and mining areas as Saarland and North-Rhine Westphalia.

Figure 34. **EARNINGS OF HIGH-PAID MALE WORKERS RELATIVE TO LOW-PAID MALE WORKERS**[1]

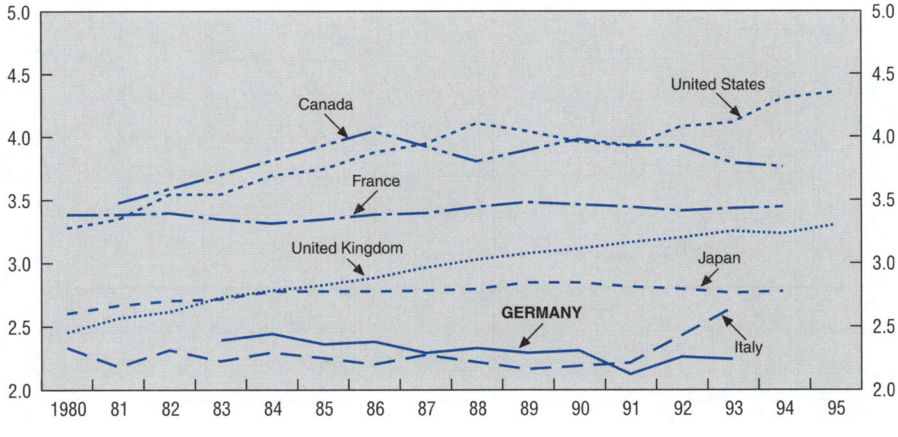

1. Ratio of upper earnings limit of the 9th decile of male workers to the upper limit of the first decile.
Source: OECD, *Employment Outlook*, 1996.

Figure 35. **REGIONAL UNEMPLOYMENT RATES AND WAGE GROWTH**

Per cent

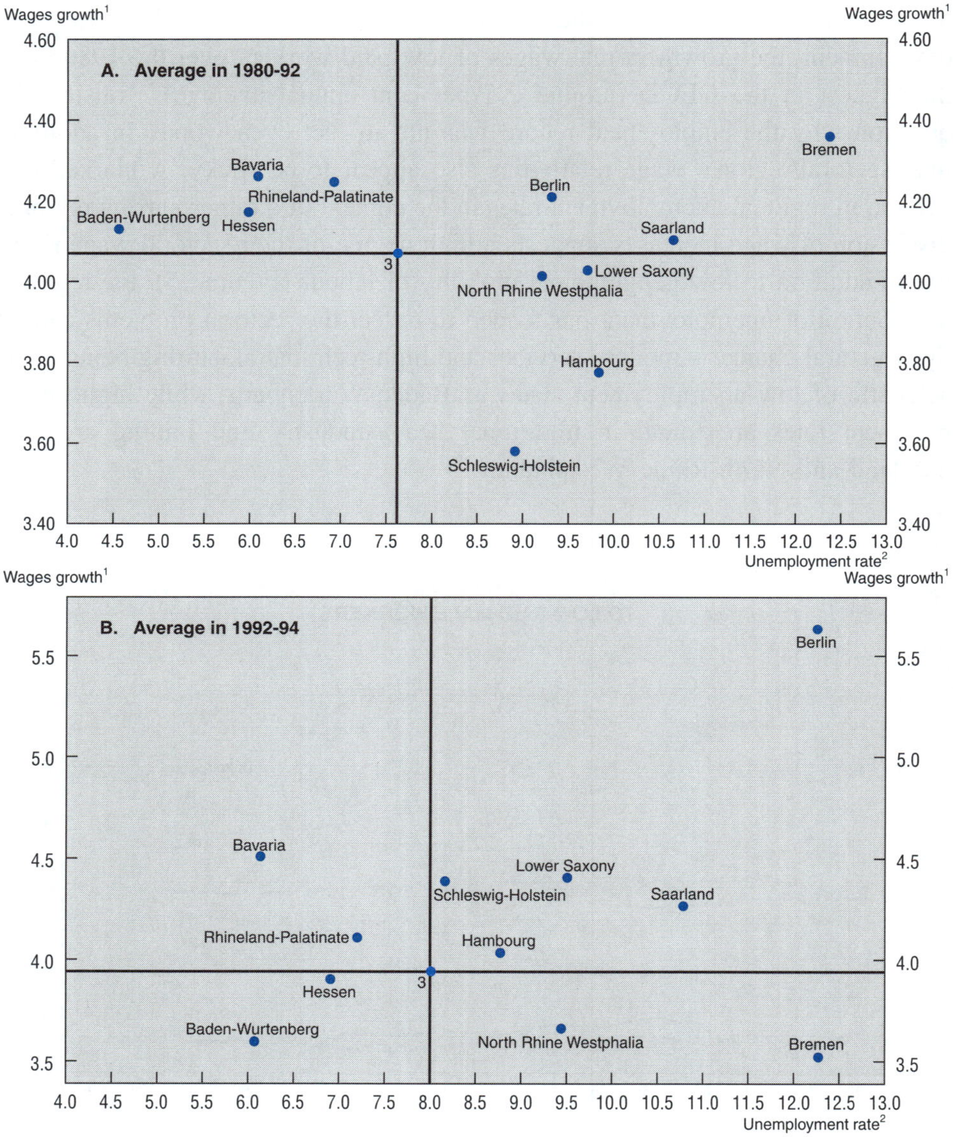

1. Blue-collar workers in industry.
2. Per cent of dependent labour force.
3. Country average.

Source: Statistisches Bundesamt, *Statistisches Jahrbuch,* various issues.

Underlying this pattern of wage development is the institution of the industry-wide wage agreement (*Flächentarifvertrag*) covering about 90 per cent of employees in western Germany.[75] Most agreements are signed for each sector at regional level, with national co-ordination assured by sectoral associations on both sides. There is no formal co-ordination between sectors, but a considerable degree of conformity is ensured by the tendency to accept pilot agreements in certain sectors – often the metal industry – as models for other parts of the labour market. Even within a sector it is customary for a pilot agreement to be established in one region, and then for other regions to take this over with minimal changes. This system of pattern bargaining may introduce an element of persistence in the form of wage staggering: as happened in 1995 with the metal agreement, adjustment to a labour market shock may be delayed by the heavy influence exerted on contracts made later in the wage round by contracts concluded earlier.

In addition to custom, the system is based on a broad legal framework. Under the federal constitution the government is excluded from a direct role in wage negotiations (*Tarifautonomie*) and the social partners are excluded from the provisions of anti-trust law. Works councils (*Betriebsrat*), which are compulsory for firms with more than five employees, can only take part in wage negotiations if allowed by the respective collective contract, though they may negotiate and discuss specific issues related to working conditions on their own initiative. The government may extend the provisions of an agreement to non-contracting parties (*Allgemeinverbindlichkeitserklärung*), though in practice this is not as important for wage agreements as for working conditions.[76] Membership of employers' associations is not compulsory and is organised on a regional basis with little direct bargaining power often accruing to the national associations. By contrast, the unions are highly centralised and exercise a key role even though only about one third of employees are members. Unlike in some other countries, the right to strike is balanced by a lock-out right on the employer side.[77] However, strike activity in Germany is very low by international standards.

Under conditions of increased international competition and rapid technological change, the current wage bargaining system may produce too little wage differentiation either regionally, by skill or by enterprise.[78] There are three reasons for this. First, bargaining covers an industry comprising many different goods markets which frequently have very little to do with one another, either in terms of profitability or labour skills. The difficult economic conditions in eastern Germany have made the contradiction even more apparent. Second, the employers' side is extremely heterogeneous, bringing together, for example, large firms and small/medium-sized enterprises. Voting rights and bargaining influence arising from greater resources give the large enterprises a disproportionate say in the outcome of the negotiations and this may be detrimental to the interests of the smaller firms which are, in aggregate, often more important for employment in the sector. Third, increased pressure to minimise costs has made firms sensitive to workplace arrangements. Industry-wide agreements, it is argued, provide too little flexibility for enterprises in this area.

A tangible result of such criticisms is that an increasing number of established firms are leaving the employers' associations and are seeking to conclude their own agreements directly. Little information is currently available about the nature of this development, but some observers believe that many contracts concern work conditions (see below) rather than wages which are for the moment taken from the industry agreements. The situation is different in the new *Länder*. About three quarters of firms (employing around a third of the work force) are not members of employers' associations and the tendency is for this proportion to increase. Nearly a third of firms, employing some 16 per cent of workers in industry, acknowledge paying wages lower than those set in industry agreements, but the actual number (both members and non-members of employers' associations alike) is believed to be much greater.[79]

If the tendency continues in both the new and old *Länder,* legal changes might be required in several areas. First, it might be useful to extend the legal powers of the works councils (*Betriebsrat*) allowing them to also finalise contracts concerning wages. Secondly, if unions were to regularly bargain with individual enterprises rather than with employers' associations, it may prove necessary to re-examine the present legal rights and obligations. In particular, the exemption from cartel law would have to be reconsidered since the balance of power, on which the current exemption rests, would cease to exist.

In response to the above pressures, enterprises are attempting to use the flexibility allowed under current arrangements, but there is also a rising tendency – albeit still in its early days and limited to special sectors – for industry agreements to set only minimum or framework conditions. With respect to the former, flexibility mainly relates to working conditions and there appears to have been a noticeable increase in the number of contracts agreed at lower levels.[80] However, the nature of industry bargaining is also changing. For example, the 1996 agreement in the textile and clothing industry contains an ''opening clause'' which allows for wage increases to be set aside if warranted by the financial state of the enterprise. Moreover, decisions at the enterprise level do not have to be approved by the union and by the employers' association. Increased wage flexibility has also been introduced in the chemical industry through opening clauses offering lower wage rates for a period to previously long-term unemployed persons. By contrast, in the building industry a minimum wage was agreed which was intended to be extended to non-contracting parties. This was part of a restrictive arrangement to protect German construction workers against low-wage competition from other EU countries (*Entsendegesetz*).[81]

In sum, while the system of wage bargaining is evolving, it does not produce a level and structure of wages compatible with sustained full employment. The role for policy has therefore to concentrate on establishing a more appropriate legal framework for collective bargaining and to ensuring that economic signals are effective. More flexibility would be possible within the existing legal framework and the aim should be to facilitate the decentralisation of wage bargaining – for example, by extending the negotiating powers of works councils – but how this will evolve will ultimately depend on the social partners. However, policy is more powerful with respect to market signals. Regulations concerning employment conditions, dismissals, early retirement, and eligibility for – and generosity of – unemployment and related social welfare benefits condition the economic pressures facing the market participants engaged in collective bargaining. In the following it is argued that these signals have been weak and need to be strengthened in order to stimulate efficient bargaining outcomes.

Increasing the flexibility of employment and working time

Hourly labour costs in Germany are amongst the highest in the world, while the adjustment speed of employment to labour demand is amongst the slowest, with overtime and short-time work – which is compensated by the social insurance system – taking up the slack (Table 26). Contributing to the increase in hourly wage costs has been the marked reduction in the work week since the mid 1980s which has not been matched by increased flexibility in working times: the incidence of flexible working practices (*i.e.* shift work, night work and weekend

Table 26. **Levels of hourly compensation costs for production workers in manufacturing**

In common currency at current exchange rates
Index, United States = 100

	1980	1985	1990	1992	1993	1994	1995[1]
United States	100	100	100	100	100	100	100
Germany[2]	**125**	**74**	**147**	**157**	**154**	**160**	**154**
Japan	56	49	86	101	114	125	114
France	91	58	102	105	97	100	97
Italy	83	59	119	121	96	95	96
United Kingdom	77	48	85	89	76	80	79
Canada	88	84	106	105	98	92	96
Portugal	21	12	25	32	27	27	29
Spain	60	36	76	83	69	67	71
EU	99	60	114	120	109	115	111
Asian NIEs	12	13	25	30	31	34	..

1. Estimate.
2. West Germany.

Source: Bureau of Labor Statistics (1995), "International Comparisons of Hourly Compensation Costs for Production Workers in Manufacturing", *Report 893,* Washington, June 1994.

work) is significantly lower than in all other European countries[82] (Table 27). As a result, the operating hours of capital equipment appear to be very low by international standards, contributing to cost pressures (Figure 36). German employers make extensive use of overtime in order to adjust their labour demand requirements. This is costly, with premia often in the range of 50 to 70 per cent. However, the reason for this pattern is to be found in industry wage agreements: while labour market regulation is significant in each area, it often only constitutes a minimum, with collective agreements specifying more restrictive conditions.[83]

Regulations are particularly restrictive with respect to fixed-term contracts, which cannot be renewed. Contracts are normally granted for up to 18 months, though contracts for 24 months are permitted under some conditions. Lifting these restrictions could have important effects: a survey concluded that between 1.5 and 3 per cent of all new hires by private firms in 1992 would not have taken place in the absence of fixed-term contracts.[84] Moreover, there was also evidence that about half the workers hired under these provisions had their contracts converted to normal ones at the end of the period.

Table 27. **Summary measures of labour market regulation**

Rank indicators[1]

	Protection of regular workers against dismissals	Regulation of fixed-term contracts	Regulation of temporary work agency organised employment	Restrictions on normal weekly hours	Restrictions on overtime, flexible weekend and night work	Summary variables: Restrictions on regular employee work	Summary variables: Restrictions on overall employment in general[2]
Belgium	4.0	11.0	8.0	10.0	5.0	4.0	5.0
Denmark	2.0	2.0	5.0	11.0	2.0	2.0	2.0
France	5.5	8.0	3.0	7.0	7.5	7.0	6.0
Germany	**7.0**	**9.0**	**6.0**	**8.5**	**6.0**	**7.0**	**7.0**
Greece	8.0	7.0	10.0	4.0	10.0	9.0	10.0
Ireland	3.0	2.0	1.5	2.0	3.5	3.0	3.0
Italy	9.0	10.0	10.0	6.0	3.5	5.0	8.0
Netherlands	5.5	4.5	4.0	8.5	7.5	7.0	4.0
Portugal	10.5	6.0	7.0	3.0	11.0	11.0	11.0
Spain	10.5	4.5	10.0	5.0	9.0	10.0	9.0
United Kingdom	1.0	2.0	1.5	1.0	1.0	1.0	1.0

1. The rank of the country with the least regulation in each column has the Rank 1. Each column is derived as the unweighted average of the ranks of individual items such as difficulty of dismissal. The summary variables are simple additions of all variables in rank form.
2. Self-employment including employers and unpaid family workers.

Source: Grubb, D. and W. Wells, (1993), ''Employment regulation and patterns of work in EC countries'', OECD *Economic Studies,* No. 21.

Figure 36. **LOW RUNNING TIMES ARE LEADING TO HIGH COSTS**

1994

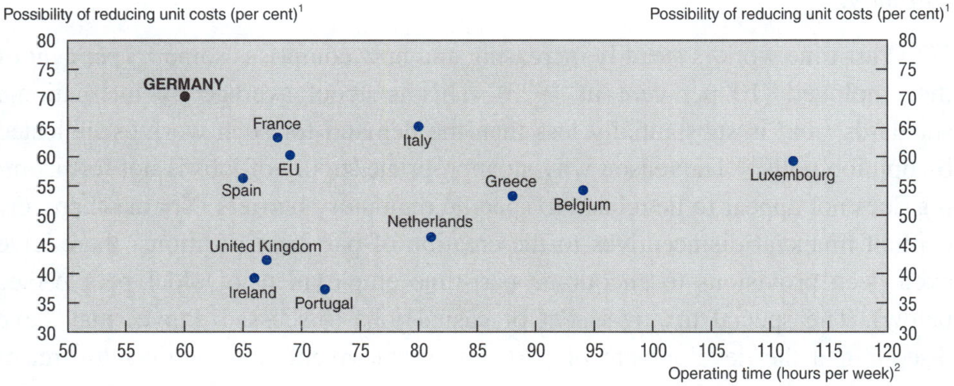

1. Percentage of firms responding affirmatively to the question which stated that they could reduce their unit costs if operating hours were extended.
2. Firms were asked about their operating hours. The answers were weighted by the number employed and then aggregated. This is the "direct method". See European Economy, page 27, for a discussion of other approaches.

Source: "Performance of the European Union Labour Market", *European Economy,* No. 3, 1995.

Casual jobs (less than 15 hours per week) earning less than DM 590 per month (DM 500 in the new *Länder*) are exempted from having to pay social security contributions and other regulations are also minimal. Although estimates of the effects of these dispensations vary widely, a recent study found that around 4.5 million persons undertook such work in 1992, mainly in the service sectors.[85] Such jobs have been particularly successful in helping to provide income opportunities for marginal workers, including housewives and students. There have, nevertheless, been criticisms on two grounds. First, some employees are deprived of social security while at the same time reducing the revenue base of the social security system. Second, the system is said to be abused, with employers splitting a full-time job into two or more posts so as to minimise costs, while employees may illegally have several such positions. These criticisms appear exaggerated. People who are employed in this manner are often covered for sickness and for other benefits by other members of their family.[86] More importantly, there is a reasonable doubt that many of these jobs would survive if full social security contributions were to be paid; estimates of lost revenues are probably biased upwards. Abuse is certainly a problem, but it is hard to see how this would be resolved by terminating the programme, an outcome which would be likely to encourage more "black" work. Attention should rather be directed to lowering the high marginal effective rates of taxation (including social security contributions) for low income/low productivity work where evasion might be stimulated currently.

Part-time work is steadily increasing and now comprises some 15 per cent of the employed (10 per cent in 1973). This is about average by international standards[87] but is substantially less than the demand for such work as indicated by opinion polls.[88] The reason why an appropriate supply of jobs is not forthcoming does not appear to be related to specific regulatory barriers. Nor are there any explicit financial disincentives to the creation of part-time positions; there have even been provisions to encourage part-time employment of older people (see below). The special tax treatment of casual jobs (discussed above) may have discouraged the development of part-time employment. The barriers to greater use of part-time arrangements rather seem to rest with the social partners themselves.

Many other regulatory barriers, legal provisions and court rulings would appear to inhibit labour flexibility and thereby ultimately reduce the level of employment. Among the two most often cited are the protection for new mothers and the extension of wage agreements to new owners. Post-natal leave is generous in Germany, extending to three months. During this time the employer is responsible for making up the difference between the previous net income of the mother and the allowance granted by the health funds (DM 25 per day). In addition, there is maternity leave extending up to three years during which time the employee has a right to return to their previous job after giving four weeks notice. Thus, the bulk of the costs falls not on the general tax payer but on specific employers. With respect to wage agreements, rulings by the courts inhibit enterprise restructuring and outsourcing. Article 613 of the Labour Code requires that all previous labour agreements be respected by new owners. This makes it difficult to restructure enterprises in receivership biasing the system towards liquidations. Moreover, the courts have also interpreted outsourcing in the same manner: for example, outsourcing cleaning to lower-cost suppliers can be prevented, unless the current employees are taken over, since it is held to constitute the transfer of a complete business operation to a new owner.

In response to the high and rising unemployment in industry, the current wage round has been marked by moves to increase work-time flexibility. A number of branches have already agreed to make the allocation of the work week more flexible (currently on average 37.5 hours, but only 35 hours in the metal industry) both within the week and over a period of up to six months to a year. The most important move concerns overtime, with the general tendency to introduce time accounts: over the period of, for example, a year, overtime above a threshold would not be associated with high penalty pay, but would be accumulated and later compensated by free time. For the unions, the scheme has the attraction of appearing to reduce overtime in favour of employment, and for the employer there would be less need to pay overtime rates. However, there are grounds to doubt that the introduction of annual time accounts will meet its goals unless carefully implemented. Research indicates that a considerable amount of overtime is worked by specific employees who cannot be easily augmented and whose additional free time would only lead to further costs. More importantly, although lowering overtime premia is important, unless the costs related to dismissals and therefore the costs of hiring – the most important barrier – are also reduced at the same time, the stimulus to further employment could remain limited.

Offsetting this picture of inflexible worktime practices is the high degree of flexibility shown by employees in moving between tasks at the factory level. Such flexibility, which has been crucial in maintaining productivity and international competitiveness, is related to the high level of training and overall education (see below). However, many observers feel that it is also related to a less definable factor, in particular, the close association between an employee and the enterprise. Whether this is a cause or a consequence of relatively low turnover rates is an open question.

Taxes and transfers

The unemployment benefits system, which consists of unemployment benefits and, on exhaustion of benefit, unemployment assistance, is discussed in detail in Chapter III. In addition, involuntary short-time work is also supported by income transfers. From the perspective of the unemployed, the system provides income replacement for an almost unlimited period (Box 4) and gives the recipient generous grounds for refusing a job offer without penalty. At the same time, the social assistance system ensures a subsistence level of income for an increasing number of families. Taken together, the incentive for active job search has been lowered, and reservation wages have been maintained at excessive levels so that working by marginal groups has been discouraged. The system has thus contributed to unemployment persistence.

Although conclusions need to remain cautious, the study commissioned by the OECD and described in Chapter III above, indicates that the three benefit systems taken together might be associated with high rates of income support in relation to the potential income from full-time employment (net replacement rate). Taking median earnings as a proxy for lifetime earnings possibilities,[89] a third of the unemployed might face net replacement rates above 80 per cent on a family income basis, and nearly two-thirds rates above 70 per cent. For those solely dependent on social assistance the situation is more difficult to summarise because work-force histories are highly variable. Nevertheless, studies indicate that net-replacement rates for some groups might also be quite high when measured by entrance wages in some of the service sectors.[90] High replacement rates diminish the incentives to work since the relatively small increase in net income may not offset either the disutility of work or the inclination to wait for a still better offer. Re-employment chances would be improved if benefits were more

Box 4. **Unemployment compensation**

Unemployment benefits are paid for six months or more, depending on the length of previous work, with the following ceilings depending on the person's age:

- Up to 41 years: 12 months of benefit after two years of work.
- 42-43 years: 18 months of benefits after three years and four months of work.
- 44-48 years: 22 months of benefits after three years and eight months of work.
- 49-53 years: 26 months of benefits after four years and four months of work.
- From 54 years: 32 months of benefits after five years and four months of work.

Work experience is calculated over the preceding seven years. One year's work and social security contributions are needed to requalify. Participation in job creation schemes serve this purpose as do some retraining schemes. Benefits are tax-free and replacement ratios based on standardised net income are 67 per cent for unemployed with at least one child, or 60 per cent otherwise up to a ceiling of 150 per cent of the average blue-collar wage.

Persons who remain unemployed after having exhausted their insurance entitlements may collect unemployment assistance indefinitely. The level of UA benefits in Germany depends on previous income and is means-tested, mainly with respect to the spouse's income. The standard rates and amounts of UA benefits are:

- 53 per cent of previous work income, or 57 per cent for persons with children.
- The average amount in 1994 was DM 1 030 per month in the old *Länder* and DM 810 in the new Länder.

Social assistance is comparable to unemployment benefits in several respects, and typically the municipalities will require the persons concerned to register at the labour office as well. Overall, only about one-third of SA recipients in Germany are treated as available for work, and thus unemployed — or fewer if one only considers those with SA as the principal income, excluding cases when SA is paid as a complement to UI or UA. Nevertheless the numbers are substantial in absolute terms: on average, over 400 000 work-available recipients relied upon SA as their main income in 1993. Social assistance is means tested against income and wealth (of the recipients and their spouses). The basic assistance for the head of household in 1995 was on average DM 525 to which must be added housing benefits (DM 486 on average) and one-time benefits (DM 84).

related to the wages applying to actual employment opportunities. For social assistance, this would imply a tightening of the "wage gap" principle which loosely determines the level of social assistance that accrues to a reference family in relation to the prospective market wage. With respect to unemployment benefits and unemployment assistance, gradually reducing replacement rates as the duration of the unemployment spell lengthens would provide an incentive to adjust reservation wages downwards.

At present, the benefits system exhibits extremely high effective marginal tax rates for certain categories of low-wage workers or households[91] as benefits are withdrawn, which reduces work incentives. Under standard conditions, a single recipient of social assistance at low levels of earnings faces an effective marginal tax rate of between 90 and 100 per cent as their labour earnings increase over a gross income range of DM 1 200. It is difficult to remedy this situation if existing benefit levels are maintained. A lowering of benefit levels could permit a more gradual withdrawal of benefits as income from employment increases. Reduced social security contributions at lower levels of income would also contribute to improved work incentives for low-wage workers.

Lost income from involuntary short-time work is replaced in the same proportion as unemployment benefits (*Kurzarbeitergeld*). However, collective agreements often provide for benefits to be topped-up by the employer to 70-90 per cent of previous earnings. The benefits were originally intended to reduce the need for cyclical layoffs by enterprises, so that benefits were paid for only six months, subject to a third of the workforce working 10 per cent fewer hours for at least four weeks. Over the years, the scheme has been extended to include short-time work in industries faced by structural adjustment, with benefit periods extended to two years under particular conditions. Such benefits were used extensively in the steel and coal industries in western Germany, often in connection with early retirement, and the benefit was extended in 1991/1992 to eastern Germany where short-time often meant working zero hours. The compensation paid in Germany in 1994 corresponded to about 135 000 full-time jobs, of which one-third were in the new *Länder*. The cyclical short-time work benefit introduces an important element of flexibility in a system characterised by high costs of employment adjustment.[92] However, the "structural" short-time work benefit hinders rather than facilitates adjustment.[93]

Since reunification, early retirement has reduced labour force participation among older groups significantly below the OECD average. Up to the end of 1992, workers aged 55 or older in eastern Germany could when dismissed claim a special type of unemployment benefit (*Altersübergangsgeld*) until they qualified for an early old-age pension at the age of 60 rather than a normal pension at age 65. More generally, enterprises have for some years been able to use early retirement provisions of the pension system to reduce their workforces. Since unemployment benefits are granted for up to 32 months to employees over the age of 54,[94] enterprises have found it easier to gain the acceptance of older workers to dismissal, with official unemployment benefits supplemented by a dismissal premium paid by the firm.[95] At the age of 60 rather than 65 the worker can then claim the usual old age pension early on account of unemployment. The total cost of reducing a workforce is thus reduced and the firm can avoid reference to social criteria in determining who is to be dismissed.[96] The numbers involved are large: in 1993 and 1994 the inflow into early retirement on account of unemployment rose by 60 and 30 per cent (Figure 22) respectively in western Germany, and surged in the new *Länder,* and initial estimates point to an inflow of 300 000 persons in 1995 for all Germany. In addition, the courts have confirmed that early retirement due to incapacity should be related to the state of the labour market, in particular whether the applicant is unemployed.

Early retirement has been implicitly encouraged as a means of promoting youth employment. This view was both misplaced and short-term. In practice, early retirement has been used mainly to reduce the level of enterprise workforces rather than giving rise to additional hirings of young workers. In the process, it has raised public expenditures, thereby increasing the financial burden imposed on active members of the population. Under existing arrangements, the financial burden on the pension system is primarily reflected in higher pension contributions, raising non-wage labour costs, and depressing labour demand; at the same time, higher effective marginal tax rates discourage additional work effort by marginal workers. Indeed, reducing early retirement would bring pressure to bear on both aggregate and relative wages, thereby preserving employment. However, relative wage rates might prove sluggish unless underpinned by wider reforms including changes to the pension system.

Nominal wage costs in Germany are amongst the highest in the world (Table 26), and non-wage labour costs make a significant contribution to this level. In manufacturing, supplementary labour costs totalled almost 80 per cent of normal wages per worker in 1992,[97] of which 43 per cent were statutory, with the remainder being negotiated between the social partners or agreed at company level. Statutory supplementary labour costs comprise the employers' share of social security contributions as well as sick pay. Social security contributions, which are divided equally between employers and employees, increased from

26.5 per cent of gross wages in 1970 to 41.1 per cent in mid-1996 (Figure 24). By international comparison, employers' social security contributions are high.

Sick pay is a particular burden on labour costs, and the structure of the system appears to create a moral hazard problem with respect to short-term sickness. On average, 5.5 per cent of the German workforce in industry were on sick leave in 1994, a level surpassed only by the Netherlands.[98] About a quarter of the cases reported to health insurance offices were short -term sickness of up to three days. In the first six weeks, income replacement for sickness is borne by the employers. Compensation appears to be extraordinarily generous in that net income based on the level of regular average earnings over the last three months before the sickness spell, including income from overtime, is often fully replaced.[99] For around 70 per cent of employees the provision of sick pay is regulated by collective agreements, but for the remainder – including civil servants – it is regulated by law. Legal provisions are important in other ways. Since 1994 the employer is entitled to demand a certificate from the first day of sickness, and since 1995 health funds are obliged to investigate any doubtful cases. However, an employer can only control an absence via the health fund.

The risk of moral hazard could be reduced by various measures which lead to less favourable income replacement at the beginning of a sickness spell and which increase the possibilities to control abuse. These include the introduction of uncompensated waiting days, and the deduction of a certain number of sickness days from the holiday account. In a number of OECD countries, there is a waiting period at the beginning of a sickness episode before benefits are paid and in others the maximum number of remunerated sick days per year are also specified. Adverse incentives would also be weakened if the replacement rate were lowered, in particular, if income from overtime work prior to the sickness episode was disregarded in calculating the level of the benefits: sick spells often occur after periods of high income.

As noted in Chapter III above, labour costs could be lowered if the financing of the non-insurance elements of the welfare system were to be shifted away from wage-related contributions to value-added taxes. The *OECD Jobs Study* concluded that policy makers should not expect sustainable effects on employment from substituting one tax by another. A reduction of the combined social security contribution rates below the current level of 41 per cent is needed, which will require sustained efforts to curb spending in all branches of the social security system. But if the connection between pension and other insurance contributions and future benefits were made clearer, the perceived long-run tax burden would be smaller – even if the overall "tax wedge" were unchanged. Such a measure would need to be introduced as part of a wider set of reforms to ensure that net wages would not rise in the short term.

Active labour market policies

Active labour market measures (ALMPs) comprising training, retraining and job creation, have in principle sought to facilitate structural adjustment and the reintegration of the unemployed into regular work. However, under the pressures of reunification, ALMPs have often been reduced to an additional form of social transfer. Active labour market measures have been used extensively in the new *Länder,* though they are much more modest in western Germany. Labour market spending (DM 128 billion) amounted to about 4 per cent of GDP in 1994 – the fourth highest in the OECD – while direct expenditures on ALMP were 1.1 per cent of GDP (Table 28).[100] The programmes have been significant: in eastern Germany as much as 40 per cent of the outflow from unemployment in 1994 was to ALMPs, while in the western *Länder* the figure was 14 per cent. A great deal of emphasis has been placed on facilitating the matching of supply and demand on the labour market, expenditures on public employment services amounting to around ¼ percentage point of GDP.

The Federal Labour Office (FLO) had a monopoly on job broking[101] up to 1994, although other organisations were commissioned to offer such services in particular market segments, and in 1993 filled about 300 000 vacancies, mainly of short duration. After liberalising entry about 1 500 new firms began operation, but by the end of 1994 they had brokered relatively few positions (*i.e.* 7 000). The Federal Labour Office remains the most important institution, providing services to all job seekers. It does not discriminate in favour of the unemployed, although until the recent introduction of a new computer system vacancies have not generally been openly announced. The number of vacancies notified to the FLO in 1994 was around 35 per cent of new hirings, but in eastern Germany the share was as high as 75 per cent, reflecting the important role of job creation measures. The trend has gradually been increasing in western Germany. The actual number of placements were smaller: 28 per cent of new hirings in western Germany and 44 per cent in eastern Germany, excluding job creation measures.

Table 28. **Indicators of labour market programmes**

	Public spending (per cent of GDP)			Participants entering active labour market programmes, per year (per cent of labour force)		
	1992	1993	1994	1992	1993	1994
1. Public employment services and administration	**0.24**	**0.25**	**0.24**			
2. Labour market training	**0.65**	**0.56**	**0.42**	**4.1**	**2.0**	**1.9**
Training for unemployed adults and those at risk [1]	0.62	0.53	0.40	3.6	1.7	1.8
Training for employed adults	0.03	0.03	0.02	0.5	0.3	0.1
3. Youth measures	**0.06**	**0.07**	**0.06**	**0.6**	**0.6**	**0.6**
Measures for unemployed and disadvantaged youth	0.05	0.06	0.06	0.4	0.4	0.4
Support of apprenticeship and related forms of general youth training	0.01	0.01	0.01	0.2	0.2	0.2
4. Subsidised employment	**0.51**	**0.47**	**0.39**	**1.3**	**1.2**	**1.4**
Subsidies to market sector employment	0.07	0.07	0.06	0.2	0.2	0.2
Support of unemployed persons starting enterprises	–	–	0.01	0.1	0.1	0.1
Direct job creation	0.43	0.40	0.32	1.0	1.0	1.2
5. Measures for the disabled	**0.25**	**0.28**	**0.26**	**–**	**–**	**–**
Vocational rehabilitation	0.14	0.15	0.14	0.3	0.3	0.3
Work for the disabled	0.11	0.13	0.12	–	–	–
6. Unemployment compensation	**1.48**	**1.99**	**2.03**			
7. Early retirement for labour market reasons [2]	**0.47**	**0.59**	**0.49**			
Total	**3.65**	**4.20**	**3.84**	**6.3**	**4.1**	**4.2**
of which: Spending on active measures (Categories 2-5)	1.45	1.37	1.13			

1. Including all participants in retraining in Germany.
2. Excluding pensions justified by invalidity etc.

Source: *The public employment service in Austria, Germany and Sweden,* OECD, forthcoming.

However, surveys of employers point to a more limited role: the FLO was the most important source of information in only 13 per cent of cases although for unskilled jobs the rate was 21 per cent.[102]

Most ALMP training and retraining programmes were designed within the framework of the vocational training system, based on standardised exams and nationally recognised skills. Adult training dominates the ALMP programmes in the old States and this was also true in the new *Länder* until 1992. Prior to 1993, up to 30 per cent of participants on training courses were still employed and not at risk of becoming long-term unemployed. In order to control costs, new legislation restricts the categories of the employed with access to retraining so that their share has now been reduced to about 10 per cent. The authorities have now taken steps to control some undesirable aspects of the schemes. The programme has been heavily cut in the new *Länder* due to growing concerns about the effectiveness of training in a situation where it seemed to be used too much for maintaining employment and income rather than for skill acquisition. Training allowances were some 5 percentage points higher than unemployment benefits, but this differential was eliminated in 1994. More recently, the authorities have begun to develop a new type of course lasting only three to four months with a view to the special needs of the unemployed.

Subsidised work schemes have been used on a particularly large scale in eastern Germany, but have been of lesser importance in the old states. Work programmes (ABM) are generally reserved for workers who have been unemployed for six months or more and who receive either unemployment benefits or unemployment assistance; however, the latter are in fact under-represented, indicating that up to now the ABM projects have not, in practice, been directed towards the long-term unemployed. In addition, there is a special scheme for the east covering, *inter alia,* social services, environmental improvements and youth assistance, and in 1994 this was extended to the old states. Job creation projects are mostly implemented by municipalities. For all work programmes the project must be in the public interest and additional to the ordinary activities of the governmental body. Employment conditions resemble normal employment contracts, but participants are expected to continue job search. The job availability requirement for participants was sharpened in 1994, a job refusal being sanctioned by removal not only from the project but also by stopping unemployment benefits for a period. Most workers, however, stay in the schemes for the full twelve months, which also requalifies them for benefits.

As noted in the previous *Survey,* ALMPs are relatively expensive: the total outlay per person per day is higher than the level of unemployment benefits (Table 29). Wages paid to participants on job creation schemes have traditionally followed those in comparable market sector jobs, but these rules have now been altered to encourage less expensive contracts. While the general ABM scheme allows a 50 to 75 per cent wage subsidy, since 1994 the subsidy is applicable only to that part of an ABM wage that does not exceed 90 per cent of the pay for comparable unsubsidised work. For the special schemes, the subsidy corresponds to the average unemployment benefit in the region as long as this does not exceed 90 per cent of the comparable market wage. As a result of these changes, and the high proportion of workers in eastern Germany where wage levels are relatively lower, the cost of direct job creation schemes has declined recently.

There are also a number of programmes expressly targeted at the long-term unemployed which include subsidies to private sector employers. These include:

Table 29. **Active labour market measures are relatively expensive**

As per cent of GDP per capita

	Spending per year per fully occupied participant place				Spending per participant entering programmes			
	Average of 1988 to 1990[1]	1992	1993	1994	1990	1992	1993	1994
Training of unemployed adults	77	100	106	88	49	36	66	47
Direct job creation	98	75	100	65	93	93	85	58
Vocational rehabilitation	98	79	98	–	95	88	121	115
Unemployment benefits	–	–	–	**42**	–	–	–	–

	1985	1990	1993
Cost per participant in job creation/average wage (%)	72	69	85

1. Western Länder.

N.B.: The figures for any single year can be biased by variations in the timing of expenditure for ongoing programmes, and by changes in programme volume from one year to the next. The intake of participants fell in 1993.

Source: OECD.

- A wage subsidy for workers aged 50 years or more who have been unemployed for a year. Subsidised work must be additional to that which would otherwise have been undertaken. The subsidy can be paid for five years and is 50 to 75 per cent in the beginning with annual decreases. The subsidy covered 20 000 workers in western Germany in 1994, and 9 500 in eastern Germany.
- A 50 to 70 per cent subsidy for one year to employers hiring persons classified as difficult to place. The work does not have to be additional and is available for both the private and public sector. Around 20 000 workers were covered by the scheme in 1994, of which 65 per cent were long-term unemployed.

While a judgement must remain provisional, it appears that ALMPs have been less successful in reducing unemployment and promoting reintegration than in providing additional income support for the unemployed. Such support might prevent them from losing contact with the labour market, but there is no reliable evidence for this. It is nevertheless important to differentiate between training/retraining on the one hand and job creation measures on the other. With respect to the former, among those previously unemployed who finished training[103] in 1992, only 26 per cent in western Germany (33 per cent in eastern Germany) were still drawing benefits six to nine months later[104] – although for retraining the proportion was about a third lower – and most found jobs relatively quickly. However, these figures do not say anything about the impact of training *per se,* since there is no control group of comparable individuals against which to evaluate the programme's effect and, as noted above, training programmes were provided most intensively to short-term rather than the long-term unemployed.

Most studies indicate that only around 30 per cent of participants in job-creation measures found regular work at the end of a project, while even two and a half years later only 40 per cent were either employed or taking part in a further job creation measure.[105] The effectiveness of the measures in terms of workforce participation appears to decline over time. One possible reason for these disappointing results is that the projects often bear little relation to the needs of the participants: one study found that whereas a third of the projects concerned gardening and other horticultural activities, only 9 per cent of participants had previously been employed in these occupations. One half of job creation measures were in occupations which concerned less than 10 per cent of the unemployed. The main reason for this deficiency in meeting the reintegration needs of the unemployed is that projects must be in the public interest and be additional to normal activities. As a result, job creation measures in effect serve to extend benefits, but with the negative side-effects that job search is reduced and uneconomic reservation wages are supported. Programmes directly targeted at particular groups appear to be more effective.[106] This applies to the programmes oriented toward the difficult-to-place long-term unemployed which pay direct wage subsidies to public and private employers. Costs are on average only DM 15 000 per person, much less than in other programmes, while two-thirds of those hired under the scheme were still employed a year and a half after the start of the subsidy.

Increasing the knowledge base, efficiency and innovative capacity

Upgrading skills and competencies

One of the reasons for the extraordinarily stable and compressed relative wage structure (Figure 34) is the education system which has been successful in meeting the increasing demand for skilled workers (Figure 32) and in permitting greater opportunities for the less skilled. The German labour force is, indeed, highly qualified. An effective dual system of vocational education provides approximately 70 per cent of each generation of young people with relevant and recognised vocational qualifications.[107] About a quarter of each age cohort participates in higher education, and of those about a third have previously completed vocational education and training. The vocational system appears to result in a high level of specialisation and inflexibility, but this impression is misleading. A high proportion of training is of a general nature and for this reason over a half of workers with such training find jobs in work different from the one in which they are formally qualified. While the unemployment problem is worst for unskilled older workers, the education system has been extraordinarily successful in equipping early school leavers and those who do not acquire vocational qualifications with skills and competencies permitting them to be relatively more productive than in other countries.[108] It is partly for this reason that the unemployment consequences of high wage growth for low paid workers have not been much worse.

Despite its evident success, the dual system is under pressure from several directions. In the new *Länder,* enterprises provide insufficient training places, so that the federal and state governments are now financing 14 000 training places.

Moreover, in the whole of Germany, there has been a continuing decline in the number of enterprises offering training places.[109] However, the most difficult challenge to the dual system arises from the relatively recent tendency for growing numbers of young people to undertake higher education.[110] The system needs to adapt to these changed preferences but this is proving difficult due in part to the complex decision making structure. In addition, the pathways between secondary vocational and academic studies can be blocked, and those into and between tertiary technical studies (*Fachhochschulen*) and academic studies (*universities*) remain to be clarified.

The experience with the higher education system is mixed. The polytechnics (*Fachhochschulen*) are characterised by an orientation toward practical work requirements, short study periods, and streamlined study programmes. The relationships with industry are close. The university sector, however, frequently is criticised for being divorced from the needs of the economy and not competitive, and because studies extend over too long a period of time. The federal government and *Länder* have agreed that reform is urgent and a progress report on likely measures is to be presented in 1996.

Product market competition

While strong competition is ensured in the internationally exposed sectors of the economy by open markets and effectively enforced competition policy, public utilities and significant branches of the service sector remain protected and Germany has been slow to introduce single-market legislation, particularly in the area of public procurement. Protection in services and in utilities raises prices for industrial and private consumers, while raising barriers to new entrants in potential employment growth areas (transport, telecommunication, etc.). The result will be to reduce employment and growth in the economy as a whole. An indication of the magnitude of the problem can be gained by international price comparisons. Electricity and gas prices in Germany are significantly above the average in Europe, and are much higher than in North America (Figure 37), while in road haulage prices fell by some 30 per cent following deregulation of prices in 1994. Price comparisons, however, only inadequately reflect the efficiency losses which might be involved for these also depend on the elasticity of supply. Thus the high road haulage prices fostered an increased use by firms of their own transport vehicles, which are nevertheless not permitted to pick up other cargoes. Efficiency losses are thus high.

Figure 37. **ELECTRICITY AND NATURAL GAS PRICES FOR INDUSTRY**[1]

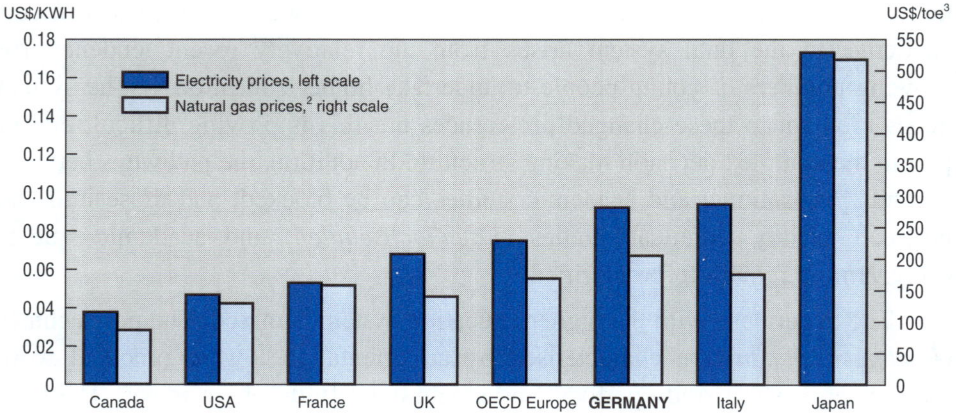

Cross country comparison is impaired by the fluctuation of the exchange rate.
1. In 1994.
2. Net calorofic value basis.
3. Toe: ton of oil equivalent = 10**7 kcal.
Source: IEA Statistics (1996).

Airlines and long-distance haulage have been controlled in order to protect the railways. In line with European competition policy, air transport has now been substantially liberalised and Lufthansa, the dominant airline, has been partially privatised. Even though competition remains restricted by the method of allocating landing slots, Lufthansa's efficiency has improved and prices have declined.[111] It remains to be seen whether the change in energy policy toward direct subsidies for coal mines, thereby allowing generators to buy coal at world prices, will translate into lower electricity prices.

Despite a large number of generating and distribution companies, competition is virtually absent in the electricity industry. This is due to exclusivity clauses in concession agreements between municipalities and utilities, and demarcation contracts between producers in different regions not to compete in their respective geographical zones. A similar situation exists in the gas industry.[112] Exclusivity clauses and demarcation contracts reinforce each other, the former making it useless for final customers to shop around, and the latter preventing companies from competing for customers. These agreements imply that third-party access provisions in the competition law are of little practical importance, but they are in any case very restrictive. The Federal government and the competition authorities have proposed to make demarcation contracts illegal, thus abolishing the exemption of utilities from general competition law and bringing legislation into line with EU law, while ending exclusivity clauses in concession contracts. However, concession fees are an important source of local government finance.

Local governments are currently under little competitive pressure to economise in the provision of public services. As a result, charges for garbage disposal and sewage rose by around 8 per cent in 1995, far above the increase of wage costs. *Länder* are responsible for the regulatory framework, which is generally cost plus, and there is no requirement for market testing. In addition, non-profit organisations are extended preferential treatment in the provision of a wide range of social services discouraging the development of alternative, potentially more efficient, suppliers. Until value-added taxes are also paid by public organisations market testing would in any case be impractical. The government committed itself to establishing equal VAT treatment during preparation of the 1996 budget, but the possibility of large tax refunds to public enterprises in the new *Länder,* which up to that time could not claim refunds, led to a postponement. Public procurement has still not been regularised along the lines required by the European Union.

The dynamism of the German economy has also been retarded by a restrictive regulatory framework in three other important areas: retailing, planning approvals, and telecommunications. First, shop opening hours have been restrictive and a report commissioned by the government suggests that turnover and employment could increase following liberalisation. Moreover, the report indicated that a large number of employees were prepared to work outside the current shop opening hours.[113] Second, planning approvals have been complex and costly. For building permits, companies still complain of delays of nine to fifteen months and 40 per cent of firms in a survey[114] claimed that profits were thereby affected. Planning approvals for railways and for motorways were simplified in the new *Länder* and this measure appears to have been successful in accelerating investment decisions. Third, contestability in basic telecommunications has been limited and the old monopoly, Telekom, is still one of the few operators in Europe also to control the cable net.

A major issue which is not yet fully resolved concerns the harmonisation of the German competition law with the law and practices of the European Union. Harmonisation would lay the framework for resolving some of the competition issues in the sectors noted above. In particular, the current prohibition of horizontal cartel agreements would be strengthened and exemptions for sectors such as transport, banking, insurance, energy and agriculture would need to be eliminated. Moreover, adopting EU rules concerning abuse of dominant market position would strengthen current German practices. On the other hand, the rule-of-reason approach adopted by the German authorities with respect to vertical agreements could in some circumstances be more conducive to the promotion of competition and efficiency than European law, which focuses on eliminating barriers to inter-community trade. As noted above, with respect to electricity generation and distribution, the issues are complex but are inadequately addressed by the system of group exemptions which is an important component of European competition enforcement.

Technology and innovation

Although there is little evidence to suggest that the present high levels of unemployment are related to weaknesses in technology and innovation, there are nevertheless signs that improved performance in these areas might be an essential factor if Germany is to achieve levels of growth compatible with a sustained reduction of unemployment. Germany is characterised by a broad level of export specialisation in medium-technology products: whereas the United States and Japan have an export specialisation in 850 and 600 product groups respectively, the number of products is nearer 1 200 in Germany.[115] The primary competitors in these markets are not the newly-industrialising countries, but rather the United States, Japan, France and Italy (*i.e.* countries with a comparative advantage in technology-intensive products). Within each of these areas of specialisation, German companies are concentrated in the technology-intensive products and this is reflected in their above-average patent activity in these sectors (Figure 38). Moreover, these R&D activities appear to be quite flexible and widely dispersed over technical areas. Small and medium-sized firms appear to be quite active, accounting for 10 per cent of total patents compared with 45 per cent for large companies.[116]

Figure 38. **INDICATORS OF INNOVATION**

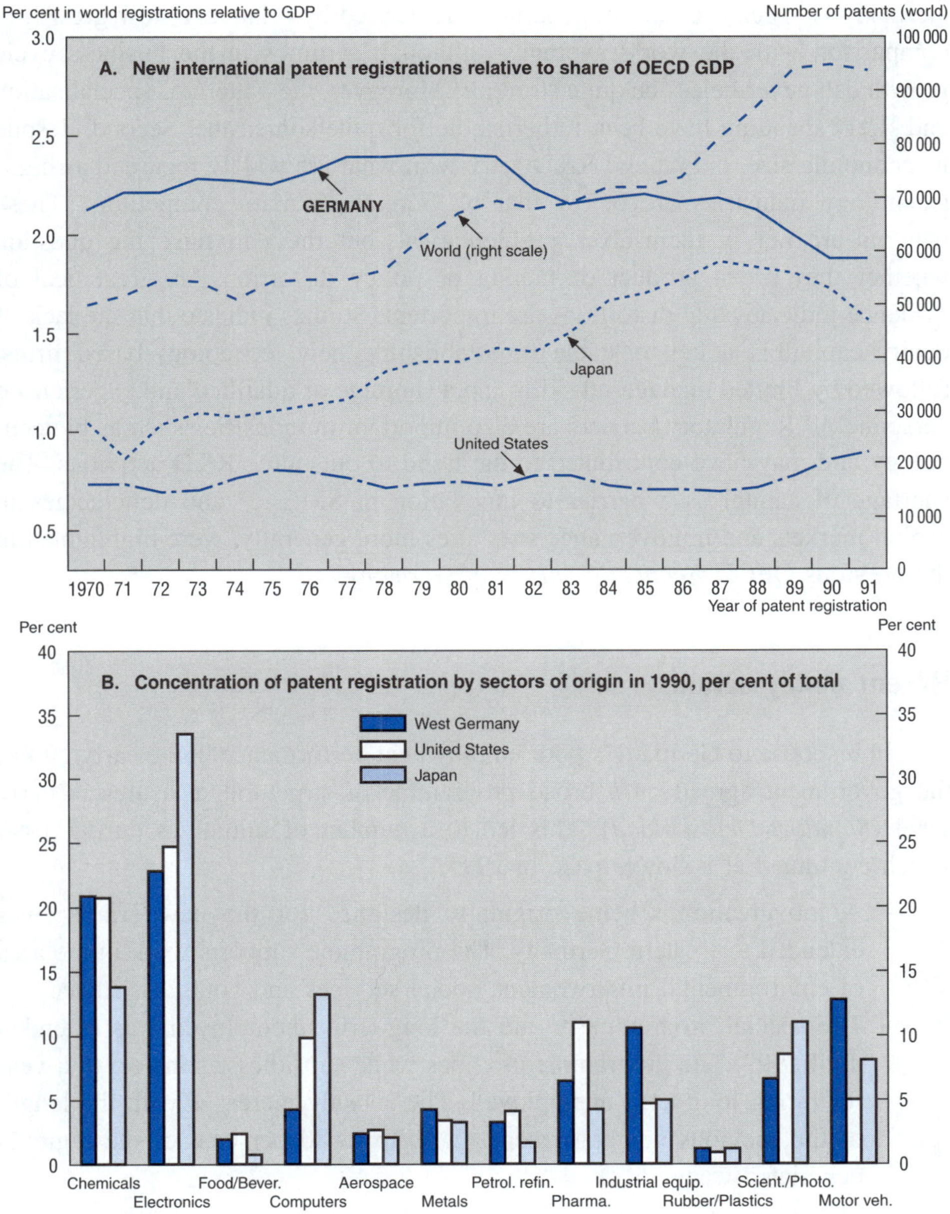

Source: OECD, IFO Patentstatistik.

Two questions, however, stand out in this pattern. First, the goods in which Germany is specialised are in general characterised by relatively slow growth in comparison with the world average – although at times in the business cycle growth can nevertheless be quite strong.[117] Moreover, the pattern of specialisation and R&D spending have been rather stable for quite some time. Second, despite its economic size, output and R&D activity in what are widely regarded as high-technology industries are below that of Germany's main competitors. These patterns are not in themselves problematical, but they do raise the question whether they are a product of market or policy distortions. A great deal of evidence indicates that distortions are important. Studies indicate that the lack of equity capital is a key obstacle to establishing new technology-based firms, followed by limited managerial skills and a shortage of qualified and experienced personnel.[118] Regulatory barriers are also important in industries such as biotechnology and may have contributed to the trend to outsource R&D activities. The shortage of capital as a barrier to innovation in SMEs,[119] and deficiencies in capital markets and in governance structures more generally, were highlighted in the previous OECD *Economic Survey of Germany*.

Recent policy actions

In response to Germany's poor employment performance in the early 1990s, the government agreed on a broad programme of structural measures in early 1994 (*Standort Deutschland*). This led to a number of initiatives during 1994 which continued at a slower pace in 1995:

- A job creation scheme originally designed for the new *Länder* was extended to western Germany. The programme supports work in the area of environmental improvement, social services and youth assistance.
- The special programme to aid the long-term unemployed was extended until 1999. The programme provides wage subsidies lasting up to a year for hiring long-term unemployed. The subsidy increases with the length of the previous unemployment spell, up to 80 per cent of the region's negotiated wages.
- In the area of science and technology, policy initiatives in 1995 have aimed to enhance government support for research and improve co-operation between the public and private sectors, with particular attention

to small and medium-sized enterprises. Several initiatives focus on strengthening the research capacity of the new *Länder* and the development and use of advanced technologies. The federal government, in conjunction with the *Länder,* is strengthening support for pre-competitive research, particularly in high-technology fields such as biotechnology and information technologies.

The 1996 income tax reform (described in Chapter III) has led to a reduction of the tax burden for low-income groups, but it does not remedy the existence of unemployment traps for social assistance recipients over a broad income band (Figure 20). Indeed, the entrance tax rate was raised by about seven percentage points. The new system of child benefits, which are not means tested, is an improvement in that it avoids the high effective marginal tax rates over some income ranges that were connected with the withdrawal of child benefits in the previous system. However, non-wage labour costs have increased with the introduction in July 1996 of the second stage of the long-term care insurance.

The government has now adopted a 50-point action plan to promote investment, growth, and employment (Box 5). Moreover, it is planning a substantial revision of the labour code with the intention of promoting active job search and improved labour-market performance. A number of decisions remain to be taken, but by the middle of 1996 a significant body of legislative proposals had already been submitted to Parliament. At the time of writing (July 1996) the following measures were under way:

– As part of the programme to raise the retirement age and discourage early retirement, part-time employment of formerly full-time workers is to be encouraged by earnings supplements paid by the federal labour office from the age of 55 onwards until retirement, provided the company compensates for reduced work hours by hiring unemployed or newly graduated apprentices. Under this condition, an employee switching from full-time to half-time employment receives tax and contribution-free transfers so as to guarantee an earnings level of 70 per cent of their former net income. In addition, contributions to the pension funds will be topped up in such a way that they correspond to gross earnings of 90 per cent of the former full-time earnings.

Box 5. **The 50-point programme to promote growth and employment (and status as of 9 July)**

The programme draws together a number of proposed initiatives and individual items of legislation covering the promotion of new enterprises, tax reform and the budget, the reduction of wage costs to stimulate employment, and the promotion of competition. Key policy proposals concerning the functioning of the labour market comprise the following:

Reducing social security contributions to under 40 per cent by 2000

- Access to early retirement is to be restricted. The entry age for early retirement because of unemployment is to be raised from 60 to 63 years in stages between 1997 and 1999. Status: Passed into law in June to take effect in August. The entry age for other schemes will also be raised. Status: Passed by lower house of Parliament. Awaiting upper house approval.
- The conditions for retirement because of incapacity will be tightened. Status: In preparation.
- The introduction of incentives to promote cost containment in the health care system is to be accelerated. Status: Law to control hospital costs passed in April. Package of measures to control health cost passed by lower house of Parliament in June, but blocked by upper house.
- The cost of sick leave, which is borne by employers for the first six weeks, is to be reduced to 80 per cent of reference wages. Status: Passed by lower house in June. To be considered by upper house in July.

Enhancing job search

- The minimum age for receiving unemployment insurance benefits for more than a year is to be increased. The job acceptability criteria for recipients of unemployment benefits will be tightened. Status: For consideration by Parliament in October.
- Social assistance payments will be reduced by at least 25 per cent if recipients reject acceptable work. Status: In effect from August.
- Clarify criteria for refusing jobs (*Zumutbarkeit*). The possibility of sequential participation in active labour market measures (training and job creation programmes) is to be abolished. Status: For consideration by Parliament in October.
- The wage base for calculating unemployment assistance is to be reduced by 3 per cent a year. Status: In force in June.
- From 1999 social assistance should be 15 per cent below the local average net wage of a low-income family. Status: Removed from legislation after negotia-

(continued on next page)

(continued)

tions. Until then benefits will be linked to the evolution of net wages in western Germany rather than to the ''needs-based'' cost-of-living index. Status: Passed by both houses of Parliament on 5 July.

Promoting employment

- Employment chances for particularly disadvantaged unemployed will be increased via targeted training programmes. The duration of fixed-term contracts will be extended from 18 to 24 months, with the possibility of three renewals within this period. Status: Passed by lower house of Parliament in June. Awaiting upper house approval.
- The employment ceiling at which job protection legislation is applicable is to be raised from 5 employees per firm to 10 employees (full-time equivalent). Status: Passed by lower house of Parliament in June. To be considered by upper house in July.
- The efficiency of both vocational training and post high school education will be increased and training within the government sector will be stepped up by 5 per cent. Status: A package of 21 revised regulations comes into force in August.
- The access of small/medium sized enterprises to risk capital is to be facilitated by changes in tax and corporate law. Status: Some tax measures form part of 1997 tax package which still requires approval by the upper house. Financial market measures under preparation for action by end of year. Tax credits will be used to support newly-established enterprises. Status: Introduced into Parliament in June. Requires approval of upper house.

- The minimum age for receiving a full pension on account of unemployment is to be increased from 60 to 63 years over a number of years, and those who retire between the ages of 60 and 63 will receive pensions actuarially reduced by 0.3 points per month. Given the generous transitory regulations included in the reform plan,[120] fiscal savings will be small initially, rising to DM 6 billion per annum by the end of the decade. Two draft bills have been introduced to Parliament to reform unemployment assistance although not in any fundamental way. Benefits will be terminated for those who have worked and paid social security contributions for less than 150 days. More importantly, it is proposed to base the entitlement level no longer exclusively on previous earnings but rather on the wages a participant would expect to receive under current conditions.

In practice, it is proposed to adjust downwards the person's last salary by 3 per cent each year, but the wage level will still be increased each year on the basis of annual increases of net wages. Both bills are currently under negotiation in the upper house of Parliament; the *Länder* fear that the reforms will increase pressure on social assistance, and therefore on their budgets.

- A bill has been passed by the lower house of Parliament to relate social assistance benefits more closely to employment opportunities. The proposal to set levels of assistance for a family of five at 15 per cent less than the earnings of lower wage and salary groups was removed from the legislation. Benefit levels for recipients who refuse a "suitable" job offer will be cut by 25 per cent.
- Shop opening hours were finally partially liberalised in July to take effect from November. Shops are now permitted to remain open till 8 o'clock on weekdays and to 4 o'clock on Saturdays.
- A law was passed in July liberalising the telecommunications market and which will also facilitate a partial privatisation of Telekom by the end of 1996. The market is to be regulated by an authority under the supervision of the Ministry of the Economy but the sector will be subject to competition law. The criteria for issuing licenses will not be as liberal as the federal government intended and Telekom will still remain in control of the cable network. In addition, the terms of access to the line network of Telekom have not been clarified and this may limit the contestability of the market.
- Proposals for new, simplified planning approvals have been submitted to Parliament. These would, *inter alia,* allow enterprises to proceed with projects which do not fundamentally change their environmental and other liabilities. Some experts believe that the new regulations might prove difficult for enterprises to use in practice.

Assessment and scope for further action

The German authorities have put forward an ambitious goal to halve unemployment by the turn of the century. In support of this objective, a package of 50 measures has been proposed (see Box 5), including changes in the labour promotion law (AFG) and in the administration of the federal labour office. The proposed measures seek to encourage more active job search while setting benefits more in line with current wage opportunities than past earnings. Attention is also directed, appropriately, toward lowering the costs of the transfer system, which will permit an overall reduction in social security charges.

Priority needs to be given now to implementing the package and to resisting any tendency to reduce the pace of reform as the economy recovers. Nevertheless, there are areas where reforms are either too modest or not at present contemplated. Further progress is needed in the following areas:

- The high net replacement rates of the unemployment assistance and social assistance schemes need to be reduced still further by relating benefits more closely to work opportunities than currently envisaged. With respect to social assistance, the reference group of a family of five appears to be of limited relevance since so few recipients come into this category, while for unemployment assistance an annual reduction in reference earnings of 3 per cent (while at the same time allowing an annual indexation to net wage developments in the economy) is inadequate. A reduction of benefits would need to be supplemented by greater work-conditional incentives. On the demand side, a restructuring of contributions so as to lower contribution rates for low income earners would be important. Moreover, the reduction of benefits could be delayed until household incomes have actually increased with the receipt of first wages.
- The criteria allowing recipients to refuse job offers (*Zumutbarkeit*) need to be tightened at the same time as net replacement rates are reduced. In particular, the right to refuse a job if the offer is below sector-wide collective wage agreements should be eliminated. In the social assistance system a major reason for dispensing with the job search requirement is difficulties related to child-minding. In view of the obligation now imposed on communities to provide such facilities, this condition should be interpreted less liberally.
- The wage-bargaining system is in a state of change. How it will evolve will ultimately depend on the social partners. The changes in the benefits system discussed above will have the effect of increasing market pressures on wage formation. In order to support a flexible response in collective agreements, the authorities would need to increase the compe-

tencies of the works councils to conclude broader enterprise-specific wage agreements and might have to re-examine other laws governing the conduct of parties in wage negotiations.

- Sick pay is extraordinarily generous by international standards. While changes might ultimately depend on the social partners, the legal basis which in part underpins collective agreements should be altered. Two areas appear crucial: the level of benefits could be related to base wages excluding overtime pay and employees could forfeit compensation for several days in order to reduce the moral hazard problems which plague the present system. Such measures are normal by international standards.
- Although the government's decision to reduce early retirement is welcome, the decision to link it to the introduction of a part-time employment scheme is questionable: it represents a continuation of the "job-sharing" philosophy under which older workers should be retired or their participation reduced in order to make way for others. One of the objectives of labour market reform should be to eliminate impediments for increased participation by older workers. Legislation needs to be passed to limit accessibility to pensions on account of incapacity by excluding from the qualifying criteria the current state of the labour market and the employment status of the applicant.
- The legal barriers to more flexible working practices need to be reviewed. Particularly important in this respect is a liberalisation of fixed-term contracts to permit renewal. Part-time work needs to be facilitated including casual jobs (so-called DM 590 jobs). Proposals to make both of these work arrangements subject to pro-rata social security contributions, although removing an implicit subsidy, would need to be closely co-ordinated with wider reforms in order to lower the risk that such jobs might simply disappear. A reduction in contribution rates for low paid workers to reduce wage costs and bring down marginal effective tax rates would be desirable.
- High and uncertain costs of dismissal remain an important barrier to hiring new workers. All aspects of dismissal protection need to be re-examined. In particular, regulations need to be redrafted to give the courts clearer guidelines as to the interpretation of economic factors in cases of unfair dismissal. Moreover, in group layoffs the social clause, which is important in determining who is to be dismissed, needs to be redefined to

give greater weight to balancing the structure and composition of the work force in terms of age, experience and skills. Legal provisions, which have been interpreted by the courts in a way which limits the flexibility of firms in contracting-out operations, need to be reformed.

- Active labour market policies and retraining measures need to be more closely focused on groups at risk. Proposals to tighten the job search requirements while participating in an ALMP project constitute a move in the right direction, as does the reduction of training allowances paid to participants on such schemes relative to market alternatives. Schemes focused on the long-term unemployed should encourage them to price themselves back into a job and for this to succeed some form of work-conditional benefit needs to be considered. However, in view of the fact that many measures are in effect income replacement schemes, participation in job creation schemes should not serve to requalify recipients for unemployment benefits.
- The rapid development of higher education makes it necessary to redefine its relationship with the dual apprenticeship system. In higher education, the university system appears to be in most need of reform in order to shorten the study period and to strengthen ties to the economy.

In addition to making labour markets more efficient, there are several areas in both manufacturing and in private and public services where there is still a clear need to strengthen competition and to promote efficiency through regulatory reform:

- Shop hours should be liberalised further. Going beyond this, there is a need to review the regulatory structure more generally. This applies particularly to the provision of local services where greater cost consciousness has to be introduced. However, in order to make market testing feasible, public and private enterprises have to be placed on the same basis with respect to value-added tax. Privatisation is moving forward at the federal level but is still held back at lower levels of government.
- Particularly important is the removal of regulatory and tax barriers which have retarded the development of venture capital. Lack of capital might have constrained the development of new enterprises and slowed technological progress. However, new subsidies in the form of tax breaks for

high-technology start-ups need to be avoided and the programmes to inject equity and funds into enterprises in the new *Länder* should be closely scrutinised, to ensure that new subsidy programmes are not being established.

- Competition in the network industries needs to be encouraged since there is evidence that efficiency is low. Legal changes might be required to better control exclusive concessions which are preventing effective third-party access in electricity and gas. In addition, regulatory arrangements may have to be more closely co-ordinated with competition policy in all the network sectors.

V. Conclusions

The pick-up in economic growth that began in 1994, and had been projected to continue in the previous *Survey,* faltered in 1995 and into 1996. The expectation of a strengthening recovery was based on the traditional pattern of German upswings, where a pick-up in export growth has been followed by accelerating private investment. This has failed to materialise this time. Investment activity deteriorated steadily during 1995, held back by stagnant investment in machinery and equipment and falling construction activity. With export demand faltering in the middle of 1995, business expectations deteriorated sharply and GDP stagnated in the second half of 1995. The dampening effects of the 1995 wage round on business confidence, together with the further appreciation of the currency in early 1995 and the lagged effects of the world-wide rise in long-term interest rates in 1994, were noted in the 1995 *Survey,* but in line with surveys of business intentions, rationalising investment was expected to remain robust. In the event, the development of the exchange rate and wage costs together with weakening growth of export markets, were more contractionary than anticipated because they compounded an already difficult profits situation. The judgement of the previous *Survey* was based on the assessment that profitability had substantially recovered in the course of 1994. However, it now appears that the rate of return on fixed investment was in fact lower than during previous recoveries, explaining the rapid revision of profit expectations, and investment intentions, as the situation deteriorated. Labour shedding, which had appeared to come to a halt at the beginning of 1995, gathered pace: overall German employment declined by 0.3 per cent, while the unemployment rate increased steadily, reaching 10.2 per cent in the first quarter of 1996.

It should be noted that the assessment of economic conditions is surrounded by more than the usual degree of uncertainty because of the statistical difficulties experienced in recent years. The immediate reason for this state of affairs was the conversion of industrial orders and production statistics to European standards at the beginning of 1995, and the extension of statistical coverage in the new *Länder*. Initially, the new series proved highly unreliable, the difficulties in interpreting incoming data underpinning the necessity that adequate resources be devoted to the provision of timely and reliable basic economic statistics. Moreover, since Germany is a major financial centre, consideration could be given to announcing a calendar for the publication of statistical releases.

The slowdown in growth was particularly marked in western Germany, but the increased integration of the new and old *Länder* has meant that growth in eastern Germany also slowed significantly as the business climate deteriorated. Some of the favourable trends noted in the previous *Survey* have continued in the new *Länder*. Exports have started to increase, albeit from a very low base, and although overall wage growth is continuing to outstrip productivity, at the enterprise level a new found realism in wage setting appears to be taking hold. But the level of bankruptcies has surged and a large number of privatised enterprises are reported to be in financial difficulties. Insofar as the construction sector is most affected and this accounts for 17 per cent of eastern GDP – an extraordinarily high ratio compared with the post-war reconstruction period in western Germany – this could reflect the start of a necessary long-term restructuring. The policy response of both the *Länder* and the federal governments to rising bankruptcies has been to establish schemes to inject equity capital into enterprises, and to financially support those which are experiencing liquidity problems. Where such firms are not fundamentally sound, these schemes risk prolonging, and even strengthening, the dependency on subsidies and state support which was noted in the previous *Survey*. Although progress has been made in the new *Länder*, growth is still not self-sustaining and the tendency to demand more transfers and subsidies appears unbroken.

Despite the disappointing 1995 wage round, inflation performance has improved significantly. Year-on-year consumer and producer price inflation have fallen to a little over 1 per cent by early 1996. Excessive wage awards have had their primary impact on the level of employment and indirectly on the level of investment, since with activity sluggish and the exchange rate strong there has been no room to pass on wage rises. The current wage round has been marked by greater realism, yielding wage increases of below 2 per cent and a more favourable trend in unit labour costs. Moreover, in the agreements signed to date working practices have been made more flexible, which should in the short run relieve cost pressures on firms, particularly agreements to replace overtime with free time later on. Also, since the start of 1996 the effective nominal exchange rate has weakened by some 4 per cent, offsetting the appreciation in 1995. This may temporarily affect import prices, but overall, taking domestic and external influences together, the prospect is for inflation of around 1½ per cent in the coming year, close to a meaningful definition of price stability.

The combination of wage restraint and depreciation of the Deutschemark should improve the profitability and competitiveness of German exports in the near term, although cost pressures on German exports remain intense. With competitiveness improving and market growth projected to strengthen, exports should provide a platform for a recovery to get under way during the second half of 1996 and to gain momentum in 1997; following a weak start to 1996 there is evidence of increasing export and domestic orders and on this basis the central projection incorporates a fairly rapid turnaround. Lower taxes and higher household incomes following the 1995 wage round may also be expected to support growth in private consumption of around 1½ per cent. But investment is projected to remain weak during 1996: cost pressures have been relieved but not removed; there is still declining demand in the construction sector, and the fall in long-term interest rates in 1995, which had followed the 1994 hikes, has been partially reversed. Growth for the year is thus likely to amount to around ½ per cent, rising perhaps to about 2½ per cent in 1997 as the traditional recovery pattern reasserts itself. This rate of expansion would be too weak to make any inroads into the high level of unemployment; but on the external side, the current account deficit is projected to narrow, reflecting an increased trade surplus. Investment could recover more sharply than projected if labour costs remain moderate and the downward drift of the Deutschemark against the currencies of Germany's main trading partners outside the ERM were to continue; such a recovery would be underpinned by the very low levels of investment in the past eighteen months and relatively high rates of capacity utilisation. Fragile business confidence could weaken private spending more than projected, and this effect would be reinforced if wage moderation appeared to be temporary. In this context, if fiscal tightening were to be stronger than currently assumed by the OECD, output might be somewhat lower, though the outlook beyond the projection period would be more favourable given, among other things, the positive effects on the investment climate.

Against the background of improving inflation prospects, monetary policy has eased significantly since the last review. Over the period since the cyclical trough in 1993, the shift in monetary stance has been initially more cautious than in previous periods of recovery, partly because the market was not discounting the need for the Bundesbank to ease monetary policy. In this situation, the policy of gradual relaxation has generally been favourably received by the markets: long-term interest rates fell in line with US rates during 1995, and by the spring of this year the yield on 10-year DM bonds was below the US equivalent. Moreover, although long-term interest rates are high relative to current inflation, on the basis of past relationships the current spread between short-term and long-term rates is consistent with the upturn incorporated into the OECD's projections. In addition, the money supply (M3) has grown rapidly during the first quarter of 1996, exceeding the Bundesbank's target, and such growth may continue in the short run as the private sector demand for credit recovers and insofar as the propensity for long-term financial asset acquisition remains weak. Although, in setting the monetary target at the end of 1995, the Bundesbank was relatively cautious in its interpretation of the economy's liquidity situation, on balance, the 1995 exchange rate appreciation having been corrected, monetary conditions now constitute a generally favourable framework for a recovery. But there is a case for interpreting monetary growth trends in a broader perspective, which would recognise that further easing in the stance of monetary policy might be appropriate if both the monetary stock and other indicators were to show weakness.

Fiscal policy is scheduled to tighten in the course of the year and especially in 1997, not only in Germany but in European countries more generally, raising questions about whether a compensating shift in the stance of monetary policy might be possible or required, and if so, when. In principle, fiscal consolidation should increase the central bank's room for manœuvre, by reducing long-term interest rates and inflation expectations. However, there is a great deal of uncertainty about the timing and degree of any short-term impact on demand, *inter alia* because much depends on the credibility of the fiscal and structural measures adopted. As a result, any strategy linking the response of monetary policy directly to the announced orientation of fiscal policy would carry significant risks. Monetary policy thus needs to adopt a wait-and-see posture.

While substantial progress was made towards fiscal consolidation during 1992-1994, 1995 saw a substantial budgetary slippage, as revenues fell short of prediction and social security spending surged. As a result fiscal policy could be in danger of losing its credibility if existing policy commitments are not fully observed. At the turn of the year, reduced growth prospects pointed to a further substantial slippage from the government's budget target in 1996 and 1997 and the probability of meeting the Maastricht budget criterion appeared to be receding. Despite actions to limit the overshoot, the general government deficit (which includes social security) is projected by the OECD to approach 4 per cent of GDP in 1996. The government's budget plans envisage a significant tightening in 1997, such that the general government deficit would be a little under 3 per cent of GDP, but achieving this will involve difficult choices. Avoiding an increase in overall contribution rates (an increase in pension contributions will be required in 1997) will necessitate strict control of transfer expenditures. At the same time, the Solidarity tax surcharge is to be reduced by a percentage point and the wealth tax is to be abolished, both of which will require offsetting actions. Incorporating only agreed and mandated policy changes, the OECD is projecting a general government deficit of around 3.4 per cent. A considerable part of the additional fiscal tightening comprises a very low wage round in both 1996 and 1997 combined with employment cuts in the public sector. A great deal of these savings (around DM 20 billion) are to be made by lower levels of government. The current wage round is a positive development in this respect. Nevertheless, the need is for both continued wage moderation and employment adjustment if the budget is to be kept on a sustained medium-term consolidation path.

The responsibility for budgetary uncertainty lies partly with conflicts between the federal and *Länder* governments, caused by difficulties in apportioning the costs of retrenchment under a Federal budget structure. The abolition of the local tax on enterprise capital has been delayed by the *Länder*. Other legislation concerning the reform of the social assistance and unemployment assistance programmes has recently been passed, but that relating to the control of health care costs is deadlocked. More generally, the stance of fiscal policy this year, and especially in 1997, will not be clear for some time, pending the agreement of the *Länder*. Federal systems have the advantage of devolving responsibility closer to the populations directly affected. But in Germany, the current system of revenue apportionment may act to protect lower levels of government from the consequences of their own spending decisions, rather than to stimulate the competitive aspects of a federal structure. In the process, it may create an upward bias in aggregate public spending and taxation.

The source of greatest public spending pressure can, however, be traced to the social security system, including factors related to increasing take-up rates, stemming in part from rising unemployment. To address these problems, the government has proposed a medium-term programme to reduce the budget deficit and lower public expenditures to pre-unification levels in relation to GDP by the year 2000. This ratio increased from slightly below 46 per cent in 1989 to 50 per cent in 1994, so the goal is clearly an ambitious one. At the same time, the level of social security contributions is to be first stabilised at its present level of 41 per cent of gross wages and then reduced to under 40 per cent. The success in containing public spending will depend on determined policy action over a wide range of programmes, including health, public pensions, subsidies and labour-market related spending.

With respect to pensions, OECD projections, which are based on a rise in the old-age dependency ratio from 21.7 at the start of the 1990s to 23.8 per cent at the end, and to 55 per cent in 2035, suggest that outlays will rise from its present level of 11.1 per cent of GDP to 12.3 per cent of GDP by the year 2020 and to 19 per cent in 2035. The increase will be dampened by the gradual increase in the retirement age, but to stabilise the contribution rate below 20 per cent while coping with future challenges the government has presented a variety of measures. These include an earlier raising of the retirement age and a lowering in the number of years of higher education which can be counted towards pension entitlements. However, in the face of future projected demographic changes, additional reform measures are still needed and a commission has been established to make additional proposals to secure the public pension system in the longer run. Raising the age of retirement and lowering the number of years of higher education which can be counted toward pension entitlements are both necessary, but not by themselves sufficient. Over the longer-term, entitlements will probably have to be restricted so that it is essential that moves be initiated now to encourage the development of supplementary pensions. In this respect the legal and tax barriers to the development of private pension funds need to be lowered.

A key to better structural budget balance is, however, lower unemployment. Poor labour market performance risks creating a vicious cycle of rising taxes and social security contributions which reduce economic growth and employment, while government budgets continue to be under pressure. To address these problems, the government announced a medium-term programme in January to encourage growth and halve unemployment by the turn of century. The programme foresees important changes in labour market and social security legislation. Consistent with the *OECD Jobs Study* view that poor labour market performance is largely a structural phenomenon, the approach to job creation also involves initiatives in the field of education and training, enterprise creation and deregulation, designed to increase labour force skills and competencies and improve the entrepreneurial climate. The announced measures constitute an important step towards implementing the *Jobs Strategy* and are evaluated below. The government has sought a consensus with the social partners. This may prove difficult to achieve but fundamental reforms are in any case needed. Since the current poor economic performance can be attributed mainly to underlying structural weakness in the economy rather than to cyclical factors, it is important to implement the package of labour market and other structural reforms in full, and not to allow the momentum to dissipate either in the face of continued economic weakness or, indeed, if conjunctural conditions improve.

Of critical importance is a reform of the taxation system which has been on the policy agenda for quite some time. Key in this respect is the personal tax system which is in urgent need of simplification, but benefits would also accrue from an overhaul of the company and wealth-tax systems:

- Marginal income-tax rates are high, in part because of a desire to achieve numerous policy objectives via tax expenditures. Disincentive effects are particularly pronounced for potential second-income earners, whose participation in the labour force is discouraged. The high tax burden may discourage work effort and entrepreneurial activity. There is thus room for rationalising the tax base and simplifying and reducing tax rates.
- With respect to the taxation of entrepreneurial income, the taxation obstacles which have prevented the development of risk capital markets – and thereby possibly the development of new technologies – need to be removed. These relate particularly to the interaction between wealth,

inheritance and income taxes, which create significant biases against incorporation and stock-market listing.
- The proposal to eliminate the local business capital tax should be implemented, since this constitutes a particularly heavy burden on new firms, and may discourage new entrants.

Tax reforms *per se* are important for their beneficial effects on incentives and the allocation of resources, particularly with respect to labour market participation. But they need to be seen in the context of an overall reduction in expenditures, including direct as well as indirect subsidies. The subsidisation of the eastern German economy has already been remarked upon. Subsidisation in the western part of the country has declined somewhat, owing to the reduction of tax breaks, but there has been an increasing focus on subsidies that tend to conserve existing structures.

Many of the key issues in the tax system concern its interaction with the transfer system and reforms in this area remain a priority. The unemployment and related benefits systems are characterised by high net replacement rates – the relationship between benefits received and probable earnings by recipients in employment – for important segments of the unemployed and by long eligibility periods for benefits. Moreover, the criteria for refusing job offers while maintaining full benefit entitlements are generous and benefit recipients have only to report once every three months to benefit offices. Taken together, the system encourages extended periods of unemployment, raises reservation wages and increases the obstacles and lowers the incentives especially for older unskilled workers to find employment. The steps taken by the government to limit the duration of unemployment assistance to four years (soon to be implemented) and to reduce reference wages by 3 per cent per annum are modest moves in the right direction, as is the linking of social assistance more closely to local earnings opportunities. Even after these reforms, the system will remain very generous. Despite recent improvements, consideration might have to be given to restricting still further the ability to refuse job offers and also to increasing the incentives for lower paid workers to take employment at rates below, or even just above, those paid by assistance programmes. In this respect, the effectiveness of the recent steps towards introducing work-dependent transfers will need to be closely monitored.

In addition to an unemployment rate of some 10½ per cent, around 5 per cent of the working-age population are either on early retirement or retraining, and given the nature of these schemes most would probably be available for normal employment. Employment is particularly discouraged by poor incentive structures relating to early retirement, and by high labour costs due in part to support by the pension system for rehabilitation and sick pay arrangements. Early retirement is superficially appealing but fosters low labour utilisation and is costly to those employed. Moreover, it helps maintain wages at uneconomic levels and discourages the development of more flexible working practices. The termination of early retirement is thus welcome. However, the "grandfathering" provisions are very generous and undue emphasis is still being given to work sharing concepts via the scheme to subsidise part time work by older persons in return for equivalent new full-time employment. The tendency to think in terms of "job sharing" needs to be avoided and measures found for people to stay engaged in the workforce for longer periods corresponding to the increase in longevity.

The social security system is burdened with some particularly costly programmes which both raise the burden of non-wage costs and distort incentives. Entitlements should be reduced, without simply shifting the burden to the Federal budget. One of the most costly items is payment for visits to spas for rehabilitation. The limitation of such entitlements to three weeks every three years represents a start to reducing the overall cost burden. Sick pay is covered by employers for the first six weeks with full replacement of recent earnings and thereafter by the compulsory health funds for up to 78 weeks. The system is expensive and establishes an incentive structure which is conducive to widespread abuse. International experience suggests that employees could cover the first few days of sickness themselves, without significantly weakening the social safety net, while the rate of replacement pay could be lowered while still remaining equitable. The legislation currently being enacted along these lines reduces sick pay by 20 per cent but only applies to a third of the workforce. Extending this to the rest of the workforce will require a reassessment on the part of employers of commitments established by collective agreements. Nevertheless, the government should exercise a leadership role in this area, both as an employer and as the regulator of the health funds to take a lead in reforms in this area.

A notable feature in the German economy is that unemployment has increased markedly with cyclical downturns and supply-side shocks, but has failed to recede fully in the subsequent recovery. Moreover, around a third of the unemployed are categorised as long-term and a half are older than 50 years, usually with lower than average occupational skills. This tendency for unemployment to persist is evidently due in part to the distorted incentives built into the tax and benefit systems, but it also relates to some degree to low wage dispersion and inflexible working practices, which reduce the demand for labour.

- The sector-wide wage bargaining system ensures a high degree of collective, short-term flexibility, but at a cost in terms of inflexible wage differentials. In this respect, the system is already under intense pressure to respond to market forces and is evolving in the direction of less centralisation. While the government has to remain detached from actual wage negotiations, it should nevertheless encourage the social partners to accept greater flexibility and assist any spontaneous moves to restructure the wage bargaining system, where necessary by changes to the legal framework. In this context, the wider use of low re-entry wages for the long-term unemployed – such as those operating in the chemical sector – would be a welcome development.
- With wage costs high and the work week comparatively short, productivity needs to be augmented by more flexible working practices. Despite significant flexibility between work tasks, Germany has been slow in adopting flexible working practices, as is illustrated by relatively low machine running times. Again, decisions in this area fall within the domain of the social partners, who should make use of the liberalised regulations on working time. These should, nevertheless, be reviewed with a view to further liberalisation.

In two other areas legal provisions are binding: dismissal legislation and fixed-term contracts. The restrictions attaching to the former probably explain the reluctance of German firms to hire and their dependence on overtime for long periods during a recovery. While individual rights need to be protected, the system has undoubtedly developed in a manner not originally intended, in part through costly decisions on the part of the courts. The system is in urgent need of being simplified and placed on a more economic footing. Raising the floor on dismissal protection from firms with more than five employees to those with ten or more is a modest step in this direction. Fixed-term contracts have undoubtedly been successful in stimulating employment. However they are currently limited to three renewals within a maximum duration of up to two years. A more liberal framework would encourage improved employment prospects for marginal groups.

Active labour market policies have not been particularly successful in dealing with the problem of long-term unemployed. When not targeted on specific groups, they have tended to be costly and their efficiency in providing the re-entry to normal employment has been limited. The proposal by the government to target these measures more effectively, which will also serve to reduce such expenditures in the new *Länder* to similar levels as in the old states by the end of the century, is thus welcome. Indeed, active labour market measures as implemented have tended to reduce job search and their role in requalifying participants for unemployment benefits should be abolished. Such measures as are retained should be focused on the needs of those groups most at risk of becoming long-term unemployed.

With respect to the policies which the *Jobs Study* identifies as necessary to create the conditions for skill enhancement, technological diffusion and product market competition, the *Survey* suggests that there is, in some of these areas, substantial scope for reform.

- With respect to skills and competencies, one of the undoubted successes of the German system has been the dual system of vocational training with time being shared between the workplace and educational institutions. However, a large and growing number of young people are moving to higher education. The relationship of the system to higher education needs to be clarified and higher education should in turn include shorter and more occupationally oriented studies.
- Although the economy has a sound R&D base and is effective in adopting new technologies in existing industries, there is concern that new opportunities are not being effectively utilised. One manifestation of this is the deficiency as regards the establishment of new firms in knowledge-intensive sectors, which could be associated either with high levels of income tax and social security contributions or excessive regulation. As noted in the previous *Economic Survey of Germany,* perhaps one of the most important factors here is the underdeveloped state of the market for risk

capital, the current bank-oriented system of finance being unsuited to collateralising investment which often has an intangible character.

– Most significantly for an economy which has a below-average record for creating service-sector jobs, there is a need for greater product market deregulation. Germany is a highly open economy with a well developed and effective competition policy, but there are sectors which remain protected or supported by subsidies. To increase competitive pressures deregulation is called for in some sectors, especially in relation to shop closing hours. The greatest challenges lie in stimulating competition in the network industries of electricity, gas, and telecommunications. Exemption from current competition laws should be reduced or eliminated and exclusive concession arrangements tightly regulated. At the local community level privatisation needs to be encouraged and market testing strengthened.

Summing up, following generally disappointing economic performance during 1995 and early 1996, the economy should recover in the course of the year, based on growing exports and supportive monetary policy. A resumption of growth should not, however, be allowed to weaken a determined effort to correct the structural problems which the downturn has once more made apparent and which have been exacerbated by the burden of unification. What is at stake is not a wholesale dismantling of the welfare system, but rather reforms to place it on a sustainable basis by improving economic performance through better incentives. This indeed was the original concept of the ''social market economy'' which Germany pioneered. The government's new programme represents an important step in the right direction, but needs to be implemented in full and will probably require reinforcing if the German economy is to exploit the full potential of a well-qualified and motivated population. Structural reforms along the lines suggested would allow this potential to develop more fully.

Notes

1. The immediate reason for this state of affairs was the conversion of industrial orders and production statistics to European standards at the beginning of 1995, and the extension of statistical coverage in the new *Länder*. Initially, the new series proved highly unreliable. More generally, adequate resources need to be devoted to the provision of timely and reliable economic statistics.
2. For a discussion of this issue see *OECD Economic Survey of Germany 1995,* pp. 31-32.
3. The capital intensity of tradeables and non-tradeables probably differs. As a result, mark-up ratios are only a crude indicator of relative rates of return on capital, which is of most concern for resource flows.
4. IFO *Strukturbericht,* Munich, 1995.
5. Deutscher Industrie- und Handelstag, *Aussenhandel und Wettbewerbsfähigkeit* 1995, Bonn, 1995.
6. Deutscher Industrie- und Handelstag, *Wirtschaftslage und Erwartungen,* Bonn, 1995.
7. For a description of the extensive changes to the structure of off-budget activities in 1995 see *OECD Economic Survey of Germany,* 1995.
8. One factor in the expected decline was the reintroduction of the solidarity income-tax surcharge to cope with the burden of restructuring the federal/state revenue sharing system.
9. See *OECD Economic Survey of Germany,* 1995.
10. This arose because contributions started in January 1995, but expenditures only began in the second quarter.
11. The Post/Telecom system, which was split into three parts in 1988, has been corporatised with the existing stock of debt, which was taken over by the three new companies, recorded as remaining outside the general government sector. This difference of approach compared to the corporatisation of the railway system, where outstanding debt was taken over by a public Fund within the general government sector, reflects the positive net worth and expected profitability of the three companies despite their debt burden.
12. Ministry of Finance, *Fünfzehnter Subventionsbericht,* Bonn, 1996.
13. For different estimates see *Strukturbericht, 1995,* IFO Institut, Munich, 1995.
14. Wage increases in 1996 have been replaced by a flat payment of DM 300 and for 1997 wages will be increased by 1.3 per cent.

15. J. Tartler, ''Sparkurs zu Lasten der Investitionen'', *Handelsblatt,* 4 January 1996. For earlier provisional planning targets see ''Finanzplannung von Bund und Ländern, 1995 bis 1999'', *Wirtschaft und Statistik,* 2 February 1996.

16. The upper house has the power to reject tax legislation and other measures within the competence of the *Länder*. Other legislation may also be rejected but the lower house may overrule this with an absolute majority of all members.

17. This has been taken into consideration since the government in fact has very little choice in eliminating the business capital tax. It is not at present levied in the new *Länder* but, by agreement with the European Commission, the tax must be extended to them in 1997 or eliminated. An extension appears out of the question. A ruling by the Constitutional Court also makes it unlikely that the wealth tax can be retained in its present form. The government aims to offset revenue losses by a number of measures including reduced depreciation allowances for enterprises. As these are subject to legislative approval they are not considered.

18. See the previous Survey for a discussion and medium-term simulations. Expenditure savings are to be equally split between a lower deficit and reduced taxes and social security contributions.

19. *Finanzpolitik 2000,* Ministry of Finance, Bonn, March 1996.

20. The federal government does issue some short-term securities but a secondary market does not exist.

21. Starting in July 1996 the Federal government will issue securities in the form of Treasury discount paper with a standard maturity of six months. The amount of Treasury discount paper with a maturity of less than one year outstanding in 1996 and 1997 respectively is not to exceed DM 20 billion, while the current practice of issuing short-term non-marketable securities (mainly *Bundesschuldscheindarlehen*) will be curtailed.

22. The target was based on projected potential output growth of 2¾ per cent, GDP inflation of 2 per cent, and a trend decline in velocity of 1 per cent.

23. See *Monthly Report,* Deutsche Bundesbank, January 1996.

24. Under normal conditions the Lombard instrument is of minor importance and mainly provides a subsidiary credit line for banks to meet unexpected short-term liquidity needs.

25. Most market participants believe that the minimum spread between the discount and repurchase rates should be 25 basis points, otherwise recourse to the discount facility would not be worthwhile.

26. This is particularly true of the United States, so that the general rise in rates could signal a stronger world economy.

27. This is a position advocated by the six leading economic institutes. See DIW, *Wochenbericht,* 18/96, Berlin, 1996.

28. For details on the methodology see ''Les indicateurs des conditions monétaires'', *Bulletin de la Banque de France,* No. 30, June 1996.

29. See *OECD Economic Survey of Germany,* 1993 for a description of the fiscal redistribution system.

30. Decisions on the supervisory board of the labour office are taken by simple majority voting.

31. Hauser, R., ''Problems of the German Welfare State after Unification'', *Oxford Review of Economic Policy,* Vol. 11 No. 3, 1995.

32. Deutsches Institut für Wirtschaftsforschung, *Transferleistungen in die neuen Bundesländer und deren wirtschaftliche Konsequenzen,* Berlin 1995.

33. According to the definition of the ''Social Budget'' published by the federal government, which includes tax expenditures and certain spending by employers, see Bundesministerium für Arbeit und Sozialordnung, *Übersicht über das Sozialrecht,* Bonn 1995.

34. The generosity of the system was somewhat reduced in 1994 when the replacement rate of former standardised net earnings was lowered from 68 per cent to 67 per cent for persons with children, and from 63 per cent to 60 per cent for persons without children.

35. For a similar argument see Pacqué, K.-H., ''Unemployment and the crisis of the German model'', *Kiel Working Papers,* No. 655, September 1994.

36. See for example, Thimann, C.L., ''Effective taxation for recipients of social assistance in Germany and the consequences of the 1996 tax reform'', *IMF Working Paper* 95/120. See also Deutsche Bundesbank, *Monthly Report,* February 1996.

37. High marginal effective tax rates can be lowered by cutting the benefit withdrawal rate, but only at the cost of extending the benefit provision up the income schedule. The effects of a 20 percentage point reduction in withdrawal rates for social assistance and housing benefits on marginal effective tax rates have been assessed in a micro simulation study commissioned by the OECD. The policy would reduce marginal effective tax rates predominantly for those who originally had high marginal effective tax rates exceeding 80 per cent. However, more than three times as many people would face higher marginal effective tax rates as a result of the reform than face lower marginal effective tax rates. Also, extending the benefits provision up the income schedule would put additional pressure on the government's budget.

38. For a study on the redistribution within the public health insurance system see Henke, K.D., and Behrens, C., *Umverteilungswirkungen der gesetzlichen Krankenversicherung,* Bayreuth, 1989.

39. Over the last years insured employees subsidised the health insurance of pensioners by more than three percentage points of their contribution rate.

40. Two cases are often cited. One is the requirement to accept people seeking asylum which places a burden on local social assistance. The second is the new federal law requiring the provision of kindergartens by the local authorities.

41. See *Von der Pensionsrückstellung zum Pensionsfonds: Eine Chance für den deutschen Finanzmarkt.* Deutsche Bank Research, Frankfurt, 1995.

42. Companies can establish funds which are regulated like insurance companies, but employees are taxed on employer contributions over DM 3 400 per year.

43. See Deutsche Bank Research, *op. cit.,* for a catalogue of specific barriers.

44. The share of the *Länder* was raised from 44 per cent in 1995 to compensate the higher financial burden of the *Länder* that resulted from the reform of the child benefit system.

45. Deutsches Institut für Wirtschaftsforschung, *Wochenbericht,* 46/95, Berlin, November 1995.
46. The employers' contribution rate to the pension fund for miners (*knappschaftliche Rentenversicherung*) is higher than for the employees.
47. Clemens, R. and L. Kokalis, "Bürokratie- ein Kostenfaktor", *Schriften zur Mittelstandsforschung,* No. 66, Bonn, 1995.
48. Short-term speculation denotes sales of real estate within two years of purchase or of other assets within six months of purchase.
49. Up to a portion of pensions representing capital gains by recipients.
50. Benefits are included as taxable income to derive the average tax rate, but are then deducted from the tax base in deriving the tax liability (*Progressionsvorbehalt*).
51. Prior to the 1996 tax reform, taxable income above the basic allowance was taxed at a constant marginal tax rate up to DM 8 153 (the lower proportional zone).
52. As a temporary solution prior to a more comprehensive tax reform, the basic allowance was lifted to around DM 11 000 (DM 22 000). Within a narrow band immediately above the subsistence income level the interim tax schedule then approached the 1992 tax schedule, implying high marginal tax rates of between 50 and 60 per cent in the transition range.
53. Taxpayers who are eligible for child allowances or child benefits can claim a further tax allowance for children attending school (*Ausbildungsfreibetrag*). It ranges from DM 1 800 for children under 18 years of age living separate from the family to DM 4 200 for children over 18 years who live separate from their families. The allowances are means tested against the income of the children above a certain threshold. Taxpayers who are single and are eligible for child allowances or child benefits also qualify for a "household tax allowance" (*Haushaltsfreibetrag*) of DM 5 616.
54. The tax credit does not accrue to non-resident shareholders
55. The definition of subsidies by the research institutes comprises transfers and tax expenditures that aid directly or indirectly the company sector, including aid to public enterprises. For details see Fritzsche, *et al., Subventionen – Probleme der Abgrenzung und Erfassung,* Munich, 1988.
56. See *Strukturbericht 1995*; IFO, Munich 1995.
57. Cash subsidies increased in 1996 because the special levy on consumers to compensate electricity producers for having to buy more expensive domestic coal was replaced by a cash subsidy. See also Chapter IV.
58. However, the maximum rate of subsidisation available to firms has been increased in 1995.
59. The distribution of net replacement ratios has been computed by family type, family income level and economic status of the head of the household or his or her spouse. Four different family types were specified: single person without children, lone parent, couple without children, and couple with children. Two types of non-working persons are considered: non-employed persons who do not receive unemployment benefits or payments from a public or private pension scheme, and unemployed persons receiving unemployment benefits or unemployment assistance. To take account of the dependence of net replacement rates on the level of income when out of work, average replacement rates have been estimated for each quintile of the household non-work income distribution.

60. Deutsche Bundesbank, *Monthly Report,* January 1996. Negotiated wages for low income groups in different sectors were used to measure the likely opportunity cost of social assistance. See also Thimann, *op.cit.*

61. A study commissioned by the OECD shows that in 1993 4 per cent of Germany's potential labour force faced an effective marginal tax rate of over 100 per cent (that is an extra unit of work made them worse off), and another 11 per cent face effective marginal tax rates of between 60 and 100 per cent (See also *OECD Employment Outlook,* Chapter II, 1996). Since these figures pertain to the actual number of hours worked, they already incorporate the responses of the employees to the incentive structure of the tax benefits system.

62. Rheinisch-Westfälisches Institut für Wirtschaftsforschung, Essen. *Das Zusammenwirken von Steuern und Sozialtransfers in den jungen Bundesländern- eine empirische analyse anhand von Fallbeispielen und Problemdarstellung,* Essen 1994.

63. This is due to the higher rates of female labour force participation in the past and to longer contribution periods.

64. This is reinforced by self-employment, agriculture and forestry being exempt from the local business tax.

65. For example, in France such taxes amounted to 1.8 per cent of GDP in 1992 and in the United Kingdom to around 2.3 per cent. In Germany the taxes – including land tax – amounted to some 1.7 per cent. (See *Bundestagsdrucksache,* 13/2238)

66. On a standardised basis the unemployment rate is somewhat lower than the headline rate: 8.4 per cent in 1994 while the national definition was 9.6 per cent. Both the numerator (unemployment) and the denominator (labour force) are defined differently under the two measures. In the national series, the unemployed include all people between the ages of 15 and 65 who live in Germany and are willing, able, and actually looking for work through a placement agency (whether drawing unemployment benefits or not), including those working only short-time (less than 18 hours per week). The labour force includes all civilian workers (employed and unemployed), *i.e.* dependent, self-employed, and family workers. The standardised series differs in the following respects: short-time workers (working more than two hours per week) are not counted as unemployed, and unemployment is measured by survey data rather than by registration statistics with employment placement agencies and military personnel are included as part of the labour force.

67. For a more detailed description of labour market developments over time, see *OECD Survey of Germany,* 1994.

68. Correcting the statistics to allow for the switch to services which are still classified as manufacturing jobs would increase the job losses in the latter and boost service growth. It would not change net flows and therefore the impact on employment and unemployment. See *Strukturberichterstattung, 1995*; IFO, Munich, 1996.

69. D. Bogai, *et al.,* ''Binnenstruktur der Langzeitarbeitlosigkeit älterer Männer und Frauen'', *MittAB,* 2/94.

70. A survey in 1995 of craft establishments found many more self-employed tradesmen than had been previously supposed.

71. The large number of registered female unemployed is reflected in a high rate of labour force participation in comparison with the old *Länder.* It is sometimes argued that labour force participation remains artificially high for historical reasons and will eventually normalise. This viewpoint is not supported by the labour force survey.

72. See for example D, Turner *et al.,* ''The role of real and nominal rigidities in macroeconoic adjustment: a comparative study of the G3 economies'', *OECD Economic Studies,* No. 21, 1993, and J. Elmeskov, ''Unemployment persistence'', *OECD Economic Studies,* No. 21, 1993. For additional comparative material see Sachverständigenrat, *Den Aufschwung Sichern; Arbeitsplätze Schaffen,* Wiesbaden, 1995.

73. Elmeskov, *op. cit.*

74. OECD, *Employment Outlook,* 1993, Chapter 5.

75. OECD, *Employment Outlook,* 1994, Chapter 5.

76. In 1994, 567 contracts had been declared generally binding covering about 1 million workers in western Germany. Most of the extensions covered work conditions, only 14 per cent covering wages. Construction, textiles and clothing, cleaning and hairdressing were the sectors most affected. W. Franz, ''Die Lohnfindung in Deutschland in einer internationalen Perspective: Ist das deutsche System ein Auslaufmodell'', *Beihefte der Konjunkturpolitik,* Heft 43, 1995.

77. Negotiating power is further balanced by Article 116 of the labour code which makes workers ineligible for unemployment benefit if they are laid off because a strike elsewhere has cut off a firm's supplies, and if they stand to benefit directly from the industrial agreement at stake in the strike. The provision increases the unions' need for strike funds.

78. Wages do of course differ between industries and between skill groups. In 1994, the average sector agreement covered 8.5 wage groups and 6.7 salary groups. For 23 agreements covering 5.5 million employees, monthly wages varied from DM 2 253 in the shoe industry to DM 4 731 in refining. In the important metal industry there were 12 wage groups in 1992, with a variation of wages from 85 per cent to 135 per cent of the middle-wage group. (Franz, 1995, *op cit.*). Although there clearly is wage differentiation, the question is whether it is sufficiently large. The pattern of unemployment would suggest that it is not, but the appropriate wage differentiation cannot be specified in advance. This is for market processes to discover, but the efficiency of this process will be importantly influenced by the institutional arrangements in the labour market.

79. ''Gesamtwirtschaftliche und unternehmerische Anpassungsfortschritte in Ostdeutschland'', *Kiel Discussion Papers,* 256/257, 1995, Tables 25 and 26.

80. There were 43 000 collective agreements registered in 1994 covering 850 and 250 professional or regional groupings in western and eastern Germany, respectively (Franz, *op. cit.,* 1995). Two thirds were concluded with employers' associations, the remainder directly with enterprises.

81. Construction companies have cut costs by subcontracting operations to firms in other countries such as Portugal and the UK. These firms send workers to Germany for extended periods paying wages and social contributions of the home country, which are substantially below those in Germany. The new legislation allows for the extension of any collectively agreed minimum wage to such foreign workers. At the time of writing (July 1996) the

German Federation of Employers had refused to accept the introduction of a minimum wage. Agreement was reached in the European Union in June to restrict the employment of workers on temporary assignment.

82. ''Performance of the European Union labour market'', *European Economy,* No. 3, 1995, Table 8*a*.

83. D. Grubb and Wells, W, ''Employment regulations and patterns of work in EC countries'', *OECD Economic Studies,* 21, 1993, Annex III.

84. Bundesministerium für Arbeit und Sozialordnung, ''Beschäftigung und Arbeitsmarkt'', *Research Report 242,* Bonn, 1994.

85. *Sozialversicherungsfreie Beschäftigung,* Bundesministerium für Arbeit und Sozialordnung, Forschungsbericht 181*a,* 1993. Of this figure, around 3 million were exclusively employed in this manner, the remainder having other jobs.

86. Unemployed remain members of the social security system during the period when they are receiving benefits.

87. *Employment Outlook,* OECD, Paris 1995, Table I.6.

88. Survey by McKinsey as quoted in U. Walwei and Werner, H., ''Mehr Teilzeitarbeit als Mittel gegen die Arbeitslosigkeit'', *Wirtschaftsdienst,* No. 3, March 1996.

89. The mobility in the income distribution ladder in Germany is relatively high. The probablity of leaving the lowest quintile is comparable to the United States and is around 40 per cent after four years. Burkhauser, R., D. Holz-Eakin, ''Changes in the distribution of wage earnings in the United States and Germany during the 1980s'', *Vierteljahrshefte zur Wirtschaftsforschung,* 1994.

90. These findings are broadly corroborated by studies which more closely specify earnings opportunities. See for example *Monthly Report,* Deutsche Bundesbank, February 1996.

91. The net replacement rate is the ratio between net family income from all sources when in work to all income including transfers and social assistance income when out of work. It is thus a useful indicator of the incentive to change labour market status. Marginal effective tax rates, by contrast, shed light on decisions which affect earnings in a marginal way such as small increase in hours of work. They compare an increase in earnings at a given income level to what is received by a worker after allowing for all benefits and taxes.

92. Construction employers could also be compensated up to 1994 for wage costs during bad weather. Since that time employers and workers share the costs for the first 20 days and after that there are benefits.

93. A case in point occurred in the steel industry where zero hours short-time work was combined with an innovative attempt to have skilled workmen spend time with independent craftsmen. The workers showed little interest in view of the wage differences, required geographical mobility, and the desire to maintain a permanent contract with the original place of work. The use of short time to promote retraining also appears to have met with limited success. See, H. Mosley, ''Kurzarbeitsprogramme in Frankreich, Deutschland, Italien und Spanien: von einer Konjunktur zu eine Strukturmaßnahme'' *Infor MISEP,* 52 Winter 1995.

94. Over the age of 58, an unemployed person may even refuse a suitable job offer and not be penalised in the form of a cut in benefits.

95. The law actually provides for sanctions against both the employer and the employee where there is collusion in dismissal, but in practice it is not often used.

96. Courts have interpreted provisions in the labour law restrictively so that it is often difficult to dismiss older workers or those with dependants unless the firm obtains a voluntary agreement.

97. Statistisches Bundesamt, 1995 (Fachserie 16.1, Arbeitskosten im Produzierenden Gewerbe). ''Normal wages'' denote wages paid excluding items like holiday and sick pay. The research institute of the German employers estimates that indirect labour costs in manufacturing in 1994 account for 82 per cent of normal wages (*Industriestandort Deutschland,* Institut der deutschen Wirtschaft, Köln, 1995).

98. *Wirtschaftswoche* No. 8, 15/02/1996.

99. Entitlements are based on gross pay and sick pay is taxable.

100. International comparison is, however, difficult since unemployment benefits in Germany are tax exempt so that gross outlays are thereby lower than in other countries.

101. For a discussion and assessment of job-broking activities see, *The public employment service in Austria, Germany and Sweden*, forthcoming, 1996, OECD, Paris.

102. Walwei, M *et al.,* ''Reform der Arbeitsvermittlung in OECD Ländern,'' *Mitteilungen aus der Arbeitsmarkt und Berufsforschung,* Vol. 27, No. 2, 1994.

103. It should also be noted that a third of the participants in western Germany, who were judged to have successfully completed the course, in fact passed no examination. The proportion was higher in the east.

104. Institut für Arbeitsmarkt und Berufsforschung der Bundesanstalt für Arbeit, ''Einarbeitung-szuschüsse'', *IAB Werkstattbericht* No.2, 1995.

105. For a summary of research findings in Germany, see C. Walter, ''Wie effizient ist die aktive Arbeitsmarktpolitik in der Bundesrepublik Deutschland'', *Die Weltwirtschaft* No. 2, 1995.

106. For more general support for this observation, see *Enhancing the effectiveness of active labour market policies,* OECD 1996.

107. *Vocational Training in Germany: Modernisation and Responsiveness,* OECD, Paris, 1994.

108. Nickell, S., ''The Low-skill Low-pay Problem: Lessons from Germany for Britain and the United States'', *Policy Studies,* 1996.

109. About 60 per cent of vocational training is undertaken by firms employing fewer than 100 persons, and in 1995 it is estimated that around DM 68 billion (1½ per cent of GDP) was spent by all enterprises on training.

110. For general background see Steedman, H., ''The economics of youth training in Germany'', *The Economic Journal* No. 103, 1993.

111. Prior to the partial privatisation, Lufthansa went through a one and a half year restructuring increasing productivity by 30 per cent. Commission Européenne *Panorama de l'industrie communautaire,* 95/96, Brussels, pp. 22-65.

112. Demarcation contracts are permitted provided they guarantee secure supplies and favourable prices. The competition authority recently lost a test case in the new *Länder* concerning gas distribution.

113. ''Überprüfung des Ladenschlußgesetzes vor dem Hintergrund der Erfahrungen in In-und Ausland'', *IFO Schnelldienst,* 24, 1995.

114. Survey undertaken by IFO. See *Wirtschaftswoche* No. 47, 16 November 1995.

115. *Strukturbericht 1995,* IFO, Munich, 1995.

116. Greuzmann C. and S. Grief, ''The relationship between R&D input and output'' in *Innovation, Patents and Technological Strategies,* OECD, Paris, 1996.

117. Constant-market-share analysis reported in the previous OECD *Survey of Germany,* (Annex II) indicated that, over the period 1980-1992, the concentration of exports on relatively fast expanding commodity categories had an overall beneficial effect on its aggregate export share. However, the commodity adaptation effect was negative, signifying that competitive gains had been concentrated on slower-growing segments of world trade. The Strukturbericht results reported here are confined to a shorter period, 1989/1992, so that the slowly growing export industries of the new *Länder* (*e.g.* ships, rolling stock) have a higher overall weight. The analysis was conducted at a much greater level of SITC disaggregation and did not attempt to ''explain'' the variation of market share.

118. Schmoch, U. *et al., Technology Transfer in Germany,* Frauhofer Institut für Systemtechnick und Innovationforschung, Karlsruhe, 1996.

119. See also *Green Book on Innovation,* European Commission, 1995.

120. Employees who are aged 55 or older in February 1996 (52 or older for miners and steel workers) will be exempted from the increase in the early retirement age.

Annex I

Summary indicators of the tax/benefit system: replacement rates

Definition of replacement rates

In summarising the influence of the unemployment benefits and social assistance systems, it is customary to compare incomes of individuals (and their households) when they are in and out of work. The resulting ratio is termed a *replacement rate* reflecting the extent to which the benefits system replaces income lost through unemployment. Policy concerns are now directed toward understanding the incentive structures facing the unemployed when considering a return to employment, and in this case the net gain in income after loss of benefits and taxes is the more relevant criterion. Replacement rates may be defined on either a gross or a net basis: the former defines incomes on a gross basis while the latter also includes the taxation and social security contribution regimes. Net replacement rates are more informative about work incentives, to which most policy discussion is directed, and are therefore used here. This annex describes the replacement rate concept utilised in Chapters III and IV and illustrates how the results may differ from other measures.

There are two main approaches to measuring replacement rates: the *household income ratio* and the *average effective tax rate*. They differ in the way they reflect non-labour income and in the definition of the wage base. For either approach, net replacement rates may be calculated for classes of persons based on entitlement regulations (*i.e.* they represent hypothetical replacement rates) or they may be derived from actual survey data about the socio-economic characteristics of households and augmented by information about the structure of entitlements.

With the household income ratio, the net replacement rate is defined as y^n/y^w, where y^n = household net income when the reference person is not working and y^w household net income when the reference person is working. Table A1.1 illustrates this concept, abstracting for simplicity from income taxes and social security contributions. In the first row it is assumed that the reference person receives benefits of 70 when unemployed and earnings of 100 when employed. There is no other income from the person's spouse. The household income ratio is 70/100 = 0.7 or 70 per cent. In the second row it is assumed that the person's spouse earns an income of 80. The spouse's income is not affected by the change in the employment status of the reference person. Under these conditions,

Table A1.1. **Different measures of replacement rates**

Case	Reference person			Spouse		Replacement rate	
	Benefits when unemployed	Earnings when employed	Gross earnings when employed	Income when reference person is unemployed	Income when reference person is employed	Ratio of household income (per cent)	Average effective tax rate (per cent)
1	70	100	100	0	0	70	70
2	70	100	100	80	80	83	70
3	70	100	100	80	70	88	80
4	70	100	120	80	70	88	83

Source : OECD.

household income in and out of work is higher by 80, so that the household income ratio is also greater: (70 + 80)/(100 + 80) = 0.83 or 83 per cent. The same principle would hold if the household received capital income or income from other sources. In line three of the table the income of the spouse is means tested: it drops from 80 to 70 when the reference person moves from unemployment into employment. This scenario is relevant if, for example, the spouse of the reference person received unemployment assistance, although the reductions in benefit income as family income rises are typically more severe than in this example). The household income ratio is now given by (70 + 80)/(100 + 70) = 0.88 or 88 per cent. The replacement ratio exceeds the one given in line two because in-work household income is comparatively lower due to the withdrawal of benefits. *Ceteris paribus,* the higher the level of the net replacement rate, the lower would be the incentive for the unemployed to seek and to accept work.

Another approach focuses on the income lost (sometimes called the ''effective tax rate'') when returning to work, which determines the net income gain. The replacement rate thus defined relates the net change in household income when a reference individual becomes employed to the gross earnings of that person in work. It is defined as: $1 - (y^w - y^n)/y$, where y^n and y^w are as defined above, and y = gross labour income of the reference person. The denominator in this case includes employer's social security contributions in the definition of income from working. Including these contributions reflects the assumption that the full burden of social security contributions falls on labour income. Table A1.1 (final column) illustrates this concept in comparison to the household income ratio, abstracting from income taxes and social security contributions. In the first row, if the reference person works, household income increases by only 30, implying an average effective tax rate on working of 70 per cent. In this case, where contributions are implicity assumed to be zero, the two different concepts imply the same replacement rate. In the second case, with additional income from another source, the average effective tax rate does not alter because benefits withdrawn as a percentage of the earnings of the reference person remain unchanged. By contrast, when measured by the household income approach the replacement rate increases. In case three, with the income of the spouse *means-tested,* the effective tax on work including withdrawn benefits increases to 80 per cent. The examples illustrate that, in contrast to the household income ratio, average effective tax rates are unaffected by income from additional sources unless it is means-tested. The fourth row incorporates the simple assumption that the employers' social security contributions are 20 per cent. This raises the average tax rate but leaves the ratio of household income unchanged.

In the present *Survey* attention has been focused on investigating the actual replacement rates for unemployed households, and especially those receiving either unemployment benefits, unemployment assistance or social assistance. The household income ratio has been used as a measure of replacement rates in preference to the average effective tax rate for two reasons, since *i)* other sources of income are fully reflected in this measure, which is important since they probably play a role in influencing the labour market behaviour of households; *ii)* the definition avoids the need to assume that employers' social security contributions fall on labour income, and thereby influence labour supply decisions. In view of the fact that other sources of income have been included, the replacement rates are higher than those reported in other studies and in Table A1.2.

Table A1.2. **Replacement rates[1] for single-earner households, 1994**

Average effective tax rate at the APW level of earnings

	Replacement rates in first month of unemployment: no social assistance Net replacement rates (after tax and other benefits)			60th month of unemployment: including social assistance Net replacement rate after tax and other benefits
	Couple, no children	Couple, 2 children	Couple, 2 children, housing benefits	Couple, 2 children, housing benefits
Australia[2,3,4]	49	64	71	71
Belgium	64	66	66	70
Canada	63	67	67	47
Denmark[5]	69	73	83	83
Finland	63	75	88	98
France	69	71	80	65
Germany	**60**	**71**	**78**	**71**
Ireland[3]	49	64	64	64
Italy	37	47	47	11
Japan[3]	43	42	42	68
Netherlands	77	77	84	80
New Zealand[3,4]	48	64	70	70
Norway	67	73	73	83
Spain	75	74	74	46
Sweden[2,5]	81	84	89	99[2]
Switzerland	77	89	89	71
United Kingdom[3]	35	51	77	77
United States[6]	60	68	68	17

Note: In the first month of unemployment it is assumed that families possess enough assets to be ineligible for social assistance. In the 60th month it is assumed that they no longer have such assets and so social assistance (SA) is assumed to be paid where it is higher than other benefits to which they may still be entitled. The replacement rates reflect a strict application of legal provisions rather than common practice, where these differ. For more details see source.

1. It is assumed that the worker is 40 years old, and started work at 18. The replacement rates are for the first month of unemployment, after waiting periods have been satisfied. This entitlement is then multiplied by 12 to give an annualised equivalent, on which tax is calculated. The person is fully unemployed. Social assistance is calculated according to a "typical rates" for the country concerned. This may involve making assumptions about housing costs.
2. Benefit amounts for couples are calculated on the basis of both spouses actively seeking work.
3. Figures for Australia, Ireland, New Zealand and the United Kingdom are for 1995. Unemployment benefits parameters for Japan are for 1996.
4. There is no social insurance in Australia or New Zealand. All figures in the table, refer to the assistance benefit.
5. Social assistance is only available when there is a "social event" such as unemployment. Low earnings are not themselves a social event.
6. The taxes and benefits are calculated using the rules applying in Detroit, Michigan. All figures include AFDC and Food Stamps. If these are treated as being equivalent to social assistance, columns 3, 4 and 5 would read 60, 59 and 59 at the level of APW.

Source: "Making work pay", *Employment Outlook,* OECD, Paris 1996.

Computing replacement rates

Replacement rates may be computed either for hypothetical households or for actual households. For the former, a *hypothetical household* with socio-economic characteristics of specific interest is analysed. For example, the group to be studied may be defined as a single earner household comprising a couple with two children. For the reference person, the level of earnings needs to be specified (for example, earnings of an average production worker), as well as the level of unearned non-transfer income. Taxes and benefits for the family under consideration are then imputed in accordance with the relevant legal provisions covering both employment and unemployment of the reference person.[1] The benefits received when unemployed may depend on the duration of unemployment (as is the case for Germany) which also needs to be specified. With the second approach, replacement rates are computed on the basis of a *household sample,* which allows for the distribution of the socio-economic characteristics of the households in the population. For a sample of employed, the information on household income, family benefits and taxes, can be used to simulate the implied replacement ratio for each household by application of a model which incorporates the relevant legal provisions. This provides a picture of the distribution of replacement rates as they prevail in the population. Summary statistics such as the average replacement rate for certain types of households can be computed, the replacement rates thus derived being interpreted as measuring the incentive to remain employed. Similarly, replacement rates may be computed from a sample of households with the reference person unemployed. In this case, family benefits and taxes would be simulated for the unemployed reference person moving into employment at a pre-specified level of earnings; since the wages of an unemployed person are not known, they need to be estimated or approximated.

Replacement rates for hypothetical households have the advantage that they are well suited for international comparisons because of the high degree of standardisation that can be achieved with respect to the socio-economic characteristics of households and the labour market transition. The OECD has undertaken such a cross-country comparison of hypothetical replacement rates as part of the *OECD Jobs Study* (Table A1.2). However, replacement rates derived from household samples have the advantage that they provide empirical information about the incidence of replacement ratios in the population. Replacement ratios on this basis have been calculated as part of the follow-up to the *Jobs Study*.

The replacement ratios reported in Chapters III and IV are based on a cross-section sample of households taken from the tenth wave of the German Socio-Economic Panel, sampled in autumn 1992 and spring 1993. Wages and benefits have been adjusted to 1995 levels. The ratios are computed for two sub-samples of households with the reference person being out-of-employment. Since potential earnings are not known, they are approximated by the earnings of full-time employees observed in a subsample. Two alternative calculations have been undertaken. First, individuals have been assumed to enter jobs at the level of the first decile of the gross earnings distribution from the sample of the full-time employed. This decile covers particularly low earning opportunities. Replacement ratios were also evaluated at the median gross earnings of the full-time employed. This scenario allows for both higher entry wages and wage increases that occur over time as individuals with a low wage job move up the income ladder. Eight types of family income are considered: labour earnings, capital income, alimony, unemployment benefits, unemployment assistance, social assistance, housing benefits, child benefits. For the first five income sources, sample information for non-working households is available. The remaining types of income are derived from the tax-benefits model. In deriving replacement rates it was assumed that, to the extent benefits are not means tested, the spouse continues to receive the same gross earnings and unearned income, regardless of the change in the partner's employment status. The tax-benefits model incorporates the 1995 benefits schedule.[2] The simulations have been conducted by the Rheinisch-Westfälisches Institut für Wirtschafsforschung (RWI).

Notes

1. Employment may be specified as full-time or part-time employment. Moreover, instead of considering unemployment, other states of not working may be of interest, such as non-participation in the labour force.
2. The 1995 tax schedule was changed in 1996. While for certain income groups the change implies a significant impact on marginal tax rates, the impact on average replacement ratios, is expected to be limited.

Annex II

The impact of tax/transfers on labour supply and unemployment duration: econometric evidence

This annex reviews empirical evidence on the impact of taxes (*i.e.* net wages) and benefits on labour supply and unemployment duration. All of the studies considered, apart from those regarding ''black market'' activity, are micro-econometric investigations and often report results in the way of policy simulations rather than by simply specifying statistically signficant coefficients. With the exception of the work of Franz (1982) they are based on samples drawn from the German Socio-economic Panel which is the most comprehensive data set for the analysis of household data available in Germany.

There is strong evidence that female labour supply is reduced by the system of split taxation. Tax splitting in Germany reduces family taxation and increases disposable family income in comparison to taxation on an individual basis. For the spouse with the higher income, the marginal tax rate decreases, while increasing for the spouse with lower income, especially for those not working. Using a structural model of married women's labour supply, Strom and Wagenhals (1991) simulated the effect on female labour force participation of abolishing split taxation while leaving other parameters of the tax schedule unchanged. According to their estimates, a change in the tax regime would increase the share of women participating in the labour market in Germany by several percentage points, and this result is also supported by Gustaffson (1992). Extending the former study, Wagenhals (1996*a*) showed that the increase in labour force participation would be particularly pronounced among women with lower income. In addition, the desired hours of work at all levels of income would increase. Spahn *et al.* (1992) considered the policy option of compensating the termination of tax-splitting by revenue-neutral increases in child allowances. Labour supply, measured as aggregate hours of work, increased as a result of the joint reform. A deficiency of all these studies is that they do not model the joint determination of the spouses' labour supply. The effect of abolishing income tax splitting on labour supply would be reduced as male labour-force participation declined, but the overall effect on labour force participation is likely to remain positive given the apparently low elasticity of male labour supply with respect to net wages.

Other studies of female labour force participation consider a broader range of taxes and benefits and conclude that while female labour supply in Germany responds positively to increases in net wages, for some groups hours of work may decline. Laisney *et al.* (1993) modelled labour supply of single mothers as a choice between non-participation in the labour market and full-time and part-time employment. Considering the 1990 tax schedule, they found that a reduction in social assistance would lead to an increase in desired female labour force participation, almost equally distributed between part-time and full-time employment. In another simulation the child allowance was increased to the level of the basic allowance. This increase led to a relatively strong tendency for full-time employees to change to part-time employment, while there was a less pronounced effect for non-participants to enter employment. The former result is attributable to an income effect, allowing single mothers to reduce their working time. They also simulated a doubling of the basic income tax allowance and concluded that it would create an incentive for working part-time, which operates in a similar manner to an increase of the basic child allowance. Wagenhals (1996*b*) investigated the potential impact of the 1996 tax reform on the labour supply of married women, and concluded that the increase in the basic tax allowance, in comparison to the 1992 tax schedule, could lead to a significant increase in labour force participation by women in low-income households. On the other hand, increased marginal tax rates implied by the 1996 tax schedule would lead to a reduction in the desired number of hours worked for women with higher earnings. However, the higher marginal tax rates would not lead to a decline in labour force participation by high-earning persons. Overall, the tax reform would increase labour force participation by married women.

Little research effort has been devoted to studying the labour supply response of men with respect to net wages. This is attributable mainly to the fact that male labour supply in terms of number of hours worked has generally been found inelastic, see *e.g.* Kaiser, H. *et al.* (1992). This finding, which is consistent with empirical evidence from other countries, may reflect the traditional role of men as the main source of household income. On the other hand, there is indirect evidence that male labour supply does nevertheless respond to broader features of the tax-transfer system. Econometric work indicates that the size of the shadow economy in Germany amounts to several percentage points of GDP and is related to the tax burden [see Kirchgässner (1983), and Schneider (1994)].

Empirical investigations, while not unambiguous, suggest that the transition from unemployment to employment is responsive to the level of income replacement and to entitlements for some transfer schemes. The research methodology normally involves estimating the (conditional) probability of moving from the state of unemployment into some other pre-defined state such as full-time employment. Hujer and Schneider (1987), Hujer, Löwenbein and Schneider (1990), Schneider (1991), and Wurzel (1990) estimate the effects of benefit entitlement and/or the level of unemployment compensation. However, only one (the study by Hujer, Löwenbein and Schneider) indicates that entitlement for unemployment assistance (*Arbeitslosenhilfe*) serves to reduce the transition rate for men to employment. The level of unemployment compensation is not statistically significant in the study by Wurzel (1993). It has been argued, however, that with insufficient information on pre-unemployment work histories, econometric estimates are likely to be biased against establishing a significantly positive impact of unemployment benefits on the duration of unemployment. Working with a larger data set, Steiner (1994) found that entitlement for unemployment compensation significantly increases unemployment duration. A marginal increase in the replacement ratio, as defined by unemployment compensation relative to previous earnings, was also found to increase unemployment duration, but the effect is small. According to Steiner (1996), entitlement for unemployment assistance appears to have a substantial effect on the transition of women out of unemployment to non-participation in the labour force.

Research suggests that the duration of benefits has a significant impact on labour market behaviour. For younger unemployed, the analysis by Wurzel (1993) indicates that exits from unemployment into employment increase before unemployment benefits are set to decline or to be exhausted. Hunt (1995) found a significant negative impact on exit rates from unemployment due to the lengthening of the benefits entitlement period (*Arbeitslosengeld*) for older unemployed following the 1980s policy reforms. The decline in exit rates was focused on two groups of the unemployed: elderly women and men aged mid-forties to early fifties. For the former, exit rates to non-participation declined, while for the latter exit rates to employment fell. Steiner (1996), also found evidence suggesting that the lengthening of benefit entitlement has increased unemployment duration for elderly women. Moreover, the transition rates of males into employment and of females into non-participation increase substantially as unemployment benefits cease.

Transfer programmes can serve to increase reservation wages, thereby lengthening the duration of unemployment, but only a few studies have investigated this question directly. Using direct sample information on desired wages of unemployed persons when entering the unemployment register Franz (1982) analysed the determinants of reservation wages. The analysis showed reservation wages to be positively related to unemployment compensation, but this effect was quantitatively weak.

References

Franz, W. ''The reservation wage of unemployed persons in the Federal Republic of Germany: theory and empirical tests'', *Zeitschrift für Wirtschafts- und Sozialwissenschaften,* Vol. 102, No. 1, 1982.

Gustafsson, S. ''Separate taxation and married women's labor supply. A comparison of west Germany and Sweden'', *Journal of population economics,* Vol. 5. No. 1, 1992.

Hunt, J. ''The effect of unemployment compensation on unemployment duratiuon in Germany'', *Journal of Labour Economics,* Vol. 13, No. 1, 1995.

Hujer, R. and H. Schneider, ''Determinanten der Arbeitslosigkeit in der Bundesrepublik Deutschland'', in: K.W. Rothschild, G. Tichy, *Arbeitslosigkeit und Arbeitsangebot in Österreich,* Vienna, 1987.

Hujer, R., O. Löwenbein, H. Schneider, ''Wages and unemployment – a microeconometric analysis for the FRG'', in: H. König, *Economics of wage determination,* Berlin, 1990.

Kaiser, H., U. van Essen, P. B. Spahn, ''Income taxation and supply of labour in West Germany'', *Jahrbücher für Nationalökonomie und Statistik,* Vol. 209, No. 1-2, 1992.

Kirchgässner, G., ''Size and development of the West German shadow economy, 1955-1980'', *Zeitschrift für die gesamte Staatswirtschaft,* Vol. 139, 1983.

Laisney F., M. Lechner, M.Staat and G. Wagenhals, ''Labour force and welfare participation of lone mothers in West Germany'', *Zentrum für Europäische Wirtschaftsforschung,* Discussion paper No. 93-26, 1993.

Schneider, F., ''Determinanen der Steuerhinterziehung und der Schwarzarbeit im internationalen Vergleich'', in Smekal, C. and E. Theurl, *Stand und Entwicklung der Finanzpsychologie,* Baden Baden, 1994.

Schneider, H., *Determinanten der Arbeitslosigkeitsdauer,* Frankfurt/Main 1991.

Spahn, P. B., H. Kaiser and T. Kassella, ''The tax dilemma of married women in Germany'', *Fiscal Studies,* Vol. 13, No. 2, 1992.

Steiner, V. ''Labour market transitions and the persistence of unemployment – West Germany 1983-1992'', *Zentrum für Europäische Wirtschaftsforschung,* Discussion paper No. 94-20, 1994.

Strøm, S. and G. Wagenhals, ''Female labour supply in the Federal Republic'', *Jahrbücher für Nationalökonomie und Statistik,* Vol. 208, No. 6, 1991.

Wagenhals G., ''Auswirkungen des Ehegattensplitting in der Bundesrepublik Deutschland – Ergebnisse einer mikroökonometrischen Analyse'', in: Seel, B. *Frauenpolitische Aspekte im Einkommensteuerrecht,* Wiesbaden, 1996*a*.

Wagenhals, G., ''Anreizwirkungen der Steuerbefreiung des Existenzminimums – eine mikroökonometrische Analyse alternativer Reformvorschläge'', *Institut für Volkswirtschaftslehre Universität Hohenheim,* Diskussionsbeitrag No. 123/1996*b*.

Wurzel, E.,''Staggered entry and unemployment durations: an application to German data'', in: Hartog, J., G. Ridder, J. Theeuwes, *Panel data and labor market studies,* Amsterdam, 1990.

Wurzel, E., *An econometric analysis of individual unemployment duration in West Germany,* Heidelberg, 1993.

Annex III

Chronology of main economic events

1995

January

Various fiscal policy measures come into force:

- Reintroduction of the solidarity income tax surcharge of 7.5 per cent of personal and company income tax,
- increase in the insurance tax from 12 to 15 per cent,
- doubling of the wealth tax from 0.5 to 1 per cent on many assets and, at the same time, increasing the wealth tax allowance from DM 70 000 to 120 000,
- abolition of the law providing special support for Berlin.

The contribution rate for the pension insurance funds is decreased from 19.2 per cent to 18.6 per cent.

The debts of the Treuhandanstalt and the Credit Fund are taken over by the newly created Inherited Debt Fund (the major part of the debts of the eastern German public housing sector are taken over by mid year); the servicing of the debt will be financed by the federal budget.

The Treuhandanstalt is abolished, having nearly fulfilled its main task of privatising the state-owned enterprises of the former GDR. The remaining tasks will be performed by various smaller successor institutions which are financed by the Federal budget.

The new Länder are fully integrated into a reformed revenue and burden sharing arrangement (Länderfinanzausgleich)

The first stage of the law providing for long-term nursing care insurance comes into force: initial contributions are equal to 1 per cent of gross wages. Employers' contributions will be compensated by the abolition of one public holiday in all Länder except Saxony, where the employees pay the full amount. Payments or benefits in kind start for people being cared for at home in April.

The new Federal Supervisory Board for Securities Trade starts operation.

March

A two year wage agreement is reached in the metal industry providing for a 3.4 per cent increase in wages and salaries from May and a further 3.6 per cent rise for the period November 1995 to the end of December 1996.

The Bundesbank reduces the discount rate from 4½ per cent to 4 per cent and the rate for fixed-rate repos from 4.85 per cent to 4.5 per cent while announcing a subsequent shift to floating rate repos.

June

Parliament passes the Federal budget for 1995, rejecting the veto of the upper house, providing for expenditures of DM 477.7 billion and a deficit of DM 49.5 billion.

July

After a mediation process, the upper and the lower houses of Parliament agree on the 1996 tax law (see January 1996).

August

The Bundesbank completes the restructuring of the minimum reserve requirements for private banks. The minimum reserve rate for sight deposits is lowered from 5 per cent to 2 per cent, equalising the rates for sight and time deposits. The minimum reserve rate for savings deposits is lowered from 2 per cent to 1.5 per cent. The crediting of cash holdings by private banks' against the minimum reserve requirements is abolished.

The Constitutional Court announces the grounds for the June 1995 decision on wealth and inheritance taxation which declared the different taxation of real estate and financial assets as unconstitutional specifying general rules for the taxation of property.

The Bundesbank lowers the discount rate from 4 to 3½ per cent and the Lombard rate from 6 to 5½ per cent.

October

Following a 1990 agreement, working hours in the metal industry are reduced to 35 hours per week.

November

Parliament passes the Federal budget for 1996 providing for spending of DM 451.3 billion and a deficit of DM 60.1 billion.

Parliament extends the regulation according to which the trade capital tax (*Gewerbekapitalsteuer*) is not levied in the new Länder until the end of 1996.

December

The Bundesbank sets the M3 target for 1996 at 4 to 7 per cent between the fourth quarter 1995 and the fourth quarter 1996. The Bank lowers the discount rate from 3½ to 3 per cent and the Lombard rate from 5½ to 5 per cent and shifts from floating rate repos to fixed interest repos (volume tender) with a rate of 3¾ per cent for the following three repurchases.

1996

January

The 1996 tax law increases the basic tax allowance for untaxed income (*Grund-freibetrag*) to DM 12 095 and to DM 24 190 for married couples (basic tax allowance according to the 1992 tax schedule: DM 5 616, respectively DM 11 232). The entrance tax rate is increased from 19 per cent to 25.9 per cent. Child allowances and child benefits are also increased but can no longer be cumulated.

The tax depreciation allowance for the construction of rented housing is cut, and benefits for acquiring homes is restructured.

The special charge for subsidisation of coal mining (*Kohlepfennig*) is abolished. Cash subsidies to the coal mines are introduced to be financed by the Federal budget.

The contribution rate for the pension insurance funds is increased from 18.6 per cent to 19.2 per cent.

The government decides a fifty point ''Action Programme for Investment and Employment''. Major policy objectives include a reduction of the solidarity tax surcharge and an enterprise tax reform in 1997, support for small and medium-sized companies (*Mittelstand*), reductions in social spending, reforms of vocational and tertiary education, and measures aiming at fostering competition, privatisation and improving the flexibility of the labour market.

February

After sharp declines in the repurchase rate the Bundesbank shifts the repurchase transactions from floating rate tenders to a fixed interest tenders (volume tender) at 3.30 per cent.

The lower house of Parliament (Bundestag) passes two bills which relate social assistance benefits and unemployment assistance benefits more closely to employment opportunities. Another approved bill restricts benefits accruing to asylum seekers. These bills are subsequently rejected by the upper house of Parliament and enter the mediation process.

The government agrees a pact to promote employment with the social partners. The non-binding statement of principles calls for moderate wage increases, improved labour market flexibility and lower social charges. A phased withdrawal of early retirement provisions is agreed in principle.

March

The Minister of Finance enacts expenditure controls for the Federal budget (*Haushaltssperre*) according to which discretionary spending above a threshold requires the approval of the Minister of Finance.

Wage agreements for a twelve months period are reached in the textile and the chemical industries, specifying wage increases of 1.5 and 2 per cent respectively. Both agreements contain commitments on the side of the employers to maintain employment. The agreement in the textile industry allows wage increases to be suspended, based on agreements on the company level, if a company is in difficulties. Both agreements provide for more flexible working time arrangements, and contain regulations which aim at reducing the overall volume of overtime by compensating for overtime work with free time.

April

The government announces a package of measures complementing the 50 point programme (see January 1996). The programme aims to reduce general government spending by almost DM 70 billion in 1997.

The Bundesbank lowers the discount rate from 3 to 2½ per cent and the Lombard rate from 5 to 4½ per cent.

The bill to control hospital budgets comes into force, back-dated to the start of the year.

May

The official tax revenue estimates for 1996 and 1997 indicate a substantial downward revision of revenues for the territorial authorities. For 1996, losses on account of lower growth rate assumptions amount to DM 22 billion in comparison to the estimates of October 1995. For 1997 lower revenues in comparison to the estimates of May 1995 amount to around DM 66 billion.

The government introduces the legislation needed to implement the 1997 tax package in the parliament. It contains bills for a reform of property taxation on the basis of the ruling of the Constitutional Court (see August 1995), and tax measures based on the government's "Action Programme for Investment and Employment" and the supplementary budget programme (see January and April 1996). Major points of the bill include:

- the abolition of the wealth tax (*Vermögensteuer*), and an accompanying reform of the inheritance and gift taxes (*Erbschaftsteuer, Schenkungsteuer*),
- a new valuation method for real estate which is more closely related to the current market value but only conducted when required,
- a reduction of the solidarity tax surcharge from 7.5 per cent to 6.5 per cent in January 1997 and to 5.5 per cent in January 1998,
- a depreciation allowance to foster investment of newly founded small and medium sized companies.

June

A wage agreement is reached for public sector employees providing for a lump sum of DM 300 in 1996 and an increase of 1.3 per cent in 1997. Sick pay is left unchanged. Moderate agreements are also finalised in banking and in the steel industry.

The proposal to increase the retirement age of women from 1997 from 60 to 65 years is withdrawn and is to come into force instead from 2000. Lost savings until the end of 2000 are put at DM 3.5 billion.

A bill raising the entry age into early retirement from 60 to 63 years in stages between 1997 and 1999 is passed into law. New legislation comes into force requiring that the wage base for calculating unemployment assistance is to be reduced by 3 per cent a year.

July

The upper house of Parliament (Bundesrat) approves a relaxation of shop opening hours. Also, a social assistance reform bill is approved. Social assistance is reduced by 25 per cent if acceptable work is refused.

The lower house of Parliament (Bundestag) passes legislation to curb spending in the pension insurance. The increase in the retirement age is phased in earlier than scheduled in the 1992 pension reform law. The retirement age for women is to be increased from 63 to the standard retirement age of 65 years between 2000 and 2005. In both cases early retirement is still possible at pensions reduced by 0.3 per cent for each month of early retirement.

The government presents the draft budget for 1997 which provides for a decrease in spending in comparison to 1996 by 2.5 per cent.

Bill to liberalise telecommunications is agreed by both houses of Parliament.

STATISTICAL ANNEX AND STRUCTURAL INDICATORS

Table A. **Selected background statistics**

	1986	1987	1988	1989	1990	1991	1992	1993	1994	1995
A. Percentage change from previous year at constant prices [1]										
Private consumption	3.5	3.4	2.7	2.8	5.4	5.6	2.8	0.5	0.9	1.7
Gross fixed investment	3.3	1.8	4.4	6.3	8.5	6.0	3.5	–5.6	4.3	1.5
Construction	3.1	0.0	3.1	4.4	4.9	2.7	9.7	0.9	7.8	1.2
Public	8.0	–1.2	0.4	3.1	–0.8	0.3	11.1	–3.3	1.8	–2.7
Residential	–0.6	–1.2	3.7	4.9	8.5	4.3	9.4	3.8	13.1	3.0
Business	6.0	2.5	3.6	4.4	2.8	1.6	9.4	–1.2	3.0	0.4
Machinery and equipment	3.7	4.5	6.3	8.8	13.2	10.0	–3.5	–14.1	–1.2	2.0
GDP at market prices	2.3	1.5	3.7	3.6	5.7	5.0	2.2	–1.2	2.9	1.9
GDP implicit price deflator	3.2	1.9	1.5	2.4	3.2	3.9	5.5	3.8	2.3	2.2
Industrial production	2.0	0.4	3.6	4.7	5.2	3.0	–2.6	–7.3	3.6	0.8
Employment	1.4	0.7	0.8	1.5	3.0	2.5	–1.8	–1.8	–0.7	–0.3
Compensation of employees (current prices)	5.2	4.2	4.0	4.5	7.8	8.0	8.0	2.0	2.2	3.2
Productivity (GDP/employment)	0.9	0.7	2.9	2.1	2.7	2.5	4.1	0.6	3.6	2.2
Unit labour costs (compensation of employees/GDP)	2.8	2.7	0.2	0.8	2.0	3.3	5.6	3.2	–0.6	1.3
B. Percentage ratios [2]										
Gross fixed investment										
As a per cent of GDP at constant prices	19.9	19.9	20.1	20.6	21.1	23.0	23.3	22.2	22.5	22.4
Stockbuilding										
As a per cent of GDP at constant prices	0.2	0.0	0.5	0.8	0.6	0.5	–0.1	–0.2	0.9	0.9
Foreign balance										
As a per cent of GDP at constant prices	5.1	4.2	4.4	5.1	5.5	–0.1	–0.7	–0.6	–0.5	–0.2
Compensation of employees										
As a per cent of GDP at current prices	56.1	56.5	55.8	54.9	54.3	56.5	56.6	56.3	54.7	54.2
Direct taxes										
As a per cent of household income	12.3	12.8	12.5	12.9	11.3	11.8	12.5	12.1	12.2	13.2
Household saving										
As a per cent of disposable income	12.3	12.6	12.8	12.4	13.8	12.7	12.8	12.2	11.6	11.5
Unemployment										
As a per cent of civilian labour force	7.7	7.6	7.6	6.9	6.2	6.7	7.7	8.9	9.6	9.4
C. Other indicator [2]										
Current balance (billion $)	40.5	46.1	49.5	57.2	48.9	–19.2	–21.5	–16.3	–21.4	–17.4

1. From 1992 all Germany.
2. From 1991 all Germany.

Source: Statistisches Bundesamt, *Volkswirtschaftliche Gesamtrechnungen, Reihe 1;* Deutsche Bundesbank, *Statistisches Beiheft zum Monatsbericht, Reihe 4.*

Table B. **Gross domestic product by origin**[1]

DM billion

	1986	1987	1988	1989	1990	1991	1992	1993	1994	1995
Current prices										
Agriculture, forestry, fishing	34.0	30.2	33.7	37.2	36.7	41.0	40.6	36.3	36.0	37.2
Mining and quarrying, energy	65.9	68.7	67.8	69.3	70.2	90.0	90.3	90.3	91.4	89.9
Manufacturing	620.4	624.7	652.7	686.0	741.6	825.6	836.5	789.1	814.5	839.5
Construction	100.1	101.7	106.3	114.7	127.6	161.5	190.1	198.3	221.0	228.3
Trade, transport, communications	269.6	279.5	294.7	311.3	346.8	415.8	438.3	439.8	450.2	462.0
Government[2]	217.1	225.8	231.9	238.6	253.2	317.6	349.3	365.4	370.2	384.6
Non-profit organisations, households	46.4	49.3	51.7	53.9	58.3	69.6	78.5	83.9	89.1	95.0
Other services	571.7	610.6	657.3	713.5	791.6	932.5	1 051.9	1 151.9	1 247.8	1 323.2
Gross domestic product at market prices	1 925.3	1 990.5	2 096.0	2 224.4	2 426.0	2 853.6	3 075.6	3 154.9	3 320.3	3 459.6
At 1991 prices										
Agriculture, forestry, fishing	35.2	32.1	34.5	35.0	36.4	41.0	48.1	45.3	43.7	45.3
Mining and quarrying, energy	64.0	67.0	66.7	69.5	69.4	90.0	86.8	84.6	83.5	83.6
Manufacturing	689.6	677.0	698.6	722.6	762.3	825.6	805.9	749.0	770.8	778.2
Construction	126.6	124.6	127.1	132.5	136.8	161.5	172.5	170.5	182.9	183.4
Trade, transport, communications	293.6	301.2	315.8	330.0	355.8	415.8	424.9	422.2	425.0	432.9
Government[2]	255.6	259.0	261.7	262.6	266.9	317.6	322.2	325.5	325.7	328.1
Non-profit organisations, households	54.2	55.8	57.5	59.1	61.6	69.6	73.4	75.5	78.7	81.1
Other services	667.4	701.8	739.1	773.1	831.3	932.5	982.7	1 010.1	1 054.8	1 090.3
Gross domestic product at market prices	2 186.1	2 218.4	2 301.0	2 384.4	2 520.4	2 853.6	2 916.4	2 882.6	2 965.1	3 022.8

1. From 1991 all Germany.
2. Central and local government, municipalities and social security.

Source: Statisches Bundesamt, *Volkswirtschaftliche Gesamtrechnungen, Fachserie 18, Reihe 1.*

Table C. **Gross domestic product by demand components**[1]

DM billion

	1986	1987	1988	1989	1990	1991	1992	1993	1994	1995
Current prices										
Private consumption	1 066.4	1 108.0	1 153.7	1 221.0	1 320.7	1 629.3	1 754.5	1 834.4	1 902.4	1 972.0
Public consumption	382.6	397.3	412.4	418.8	444.1	557.0	617.2	631.7	646.2	675.4
Gross fixed investment	373.5	385.8	409.9	448.5	507.8	656.0	709.4	689.2	729.7	751.1
Machinery and equipment	160.9	169.4	182.5	203.5	234.6	306.8	301.8	261.5	257.8	262.7
Public	6.5	7.1	7.2	8.1	8.8	13.5	14.4	12.4	10.7	10.9
Private	154.3	162.3	175.3	195.4	225.8	293.3	287.4	249.1	247.1	251.8
Construction	212.6	216.4	227.4	245.1	273.2	349.2	407.6	427.7	471.8	488.4
Public	40.8	40.9	41.7	44.3	46.8	61.5	72.8	73.0	75.5	74.5
Residential	101.8	102.6	108.6	117.9	135.9	168.2	195.4	212.5	246.9	261.2
Other private	70.0	72.9	77.1	82.8	90.6	119.5	139.4	142.3	149.4	152.7
Stockbuilding	2.9	–0.6	10.3	16.0	11.5	14.4	–2.8	–12.7	24.6	25.4
Total domestic demand	1 825.4	1 890.5	1 986.3	2 104.3	2 284.1	2 856.6	3 078.3	3 142.6	3 302.8	3 423.9
Exports of goods and services	580.5	576.6	619.8	701.4	778.9	724.1	728.8	695.9	752.7	795.7
Imports of goods and services	480.6	476.7	510.1	581.3	637.0	727.1	731.4	683.6	735.2	760.0
Gross domestic product at market prices	1 925.3	1 990.5	2 096.0	2 224.4	2 426.0	2 853.6	3 075.6	3 154.9	3 320.3	3 459.6
At 1991 prices										
Private consumption	1 190.0	1 230.6	1 264.3	1 300.2	1 370.0	1 629.3	1 675.5	1 683.7	1 698.1	1 726.2
Public consumption	445.8	452.7	462.3	454.9	465.0	557.0	584.6	581.4	585.3	597.8
Gross fixed investment	434.3	442.2	461.8	490.7	532.4	656.0	679.3	640.9	668.2	678.4
Machinery and equipment	176.1	184.0	195.7	212.8	240.9	306.8	296.2	254.5	251.6	256.6
Public	7.1	7.6	7.6	8.2	8.9	13.5	14.1	12.0	10.4	10.5
Private	169.1	176.4	188.1	204.6	232.0	293.3	282.1	242.5	241.2	246.0
Construction	258.2	258.2	266.1	277.9	291.4	349.2	383.1	386.4	416.6	421.8
Public	49.2	48.6	48.8	50.4	49.9	61.5	68.4	66.1	67.3	65.4
Residential	124.6	123.1	127.6	133.9	145.2	168.2	184.0	191.1	216.2	222.7
Other private	84.4	86.5	89.7	93.6	96.3	119.5	130.7	129.2	133.1	133.7
Stockbuilding	4.3	–0.6	12.1	18.1	15.0	14.4	–2.0	–6.8	28.1	26.7
Total domestic demand	2 074.4	2 125.0	2 200.6	2 263.8	2 382.4	2 856.6	2 937.4	2 899.2	2 979.6	3 029.1
Exports of goods and services	609.3	611.7	645.3	710.9	789.1	724.1	721.9	688.0	739.8	768.1
Imports of goods and services	497.6	518.3	544.8	590.3	651.1	727.1	742.9	704.6	754.3	774.4
Gross domestic product at market prices	2 186.1	2 218.4	2 301.0	2 384.4	2 520.4	2 853.6	2 916.4	2 882.6	2 965.1	3 022.8

1. From 1991 all Germany.

Source: Statistisches Bundesamt, *Volkswirtschaftliche Gesamtrechnungen, Fachserie 18, Reihe 1.*

Table D. **Distribution of national income**[1]

DM billion, current prices

	1986	1987	1988	1989	1990	1991	1992	1993	1994	1995
Compensation of employees	1 079.5	1 124.7	1 169.4	1 221.9	1 317.1	1 612.0	1 740.3	1 775.6	1 815.0	1 873.5
less:										
Employers' social security contributions	202.9	211.9	220.5	229.1	247.5	298.3	323.5	327.2	346.3	359.4
Employees' social security contributions	124.2	129.3	135.6	142.1	152.4	193.4	212.3	220.6	236.3	246.6
Wage tax	150.0	162.4	165.5	179.2	173.7	220.6	251.8	252.5	263.5	294.0
Net wages and salaries[2]	602.4	621.1	647.8	671.6	743.6	899.7	952.7	975.4	968.8	973.5
Income from property and entrepreneurship	418.1	425.3	466.2	516.2	575.1	612.4	625.7	616.6	684.9	742.6
less:										
Direct taxes on business and property income	73.6	69.3	75.9	89.9	80.9	94.7	100.0	103.8	90.9	81.3
Net income from property and entrepreneurship	344.5	356.0	390.3	426.3	494.2	517.7	525.8	512.9	594.0	661.2
of which:										
Retained profits	33.2	35.6	64.8	54.9	74.4	22.9	–2.1	–26.1	10.3	56.9
Accruing to Government	–23.3	–30.7	–39.9	–29.0	–29.1	–38.4	–50.5	–55.4	–59.9	–89.8
Distributed to households	334.6	351.1	365.4	400.4	448.8	533.2	578.3	594.3	643.5	694.2
Net national income at factor costs	1 497.6	1 550.0	1 635.5	1 738.1	1 892.2	2 224.4	2 366.1	2 392.3	2 499.9	2 616.0
Memorandum items:										
Household disposable income	1 215.7	1 267.6	1 323.2	1 394.3	1 532.2	1 866.0	2 010.9	2 089.4	2 151.6	2 229.3
Household saving ratio[3]	12.3	12.6	12.8	12.4	13.8	12.7	12.8	12.2	11.6	11.5

1. From 1991 all Germany.
2. Including voluntary fringe benefits.
3. Per cent of household disposable income.

Source: Statistisches Bundesamt, *Volkswirtschaftliche Gesamtrechnungen, Fachserie 18, Reihe 1.*

Table E. **Receipts and expenditure of general government: national accounts basis**[1]

DM billion, current prices

	1986	1987	1988	1989	1990	1991	1992	1993	1994	1995
Current receipts										
Income from property and entrepreneurship	33.9	27.0	19.9	31.5	34.3	38.2	49.9	48.5	53.5	40.5
Indirect taxes	236.2	245.5	257.1	278.3	302.2	358.5	389.8	409.1	443.3	446.8
Direct taxes	235.1	243.9	255.4	281.8	271.0	330.8	364.9	363.4	367.7	391.4
Social security contributions	336.8	349.9	366.5	383.2	410.5	513.1	562.7	596.3	639.4	669.9
Other current transfers received	25.5	25.0	25.5	24.9	26.1	31.4	38.5	37.5	39.4	39.8
Total current receipts	867.3	891.3	924.5	999.6	1 044.0	1 272.0	1 405.9	1 454.8	1 543.3	1 588.4
Current expenditure										
Final consumption expenditure	382.5	397.3	412.4	418.8	444.1	557.0	617.2	631.7	646.2	675.4
Wages and salaries	203.3	211.5	216.9	222.8	236.3	297.2	327.0	341.5	345.4	358.6
Goods and services	179.2	185.8	195.5	195.5	207.8	259.8	290.3	290.2	300.8	316.8
Subsidies	41.3	44.8	47.7	46.8	48.8	65.4	59.3	63.6	70.3	73.5
Debt-interest payments	57.2	57.8	59.8	60.5	63.4	76.7	100.3	103.9	113.4	130.3
Current transfers paid	353.8	371.4	392.5	409.6	472.9	556.5	605.0	661.6	700.4	736.4
Total current expenditure	834.8	871.3	912.5	935.7	1 029.2	1 255.5	1 381.8	1 460.8	1 530.2	1 615.6
Savings	32.5	20.0	12.0	63.9	14.8	16.5	24.1	–6.0	13.0	–27.1
Depreciation	13.6	14.1	14.7	15.6	16.7	20.0	21.9	23.5	24.5	25.6
Net capital transfers received	–24.1	–24.0	–23.0	–24.3	–25.7	–55.7	–45.5	–43.8	–38.1	–35.8
Gross fixed investment	47.3	48.0	48.9	52.4	55.5	75.0	87.2	85.4	86.2	85.4
Financial balance (net lending)	–25.4	–37.9	–45.2	2.7	–49.7	–94.2	–86.7	–111.6	–86.8	–122.7
As a per cent of GDP	–1.3	–1.9	–2.2	0.1	–2.1	–3.3	–2.8	–3.5	–2.6	–3.5

1. From 1991 all Germany.

Source: Statistisches Bundesamt, *Volkswirtschaftliche Gesamtrechnungen, Fachserie 18, Reihe 1.*

Table F. **Balance of payments**[1]

DM billion

	1986	1987	1988	1989	1990	1991	1992	1993	1994	1995
A. Current account										
1. Foreign trade, net	112.6	117.7	128.0	134.6	105.4	21.9	33.7	60.3	71.8	91.1
Exports (f.o.b.)	526.4	527.4	567.7	641.0	662.0	665.8	671.2	632.2	694.7	732.3
Imports (c.i.f.)	413.7	409.6	439.6	506.5	556.7	643.9	637.5	571.9	622.9	641.1
2. Supplementary trade items	–3.6	–4.0	–2.8	–3.9	–3.6	–4.5	–3.5	–5.5	–3.7	–5.8
Balance of trade	109.0	113.8	125.2	130.6	101.8	17.4	30.1	54.8	68.1	85.4
3. Services, net	–0.9	–6.5	–10.3	–7.2	–11.1	–16.4	–31.2	–41.2	–49.3	–50.3
Receipts	85.9	83.1	85.0	95.8	104.2	109.1	107.3	105.3	104.6	112.6
Expenditure	86.8	89.6	95.4	103.0	115.3	125.5	138.5	146.6	153.9	162.9
4. Factor income, net	8.6	6.0	6.6	20.9	27.2	29.7	22.5	17.8	8.2	–2.0
Receipts	49.0	53.1	59.1	81.3	101.5	118.7	121.9	125.9	124.3	137.0
Expenditure	40.4	47.2	52.6	60.4	74.3	89.0	99.4	108.0	116.1	139.0
5. Transfer payments, net	–28.9	–30.4	–34.5	–36.9	–38.8	–62.6	–54.9	–58.3	–61.4	–58.0
of which:										
Remittances of foreign workers	–7.5	–7.4	–7.5	–7.5	–7.1	–6.4	–6.8	–6.8	–7.5	–7.6
Transfers to the European Community, net[2]	–9.2	–11.1	–14.5	–14.8	–13.0	–21.3	–24.7	–26.7	–31.0	–29.1
Balance on current account	87.9	82.8	87.0	107.5	79.0	–31.9	–33.5	–26.9	–34.4	–24.9
B. Capital account										
6. Capital transfers	0.0	–0.2	0.0	0.1	–2.1	–1.0	0.9	0.8	0.3	–0.9
7. Financial transactions	–84.6	–39.2	–125.6	–134.7	–90.5	20.9	92.2	13.4	59.0	55.8
German investment abroad (increase: –):	–160.7	–86.7	–155.2	–248.6	–183.4	–106.0	–116.8	–296.1	–112.4	–183.5
Direct investment	–21.9	–17.4	–21.2	–28.5	–38.7	–39.3	–30.5	–25.3	–27.0	–50.0
Portfolio investment	–21.4	–25.0	–71.7	–50.1	–25.1	–29.9	–75.6	–53.0	–89.3	–42.8
Credit transactions	–115.5	–42.5	–60.6	–167.8	–117.5	–33.6	–8.1	–215.2	6.4	–87.4
Long-term	–10.3	–18.6	–2.5	–14.2	–43.0	–26.2	–14.1	–33.4	–26.4	–26.9
Short-term	–105.2	–24.0	–58.2	–153.6	–74.5	–7.4	5.9	–181.8	32.8	–60.5
Other investment	–2.0	–1.7	–1.7	–2.2	–2.1	–3.2	–2.6	–2.5	–2.6	–3.4
Foreign investment in Germany (increase: +):	76.1	47.5	29.7	113.9	92.9	126.9	209.0	309.4	171.5	239.4
Direct investment	2.5	3.3	2.0	13.3	4.0	6.8	4.2	2.9	1.1	12.9
Portfolio investment	72.5	32.3	7.4	45.7	19.4	71.2	122.5	235.3	45.4	84.6
Credit transactions	1.2	11.9	20.4	55.0	69.8	49.0	82.5	71.2	124.2	142.9
Long-term	12.3	2.9	1.7	14.3	20.7	–0.2	27.6	50.1	33.0	62.9
Short-term	–11.1	9.0	18.7	40.7	49.2	49.1	54.9	21.1	91.2	79.9
Other investment	–0.1	0.0	–0.0	–0.1	–0.4	–0.1	–0.2	–0.0	0.8	–1.0
8. Unclassifiable transactions	2.8	–2.2	3.9	8.0	24.6	12.3	9.1	–23.0	–12.7	–12.3

Table F. **Balance of payments**[1] *(cont.)*

DM billion

	1986	1987	1988	1989	1990	1991	1992	1993	1994	1995
C. Change in the Bundesbank's net external assets (transaction values) (increase: +)	6.0	41.2	–34.7	–19.0	11.0	0.3	68.7	–35.8	12.2	17.8
9. Balancing item of the Bundesbank	–3.2	–9.3	2.2	–2.6	–5.1	0.5	–6.3	1.5	–3.7	–2.7
D. Change in the Bundesbank's net external assets (balance sheet values) (increase: +)	2.8	31.9	–32.5	–21.6	5.9	0.8	62.4	–34.2	8.6	15.1

1. From July 1990 including the external transactions of the former German Democratic Republic.
2. Excluding collection expenses, EAGGF (Guidance Funds) and Regional Fund.

Source: Deutsche Bundesbank, *Statistisches Beiheft zum Monatsbericht, Reihe 4.*

Table G. **Imports and exports of goods by regions**

DM billion

	1986	1987	1988	1989	1990	1991	1992	1993	1994	1995
					Imports, f.o.b.					
OECD	325.3	325.9	351.7	404.7	442.4	509.5	505.8	436.5	470.6	477.3
EU	241.9	242.6	258.9	295.1	328.9	381.3	378.5	317.1	343.9	344.9
Austria	15.8	16.6	18.5	20.6	23.9	26.7	27.7	25.9	28.6	22.8
Belgium-Luxembourg	28.9	28.8	30.9	34.7	39.8	45.8	44.8	34.1	38.5	41.0
France	46.6	46.8	52.5	60.2	65.6	79.0	76.5	65.8	69.6	68.2
Italy	37.6	38.7	40.0	45.0	51.9	59.7	58.4	48.0	51.9	52.7
Netherlands	46.9	44.1	45.3	51.9	56.2	63.0	62.1	51.0	52.5	53.8
Sweden	9.5	9.4	10.2	12.2	12.6	13.8	13.4	11.9	13.3	12.2
United Kingdom	28.7	28.6	29.7	34.0	36.5	42.3	42.6	35.4	38.9	40.0
Other European countries	27.8	28.2	29.7	33.2	37.1	40.2	41.4	39.8	43.5	46.5
Switzerland	18.0	18.8	19.6	21.0	23.4	25.2	25.4	23.9	26.3	27.5
Other OECD	55.6	55.1	63.1	76.4	76.4	88.0	86.0	79.6	83.2	85.9
Japan	25.0	25.9	29.6	33.3	33.2	40.7	38.4	34.9	34.6	35.7
United States	26.1	24.6	28.4	37.1	36.9	40.9	41.5	39.3	42.9	43.5
Central and Eastern European countries [1]	16.2	13.8	13.9	17.1	23.7	29.9	31.8	32.6	40.1	47.0
Non-oil developing countries	41.2	39.7	45.3	51.5	55.0	63.0	58.5	58.1	62.9	66.5
OPEC	12.1	10.5	9.9	11.4	13.2	13.8	14.0	12.8	11.9	10.1
China	2.7	3.4	4.2	5.8	7.7	11.3	11.1	13.4	14.9	15.9
Dynamic Asian economies	15.7	18.2	20.9	23.2	25.6	31.9	30.0	31.2	33.8	36.4
Total imports	404.8	400.6	432.7	499.4	551.7	637.7	630.2	567.0	616.0	634.6
					Exports, f.o.b.					
OECD	428.1	435.7	474.3	533.5	537.9	538.1	538.1	485.5	531.3	552.3
EU	312.9	324.9	362.4	414.3	413.8	421.2	424.7	368.1	401.3	414.6
Austria	28.1	28.3	32.3	35.9	37.5	40.2	40.4	37.7	40.1	39.6
Belgium-Luxembourg	36.3	38.1	41.3	45.5	47.5	48.2	49.0	42.5	46.5	46.6
France	61.2	62.5	70.6	83.8	84.2	87.5	86.9	77.4	83.2	84.3
Italy	42.5	45.5	51.4	59.6	60.0	61.2	62.3	46.9	52.4	54.4
Netherlands	44.6	45.3	48.8	54.2	54.7	56.3	56.1	48.8	52.6	54.0
Sweden	14.8	15.8	16.8	18.5	17.0	15.0	14.7	12.8	15.5	17.7
United Kingdom	44.3	46.3	52.7	59.1	54.7	50.5	50.9	50.0	55.4	58.2
Other European countries	43.1	43.6	45.4	49.6	52.1	51.4	49.1	48.6	50.5	56.3
Switzerland	31.0	32.1	34.8	38.8	38.9	38.0	35.7	34.1	37.2	39.7
Other OECD	72.2	67.2	66.5	69.5	72.1	65.4	64.3	68.8	79.6	81.4
Japan	8.5	10.3	12.9	15.0	17.2	16.3	14.5	15.2	17.3	18.4
United States	54.3	48.8	45.2	44.9	46.4	41.0	41.9	45.7	53.2	53.6
Central and Eastern European countries [1]	17.3	15.7	17.9	23.1	36.8	36.9	35.8	40.5	45.1	50.8
Non-oil developing countries	42.7	42.7	44.7	52.0	53.3	56.4	59.3	64.1	74.8	83.1
OPEC	17.6	14.0	15.3	16.3	18.3	21.4	23.0	18.4	17.7	17.0
China	6.1	4.9	4.9	4.6	4.0	4.0	5.7	9.5	10.2	10.6
Dynamic Asian economies	12.5	13.4	16.3	20.2	22.3	25.1	26.2	30.2	37.2	42.0
Total exports	522.4	522.2	566.8	640.5	663.8	667.6	671.6	632.7	696.0	732.6

1. Poland, ex-USSR, former Czechoslovakia and Hungary.

Source: Deutsche Bundesbank, *Statistisches Beiheft zum Monatsbericht, Reihe 4.*

Table H. **Foreign trade by main commodity groups – customs basis**[1]

DM billion

	1986	1987	1988	1989	1990	1991	1992	1993	1994	1995
	Imports, c.i.f.									
SITC classification										
0. Food and live animals	42.7	40.1	41.4	43.8	46.4	53.4	54.7	46.8	52.4	52.4
1. Beverages and tobacco	4.5	4.5	4.4	4.7	5.4	6.6	6.7	6.0	6.5	6.2
2. Crude materials, except fuels	26.5	25.1	28.5	33.5	29.5	28.6	28.5	23.1	27.6	28.4
3. Mineral fuels, lubricants and related materials	48.2	39.5	33.5	38.3	45.5	53.6	47.5	44.9	43.2	40.6
4. Animal and vegetable oils, etc.	1.5	1.2	1.5	1.7	1.5	1.6	1.7	1.5	1.9	1.9
5. Chemicals	38.3	38.5	42.6	47.7	49.7	54.2	54.6	46.9	55.0	59.3
6. Manufactured goods classified chiefly by material	73.4	71.6	80.5	94.6	98.3	106.7	106.2	86.2	100.2	108.3
7. Machinery and transport equipment	109.0	114.3	128.1	154.4	178.1	225.7	220.5	187.5	208.9	217.9
8. Miscellaneous manufactured articles	55.9	61.5	65.7	73.3	83.1	102.7	103.3	94.2	99.2	94.6
9. Other	13.6	13.2	13.4	14.4	13.1	10.9	13.8	29.5	22.1	24.7
0-9. **Total imports**	413.7	409.6	439.6	506.5	550.6	643.9	637.5	566.5	617.0	634.3
	Exports, f.o.b.									
SITC classification										
0. Food and live animals	21.7	21.1	23.6	26.0	25.1	29.2	29.7	27.8	29.3	29.3
1. Beverages and tobacco	3.4	3.1	3.2	3.6	3.7	4.2	4.7	4.5	5.3	4.9
2. Crude materials, except fuels	9.2	9.2	10.6	12.4	11.7	12.5	12.5	10.8	13.0	13.8
3. Mineral fuels, lubricants and related materials	8.6	7.1	6.9	7.9	8.2	8.3	8.2	7.5	7.8	6.7
4. Animal and vegetable oils, etc.	1.7	1.3	1.6	1.8	1.5	1.5	1.5	1.6	1.9	2.1
5. Chemicals	67.7	68.6	76.9	83.1	81.7	84.8	84.7	80.7	92.8	98.1
6. Manufactured goods classified chiefly by material	95.1	93.4	102.6	117.2	113.5	113.2	111.0	100.4	111.2	120.7
7. Machinery and transport equipment	251.3	254.6	272.8	311.7	317.2	325.9	333.1	303.5	338.4	360.8
8. Miscellaneous manufactured articles	55.9	56.8	62.4	69.7	71.7	74.4	75.5	68.7	72.3	72.6
9. Other	11.7	12.1	7.0	7.7	8.4	11.6	10.2	23.1	18.5	18.8
0-9. **Total exports**	526.4	527.4	567.7	641.0	642.8	665.8	671.2	628.4	690.6	727.7

1. From 1991 all Germany.

Source: Statistisches Bundesamt, *Aussenhandel, Fachserie 7.*

Table I. **Money and credit**[1]

End of period, DM billion

	1986	1987	1988	1989	1990	1991	1992	1993	1994	1995
Consolidated balance sheet of the banking system:										
I. Bank lending to domestic non-banks	2 131.3	2 214.2	2 346.9	2 483.9	2 888.6	3 160.6	3 497.5	3 839.8	4 149.0	4 446.5
Bundesbank	16.8	13.9	14.5	13.9	13.5	13.7	19.3	13.4	11.9	9.6
Credit institutions	2 114.6	2 200.3	2 332.4	2 470.1	2 875.0	3 147.0	3 478.2	3 826.4	4 137.2	4 436.9
To public sector	471.6	500.5	541.4	547.2	603.6	629.2	739.3	840.4	926.2	1 067.5
To private sector	1 643.0	1 699.8	1 790.9	1 922.8	2 271.5	2 517.8	2 739.0	2 986.0	3 210.9	3 369.4
Short-term	342.1	325.8	341.5	375.2	521.0	575.8	571.2	544.2	549.1	584.0
Medium- and long-term	1 300.9	1 374.0	1 449.5	1 547.6	1 750.5	1 941.9	2 167.8	2 441.8	2 661.9	2 785.5
II. Net foreign assets	227.4	270.8	255.9	288.4	325.4	334.4	338.1	414.0	287.5	280.7
Bundesbank	67.7	99.8	67.1	45.8	51.8	52.5	114.8	80.4	89.2	104.3
Credit institutions	159.7	171.1	188.8	242.6	273.6	281.9	223.3	333.7	198.3	176.4
III. Domestic monetary capital holdings	1 266.0	1 339.5	1 369.6	1 482.9	1 670.9	1 852.8	1 988.5	2 146.1	2 338.1	2 561.3
Time deposits (more than 4-year notification)	362.4	406.2	452.6	491.3	524.9	560.1	564.3	603.1	669.5	726.1
Public sector	155.2	160.2	165.2	169.3	173.7	185.4	173.3	178.6	187.5	192.7
Private sector	207.2	246.1	287.5	322.0	351.1	374.7	391.1	424.5	481.9	533.4
Saving deposits and certificates	781.8	801.5	777.5	835.6	955.7	1 080.8	1 184.6	1 280.9	1 382.3	1 526.4
Share capital and reserves	121.8	131.7	139.4	156.0	190.3	211.9	239.5	262.1	286.3	308.8
IV. Public sector claims on the Bundesbank	1.1	4.7	3.5	6.9	19.1	12.7	0.4	13.5	3.0	2.2
V. Other items, net	–480.7	–495.2	–533.6	–505.9	–536.3	–544.9	–650.2	–775.0	–812.7	–906.0
VI. (M2 = I + II – III – IV + V)	610.9	645.6	696.1	776.6	987.6	1 084.5	1 196.5	1 319.2	1 282.7	1 257.7
VII. Time deposits (less than 4-year notification)	252.2	260.5	269.1	325.8	403.3	480.5	527.0	592.9	518.6	441.6
Money supply (M1 = VI – VII)	358.7	385.2	427.0	450.7	584.3	604.0	669.6	726.3	764.1	816.1
Sight deposits	246.6	261.1	284.4	303.8	425.8	432.3	469.1	514.3	538.2	578.6
Currency in circulation	112.2	124.1	142.6	146.9	158.6	171.8	200.5	212.0	225.9	237.5
Memorandum items:										
Central bank money[2]	167.7	188.7	207.2	216.6	246.1	266.3	305.0	294.3	280.9	271.9
M3	1 050.7	1 112.4	1 189.6	1 255.6	1 503.0	1 597.7	1 718.7	1 906.7	1 937.0	2 007.4

1. From July 1990 the time series cover the entire Deutsche Mark currency area.
2. Defined as currency in circulation plus minimum reserves on domestic bank liabilities at current reserve ratios. Data reported here are averages of daily figures for December.

Source: Deutsche Bundesbank, *Monatsbericht.*

Table J. **Population and employment**[1]

	1986	1987	1988	1989	1990	1991	1992	1993	1994	1995
	Thousands									
Population	61 066	61 077	61 449	62 063	63 253	79 984	80 595	81 180	81 423	..
Working-age population (15-64 years)	42 798	42 826	42 960	43 258	43 947	54 743	54 998	55 406	55 341	..
Labour force, total	29 188	29 386	29 608	29 799	30 369	39 165	38 837	38 632	38 651	38 448
Self-employed	3 050	3 016	3 001	3 011	3 026	3 424	3 485	3 533	3 588	3 639
Dependent employment, total	23 910	24 141	24 365	24 750	25 460	33 139	32 373	31 680	31 365	31 197
Nationals	22 340	22 564	22 755	23 072	23 685	..	..	..	..	..
Foreigners	1 570	1 577	1 610	1 678	1 775	..	..	..	..	..
Employment, total	26 960	27 157	27 366	27 761	28 486	36 563	35 858	35 213	34 953	34 836
	Per cent of civilian employment									
Agriculture, forestry, fishing	4.4	4.2	4.0	3.7	3.5	3.9	3.4	3.2	3.0	2.9
Industry	40.6	40.3	39.8	39.8	39.7	39.5	37.9	36.7	35.9	35.5
Commerce and communications	18.5	18.5	18.6	18.6	18.7	18.6	19.0	19.1	19.0	18.8
Other	36.5	37.1	37.6	37.9	38.1	38.0	39.7	41.0	42.1	42.8
	Thousands									
Unemployment	2 228	2 229	2 242	2 038	1 883	2 602	2 979	3 419	3 698	3 612
Short-time workers	197	278	208	108	56	1 761	653	948	372	199
Vacancies	154	171	189	251	314	363	356	279	285	321
	Per cent of dependent labour force									
Unemployment	7.6	7.6	7.6	6.8	6.2	6.6	7.7	8.9	9.6	9.4
Vacancies	0.5	0.6	0.6	0.8	1.0	0.9	0.9	0.7	0.7	0.8

1. From 1991 all Germany.

Source: Statistisches Bundesamt, *Wirtschaft und Statistik* and *Volkswirtschaftliche Gesamtrechnungen, Fachserie 18 Reihe 1;* and OECD, *Labour Force Statistics.*

Table K. **Wages and prices in western Germany**

Indices 1985 = 100

	1986	1987	1988	1989	1990	1991	1992	1993	1994	1995
Wages and productivity, whole economy										
Monthly contractual pay rates	103.8	107.3	110.2	113.2	118.2	125.6	133.2	138.2	140.8	146.5
Monthly gross wages and salaries per employee	103.6	106.9	110.1	113.3	118.7	125.6	132.8	136.6	139.3	143.8
Output per employee	100.9	101.7	104.7	106.9	109.8	112.5	113.4	113.0	117.1	119.8
Unit labour costs	102.7	105.1	105.3	106.0	108.2	111.7	117.3	120.9	119.9	121.3
Wages and productivity, manufacturing										
Hourly contractual pay rates, blue collar	103.7	108.0	111.9	116.1	121.6	129.5	138.4	145.4	149.3	154.2
Hourly gross earnings, blue collar	103.5	107.7	112.1	116.5	122.6	130.0	137.1	144.0	148.5	154.4
Hours worked, blue collar	100.8	99.2	99.1	100.7	102.3	102.0	99.4	89.7	85.8	..
Output per man-hour	101.4	103.4	107.8	111.8	115.9	119.7	120.7	123.4	133.1	..
Unit labour costs[1]	103.7	106.8	106.4	107.5	110.5	115.2	120.9	125.2	117.6	..
Prices										
Agricultural producer prices	94.3	91.7	91.8	99.8	94.7	94.1	91.9	84.7	86.5	87.1
Industrial producer prices	97.4	95.0	96.2	99.3	100.9	103.4	104.9	104.9	105.5	107.2
Costs of dwelling construction	101.4	103.2	105.5	109.3	116.4	124.2	131.3	137.3	140.1	143.4
GDP deflator	103.2	105.0	106.7	109.3	112.8	117.1	123.5	128.1	131.1	134.1
Private consumption deflator	99.4	99.9	101.2	104.2	107.0	111.0	116.2	120.9	124.3	126.7
Consumer prices										
Including food	99.8	100.1	101.3	104.2	107.0	110.9	115.3	119.4	122.6	124.7
Excluding food	101.8	102.4	103.9	107.0	109.8	114.0	118.8	123.5	127.1	129.4
Foreign trade prices										
Exports	98.2	97.3	99.3	102.1	102.2	103.5	104.5	104.8	105.8	..
Imports	84.3	79.8	80.8	84.4	82.5	82.8	80.1	78.5	79.1	..

1. Including mining and quarrying.

Source: Statistisches Bundesamt.

Table L. **Structure of output and performance indicators in western Germany**

	1990	1991	1992	1993	1994	1995	1990	1991	1992	1993	1994	1995
	Share of GDP						Share of total employment					
A. Structure of output (constant prices)												
Agriculture, hunting, forestry and fishing	1.4	1.3	1.5	1.4	..	..	3.5	3.3	3.2	3.0	2.9	2.8
Energy, water supply, mining	2.8	2.8	2.7	2.7	2.6	2.6	1.6	1.6	1.5	1.5	1.5	1.5
Manufacturing	30.2	29.9	28.5	26.8	26.7	26.4	31.4	31.0	30.2	28.9	27.9	27.2
Construction	5.4	5.2	5.2	5.1	5.2	5.0	6.7	6.6	6.6	6.8	7.0	7.0
Traded services	26.4	26.6	26.7	27.6	27.6	27.9	21.8	22.2	22.4	22.6	22.7	22.4
Non-traded services	17.4	18.1	19.0	20.0	20.2	20.7	15.5	16.0	16.6	17.4	18.2	18.7
Total traded goods and services	83.7	83.8	83.7	83.6	82.3	..	80.5	80.7	80.6	80.2	80.2	79.5
General government non-traded sector	11.0	10.1	10.3	10.6	10.4	10.2	15.1	14.8	14.7	15.0	15.2	15.0
	Productivity growth						Share of total investment					
B. Economic performance (constant prices)												
Agriculture, hunting, forestry and fishing	7.6	–4.0	26.7	–3.2	..	..	2.6	2.4	2.1	1.8	1.7	..
Energy, water supply, mining	1.1	8.2	0.9	–0.2	1.6	5.5	4.6	4.2	4.5	4.3	4.3	..
Manufacturing	2.7	2.3	–1.0	–2.2	7.8	2.7	21.9	21.3	18.6	14.1	13.0	..
Construction	–0.9	–0.7	1.2	–4.3	1.6	–1.7	1.6	1.6	1.8	1.7	1.5	..
Traded services	2.7	1.6	0.0	2.0	3.6	4.7	43.7	43.1	42.4	40.7	..	..
Non-traded services	2.9	2.7	1.9	0.7	0.5	1.1	21.1	21.1	18.5	15.7	..	..
Total traded goods and services	2.7	2.3	0.8	0.1	2.5	..	95.5	93.7	87.9	78.3	20.5	..
General government non-traded sector	–0.4	1.6	3.0	1.0	0.8	1.2	11.5	10.8	10.5	9.9	9.6	..
			1986	1987	1988	1989	1990	1991	1992	1993	1994	1995
C. Other indicators (current prices)												
Total R&D expenditure as % of total GDP			2.7	2.9	2.9	2.9	2.8	2.6	2.5	2.4	2.3	2.3
R&D as % of GDP in business enterprise sector			2.5	2.6	2.6	2.6	2.5	2.3	2.1	..	..	..
Government-funded R&D as % of total			35.3	34.7	34.2	34.1	34.1	35.8	36.0	36.7	37.2	37.1

Source: Statistisches Bundesamt, *Volkswirtschaftliche Gesamtrechnungen, Fachserie 18 Reihe 1;* OECD, *Main Science and Technology Indicators.*

Table M. **Labour market indicators in western Germany**

A. TREND

	Peak		Trough		1991	1992	1993	1994	1995
Standardised unemployment rate	1983:	7.7	1980:	3.0	4.2	4.6	6.1	6.9	6.9
Unemployment rate (Mikrozensus)									
Total	1985:	9.3	1979:	3.8	6.3	6.6	8.2	9.2	9.3
Male	1985:	8.6	1979:	2.9	5.8	6.2	8.0	9.2	9.3
Female	1986:	10.6	1980:	5.2	7.0	7.2	8.4	9.2	9.2
Youth[1]	1983:	9.1	1980:	3.2	4.5	5.0	6.4	7.3	8.0
Share of long-term unemployment[2]	1988:	32.6	1980:	12.9	28.3	26.6	25.9	32.5	33.3
Registered vacancies (thousands)	1991:	331.0	1983:	76.0	331	324	243	234	267
Length of working week (1990 = 100)[3]	1981:	105.1	1994:	83.9	99.8	97.2	87.7	83.9	..

B. STRUCTURAL AND INSTITUTIONAL FEATURES

	1987	1988	1989	1990	1991	1992	1993	1994	1995
Labour force (% change)	0.7	0.8	0.7	2.2	1.7	1.2	0.0	–0.3	–0.5
Participation rate[4]									
Total	68.6	68.9	68.9	69.1	71.2	70.4	69.6	..	..
Males	82.5	82.2	81.5	80.8	80.6	79.3	78.0	..	..
Females	54.5	55.4	56.0	57.0	61.6	61.2	60.8	..	..
Employment/total population	44.3	44.4	44.6	45.0	45.6	45.4	44.2	43.5	..
Employers, self-employed									
and family workers (as % of total)	11.1	11.0	10.9	10.6	10.5	10.4	10.6	10.8	..
Wage-earners and salaried employees (as % of total)	88.9	89.0	89.1	89.4	89.5	89.6	89.4	89.2	89.3
Civilian employment by sector (% change)									
Agriculture	–4.4	–4.2	–4.6	–3.2	–2.5	–4.1	–5.3	–5.0	–5.4
Industry	–0.2	–0.2	1.2	2.8	1.3	–1.3	–4.7	–3.8	–1.9
Services	1.8	1.9	2.0	3.5	3.7	2.7	0.8	0.6	0.2
of which: General government	1.1	0.5	0.6	0.7	0.0	0.8	–0.2	–0.3	–0.9
Total	0.7	0.8	1.5	3.0	2.5	0.9	–1.5	–1.2	–0.7
Civilian employment by sector (as % of total)									
Agriculture	4.2	4.0	3.8	3.7	3.6	3.4	3.3	3.1	2.9
Industry	40.3	40.2	40.7	41.8	42.3	41.8	39.8	38.3	37.6
Services	55.6	56.6	57.8	59.8	62.0	63.7	64.1	64.5	64.7
of which: General government	15.6	15.7	15.8	15.9	15.9	16.1	16.0	16.0	15.8

Table M. **Labour market indicators in western Germany** *(cont.)*

	B. STRUCTURAL AND INSTITUTIONAL FEATURES								
	1987	1988	1989	1990	1991	1992	1993	1994	1995
Short-time workers[5]	1.0	0.8	0.4	0.2	0.5	1.0	2.6	1.0	0.4
Non-wage labour costs[6]	16.4	16.5	16.5	16.4	17.0	17.0	17.3	18.3	18.5

1. 15-19 year old.
2. People looking for a job one year or more as a percentage of total registered unemployment.
3. Hours worked by wage-earners in manufacturing.
4. Labour force as a percentage of population from 15 to 64 years.
5. Short-time workers as percentage of total employment.
6. Employers' social security contributions as a percentage of total wage, from 1991 all Germany.

Source: Statistisches Bundesamt; Bundesanstalt für Arbeit, *Amtliche Nachrichten, Jahreszahlen;* OECD, *National Accounts, Labour Force Statistics* and *Main Economic Indicators.*

Table N. **Public sector**[1]

	1990	1991	1992	1993	1994	1995
Budgetary indicators: general government accounts (% of potential GDP)						
Primary receipts (excluding interest)	40.7	41.2	42.8	41.4	42.6	42.0
Primary expenditure (excluding interest)	40.8	42.4	43.0	42.4	42.4	42.6
Primary budget balance	–0.1	–1.2	–0.2	–1.0	0.2	–0.6
General government budget balance	–2.1	–3.3	–2.8	–3.5	–2.5	–3.5
Structure of expenditure and taxes (% of GDP)						
General government expenditure[2]	45.8	48.6	49.2	50.4	49.7	50.2
Consumption	18.3	19.5	20.1	20.0	19.5	19.5
Subsidies	2.0	2.3	1.9	2.0	2.1	2.1
Investment	2.3	2.6	2.8	2.7	2.6	2.5
General government revenue[3]	43.7	45.3	46.4	46.9	47.2	46.7
Direct taxes	11.0	11.5	11.8	11.4	10.9	11.2
Indirect taxes	12.5	12.6	12.7	13.0	13.4	12.9
Social security contributions	16.8	17.9	18.2	18.8	19.2	19.3
Other indicators[4]						
Income tax as a per cent of total tax	39.9	41.8	42.6	41.5	40.6	42.2
Income tax elasticity	–0.3	1.2	1.5	–0.1	1.0	2.0[5]
Tax rates (%)						
Average effective personal income tax rate	21.4	21.9	22.7	22.1	22.4	23.3
Average rate of employees' social secutity contribution paid[6]	17.8	18.2	18.3	18.3	19.4	. .
Standard VAT rate	14.0	14.0	14.0	15.0	15.0	15.0

1. From 1991 all Germany.
2. Defined as current disbursements plus gross investment plus net capital transfers paid.
3. Defined as tax and non-tax receipts plus consumption of fixed capital.
4. Households. Income tax elasticity is with respect to household disposable income.
5. The increase in the tax elasticity is due to the introduction of the solidarity tax surcharge.
6. For an unmarried average production worker, per cent of gross earnings.

Source: OECD, *National Accounts* and *The Tax/Benefit position of production workers;* Deutsche Bundesbank, *Monatsbericht.*

Table O. **Financial markets**[1]

	1970	1975	1980	1985	1990	1992	1993	1994	1995
Structure of financial flows[2]									
Share of intermediated financing in total financing	88.9	73.2	88.6	59.4	57.4	50.5	51.5	58.4	83.8
Financial institutions' share of financial assets	45.2	50.3	44.1	44.3	43.4	44.9	48.1	50.3	52.7
Structure of private non-financial sector's portfolio:									
Deposits	55.4	61.2	44.9	43.6	36.4	50.9	58.9	9.3	36.0
Bonds and bills[3]	12.1	7.4	15.5	17.0	31.7	22.6	5.6	49.9	22.3
Equities	5.1	3.6	3.9	2.8	8.2	2.6	1.7	3.8	3.0
Non-financial corporate financial structure	100.0	100.0	100.0	100.0	100.0	100.0	100.0	100.0	100.0
Own-financing	56.7	67.0	58.1	67.3	60.8	54.3	57.6	62.0	66.9
Debt and equity	43.3	33.0	41.9	32.7	39.2	45.7	42.4	38.0	33.1
Long-term debt	22.9	30.6	19.0	20.5	19.9	36.7	42.8	27.4	13.6
Equity	2.2	3.2	2.3	2.5	4.8	2.2	2.4	4.2	5.6
Short-term debt	18.3	–0.8	20.6	9.7	14.6	6.7	–2.9	6.4	13.9
Internationalisation of markets									
Foreign business of the banking sector[4]									
Assets	6.5	7.1	7.4	8.8	11.8	11.0	12.7	11.4	11.6
Liabilities	4.1	4.0	6.1	5.7	6.5	7.2	7.6	8.5	9.2
International banking networks:									
Foreign banks in Germany[5]	. .	. .	. .	127	177	186	194	197	. .
German bank branches abroad (without subsidiaries)	. .	44	88	118	177	199	228	241	. .
Share of long-term capital transactions:									
Net purchases of domestic bonds by non-residents[6]	. .	–6.8	0.5	29.8	8.1	41.5	53.3	6.9	36.4
Net purchases of foreign bonds by residents[6]	6.8	2.7	13.7	26.0	10.0	2.6	3.2	9.0	10.7
Efficiency of markets									
Divergence between Euro rates and domestic interest rates[7]	–0.98	–0.42	–0.42	–0.14	–0.05	–0.23	–0.04	–0.02	–0.09

1. From 1991 all Germany.
2. Credits from domestic and foreign banks as percentage of total funds raised on the credit market by domestic non-financial sectors.
3. 1991-1994 including investment certificates.
4. As a percentage of deposit banks' balance sheets.
5. Number of branches and subsidiaries.
6. As a percentage of total purchases.
7. Three-month Euro-DM interest rate minus three-month interbank rate.

Source: Deutsche Bundesbank, *Monatsberichte* and *Statistisches Beiheft zum Monatsbericht, Zahlungsbilanzstatistik.*

BASIC STATISTICS:

INTERNATIONAL COMPARISONS

	Units	Reference period[1]	Australia	Austria
Population				
Total	Thousands	1994	17 840	8 031
Inhabitants per sq. km	Number	1994	2	96
Net average annual increase over previous 10 years	%	1994	1.4	0.6
Employment				
Total civilian employment (TCE)[2]	Thousands	1994	7 680 (93)	3 737
of which: Agriculture	% of TCE	1994	5.3 (93)	7.2
Industry	% of TCE	1994	23.7 (93)	33.2
Services	% of TCE	1994	71 (93)	59.6
Gross domestic product (GDP)				
At current prices and current exchange rates	Bill. US$	1994	331.6	198.1
Per capita	US$	1994	18 588	24 670
At current prices using current PPP's[3]	Bill. US$	1994	327.9	162.3
Per capita	US$	1994	18 382	20 210
Average annual volume growth over previous 5 years	%	1994	2.2	2.5
Gross fixed capital formation (GFCF)	% of GDP	1994	21.4	24.8
of which: Machinery and equipment	% of GDP	1993	9.8	8.7
Residential construction	% of GDP	1993	5.2	6.3
Average annual volume growth over previous 5 years	%	1994	0.8	3.7
Gross saving ratio[4]	% of GDP	1994	16.8	25.3
General government				
Current expenditure on goods and services	% of GDP	1994	17.5	
Current disbursements[5]	% of GDP	1993	36.9	48.4
Current receipts	% of GDP	1993	33.5	48.6
Net official development assistance	% of GNP	1993	0.34	0.31
Indicators of living standards				
Private consumption per capita using current PPP's[3]	US$	1993	10 803	10 546
Passenger cars, per 1 000 inhabitants	Number	1990	430	382
Telephones, per 1 000 inhabitants	Number	1991	464	432
Television sets, per 1 000 inhabitants	Number	1991	480	478
Doctors, per 1 000 inhabitants	Number	1993	2.2 (91)	2.3
Infant mortality per 1 000 live births	Number		6.1	6.5
Wages and prices (average annual increase over previous 5 years)				
Wages (earnings or rates according to availability)	%	1994	3	5.5
Consumer prices	%	1994	3	3.4
Foreign trade				
Exports of goods, fob*	Mill. US$	1994	47 363	44 881
As % of GDP	%	1994	14.3	22.7
Average annual increase over previous 5 years	%	1994	5	6.7
Imports of goods, cif*	Mill. US$	1994	49 731	55 071
As % of GDP	%	1994	15	27.8
Average annual increase over previous 5 years	%	1994	4	7.2
Total official reserves[6]	Mill. SDRs	1994	7 730	11 523
As ratio of average monthly imports of goods	Ratio	1994	1.9	2.5

* At current prices and exchange rates.
1. Unless otherwise stated.
2. According to the definitions used in OECD *Labour Force Statistics.*
3. PPPs = Purchasing Power Parities.
4. Gross saving = Gross national disposable income minus private and government consumption.
5. Current disbursements = Current expenditure on goods and services plus current transfers and payments of property income.
6. Gold included in reserves is valued at 35 SDRs per ounce. End of year.

EMPLOYMENT OPPORTUNITIES

Economics Department, OECD

The Economics Department of the OECD offers challenging and rewarding opportunities to economists interested in applied policy analysis in an international environment. The Department's concerns extend across the entire field of economic policy analysis, both macroeconomic and microeconomic. Its main task is to provide, for discussion by committees of senior officials from Member countries, documents and papers dealing with current policy concerns. Within this programme of work, three major responsibilities are:

- to prepare regular surveys of the economies of individual Member countries;
- to issue full twice-yearly reviews of the economic situation and prospects of the OECD countries in the context of world economic trends;
- to analyse specific policy issues in a medium-term context for the OECD as a whole, and to a lesser extent for the non-OECD countries.

The documents prepared for these purposes, together with much of the Department's other economic work, appear in published form in the *OECD Economic Outlook, OECD Economic Surveys, OECD Economic Studies* and the Department's *Working Papers* series.

The Department maintains a world econometric model, INTERLINK, which plays an important role in the preparation of the policy analyses and twice-yearly projections. The availability of extensive cross-country data bases and good computer resources facilitates comparative empirical analysis, much of which is incorporated into the model.

The Department is made up of about 80 professional economists from a variety of backgrounds and Member countries. Most projects are carried out by small teams and last from four to eighteen months. Within the Department, ideas and points of view are widely discussed; there is a lively professional interchange, and all professional staff have the opportunity to contribute actively to the programme of work.

Skills the Economics Department is looking for:

a) Solid competence in using the tools of both microeconomic and macroeconomic theory to answer policy questions. Experience indicates that this normally requires the equivalent of a Ph.D. in economics or substantial relevant professional experience to compensate for a lower degree.

b) Solid knowledge of economic statistics and quantitative methods; this includes how to identify data, estimate structural relationships, apply basic techniques of time series analysis, and test hypotheses. It is essential to be able to interpret results sensibly in an economic policy context.

c) A keen interest in and extensive knowledge of policy issues, economic developments and their political/social contexts.

d) Interest and experience in analysing questions posed by policy-makers and presenting the results to them effectively and judiciously. Thus, work experience in government agencies or policy research institutions is an advantage.

e) The ability to write clearly, effectively, and to the point. The OECD is a bilingual organisation with French and English as the official languages. Candidates must have excellent knowledge of one of these languages, and some knowledge of the other. Knowledge of other languages might also be an advantage for certain posts.

f) For some posts, expertise in a particular area may be important, but a successful candidate is expected to be able to work on a broader range of topics relevant to the work of the Department. Thus, except in rare cases, the Department does not recruit narrow specialists.

g) The Department works on a tight time schedule with strict deadlines. Moreover, much of the work in the Department is carried out in small groups. Thus, the ability to work with other economists from a variety of cultural and professional backgrounds, to supervise junior staff, and to produce work on time is important.

General information

The salary for recruits depends on educational and professional background. Positions carry a basic salary from FF 305 700 or FF 377 208 for Administrators (economists) and from FF 438 348 for Principal Administrators (senior economists). This may be supplemented by expatriation and/or family allowances, depending on nationality, residence and family situation. Initial appointments are for a fixed term of two to three years.

Vacancies are open to candidates from OECD Member countries. The Organisation seeks to maintain an appropriate balance between female and male staff and among nationals from Member countries.

For further information on employment opportunities in the Economics Department, contact:

Administrative Unit
Economics Department
OECD
2, rue André-Pascal
75775 PARIS CEDEX 16
FRANCE

E-Mail: compte.esadmin@oecd.org

Applications citing ''ECSUR'', together with a detailed *curriculum vitae* in English or French, should be sent to the Head of Personnel at the above address.

MAIN SALES OUTLETS OF OECD PUBLICATIONS
PRINCIPAUX POINTS DE VENTE DES PUBLICATIONS DE L'OCDE

AUSTRALIA – AUSTRALIE
D.A. Information Services
648 Whitehorse Road, P.O.B 163
Mitcham, Victoria 3132 Tel. (03) 9210.7777
Fax: (03) 9210.7788

AUSTRIA – AUTRICHE
Gerold & Co.
Graben 31
Wien I Tel. (0222) 533.50.14
Fax: (0222) 512.47.31.29

BELGIUM – BELGIQUE
Jean De Lannoy
Avenue du Roi, Koningslaan 202
B-1060 Bruxelles Tel. (02) 538.51.69/538.08.41
Fax: (02) 538.08.41

CANADA
Renouf Publishing Company Ltd.
1294 Algoma Road
Ottawa, ON K1B 3W8 Tel. (613) 741.4333
Fax: (613) 741.5439
Stores:
61 Sparks Street
Ottawa, ON K1P 5R1 Tel. (613) 238.8985
12 Adelaide Street West
Toronto, ON M5H 1L6 Tel. (416) 363.3171
Fax: (416)363.59.63

Les Éditions La Liberté Inc.
3020 Chemin Sainte-Foy
Sainte-Foy, PQ G1X 3V6 Tel. (418) 658.3763
Fax: (418) 658.3763

Federal Publications Inc.
165 University Avenue, Suite 701
Toronto, ON M5H 3B8 Tel. (416) 860.1611
Fax: (416) 860.1608

Les Publications Fédérales
1185 Université
Montréal, QC H3B 3A7 Tel. (514) 954.1633
Fax: (514) 954.1635

CHINA – CHINE
China National Publications Import
Export Corporation (CNPIEC)
16 Gongti E. Road, Chaoyang District
P.O. Box 88 or 50
Beijing 100704 PR Tel. (01) 506.6688
Fax: (01) 506.3101

CHINESE TAIPEI – TAIPEI CHINOIS
Good Faith Worldwide Int'l. Co. Ltd.
9th Floor, No. 118, Sec. 2
Chung Hsiao E. Road
Taipei Tel. (02) 391.7396/391.7397
Fax: (02) 394.9176

DENMARK – DANEMARK
Munksgaard Book and Subscription Service
35, Nørre Søgade, P.O. Box 2148
DK-1016 København K Tel. (33) 12.85.70
Fax: (33) 12.93.87

J. H. Schultz Information A/S,
Herstedvang 12,
DK – 2620 Albertslung Tel. 43 63 23 00
Fax: 43 63 19 69
Internet: s-info@inet.uni-c.dk

EGYPT – ÉGYPTE
Middle East Observer
41 Sherif Street
Cairo Tel. 392.6919
Fax: 360-6804

FINLAND – FINLANDE
Akateeminen Kirjakauppa
Keskuskatu 1, P.O. Box 128
00100 Helsinki

Subscription Services/Agence d'abonnements :
P.O. Box 23
00371 Helsinki Tel. (358 0) 121 4416
Fax: (358 0) 121.4450

FRANCE
OECD/OCDE
Mail Orders/Commandes par correspondance :
2, rue André-Pascal
75775 Paris Cedex 16 Tel. (33-1) 45.24.82.00
Fax: (33-1) 49.10.42.76
Telex: 640048 OCDE
Internet: Compte.PUBSINQ@oecd.org

Orders via Minitel, France only/
Commandes par Minitel, France exclusivement :
36 15 OCDE

OECD Bookshop/Librairie de l'OCDE :
33, rue Octave-Feuillet
75016 Paris Tél. (33-1) 45.24.81.81
(33-1) 45.24.81.67

Dawson
B.P. 40
91121 Palaiseau Cedex Tel. 69.10.47.00
Fax: 64.54.83.26

Documentation Française
29, quai Voltaire
75007 Paris Tel. 40.15.70.00

Economica
49, rue Héricart
75015 Paris Tel. 45.75.05.67
Fax: 40.58.15.70

Gibert Jeune (Droit-Économie)
6, place Saint-Michel
75006 Paris Tel. 43.25.91.19

Librairie du Commerce International
10, avenue d'Iéna
75016 Paris Tel. 40.73.34.60

Librairie Dunod
Université Paris-Dauphine
Place du Maréchal-de-Lattre-de-Tassigny
75016 Paris Tel. 44.05.40.13

Librairie Lavoisier
11, rue Lavoisier
75008 Paris Tel. 42.65.39.95

Librairie des Sciences Politiques
30, rue Saint-Guillaume
75007 Paris Tel. 45.48.36.02

P.U.F.
49, boulevard Saint-Michel
75005 Paris Tel. 43.25.83.40

Librairie de l'Université
12*a*, rue Nazareth
13100 Aix-en-Provence Tel. (16) 42.26.18.08

Documentation Française
165, rue Garibaldi
69003 Lyon Tel. (16) 78.63.32.23

Librairie Decitre
29, place Bellecour
69002 Lyon Tel. (16) 72.40.54.54

Librairie Sauramps
Le Triangle
34967 Montpellier Cedex 2 Tel. (16) 67.58.85.15
Fax: (16) 67.58.27.36

A la Sorbonne Actual
23, rue de l'Hôtel-des-Postes
06000 Nice Tel. (16) 93.13.77.75
Fax: (16) 93.80.75.69

GERMANY – ALLEMAGNE
OECD Bonn Centre
August-Bebel-Allee 6
D-53175 Bonn Tel. (0228) 959.120
Fax: (0228) 959.12.17

GREECE – GRÈCE
Librairie Kauffmann
Stadiou 28
10564 Athens Tel. (01) 32.55.321
Fax: (01) 32.30.320

HONG-KONG
Swindon Book Co. Ltd.
Astoria Bldg. 3F
34 Ashley Road, Tsimshatsui
Kowloon, Hong Kong Tel. 2376.2062
Fax: 2376.0685

HUNGARY – HONGRIE
Euro Info Service
Margitsziget, Európa Ház
1138 Budapest Tel. (1) 111.62.16
Fax: (1) 111.60.61

ICELAND – ISLANDE
Mál Mog Menning
Laugavegi 18, Pósthólf 392
121 Reykjavik Tel. (1) 552.4240
Fax: (1) 562.3523

INDIA – INDE
Oxford Book and Stationery Co.
Scindia House
New Delhi 110001 Tel. (11) 331.5896/5308
Fax: (11) 332.5993
17 Park Street
Calcutta 700016 Tel. 240832

INDONESIA – INDONÉSIE
Pdii-Lipi
P.O. Box 4298
Jakarta 12042 Tel. (21) 573.34.67
Fax: (21) 573.34.67

IRELAND – IRLANDE
Government Supplies Agency
Publications Section
4/5 Harcourt Road
Dublin 2 Tel. 661.31.11
Fax: 475.27.60

ISRAEL – ISRAËL
Praedicta
5 Shatner Street
P.O. Box 34030
Jerusalem 91430 Tel. (2) 52.84.90/1/2
Fax: (2) 52.84.93

R.O.Y. International
P.O. Box 13056
Tel Aviv 61130 Tel. (3) 546 1423
Fax: (3) 546 1442

Palestinian Authority/Middle East:
INDEX Information Services
P.O.B. 19502
Jerusalem Tel. (2) 27.12.19
Fax: (2) 27.16.34

ITALY – ITALIE
Libreria Commissionaria Sansoni
Via Duca di Calabria 1/1
50125 Firenze Tel. (055) 64.54.15
Fax: (055) 64.12.57

Via Bartolini 29
20155 Milano Tel. (02) 36.50.83

Editrice e Libreria Herder
Piazza Montecitorio 120
00186 Roma Tel. 679.46.28
Fax: 678.47.51

Libreria Hoepli
Via Hoepli 5
20121 Milano Tel. (02) 86.54.46
Fax: (02) 805.28.86

Libreria Scientifica
Dott. Lucio de Biasio 'Aeiou'
Via Coronelli, 6
20146 Milano Tel. (02) 48.95.45.52
Fax: (02) 48.95.45.48

JAPAN – JAPON
OECD Tokyo Centre
Landic Akasaka Building
2-3-4 Akasaka, Minato-ku
Tokyo 107 Tel. (81.3) 3586.2016
Fax: (81.3) 3584.7929

KOREA – CORÉE
Kyobo Book Centre Co. Ltd.
P.O. Box 1658, Kwang Hwa Moon
Seoul Tel. 730.78.91
Fax: 735.00.30

MALAYSIA – MALAISIE
University of Malaya Bookshop
University of Malaya
P.O. Box 1127, Jalan Pantai Baru
59700 Kuala Lumpur
Malaysia Tel. 756.5000/756.5425
Fax: 756.3246

MEXICO – MEXIQUE
OECD Mexico Centre
Edificio INFOTEC
Av. San Fernando no. 37
Col. Toriello Guerra
Tlalpan C.P. 14050
Mexico D.F. Tel. (525) 665 47 99
Fax: (525) 606 13 07

Revistas y Periodicos Internacionales S.A. de C.V.
Florencia 57 - 1004
Mexico, D.F. 06600 Tel. 207.81.00
Fax: 208.39.79

NETHERLANDS – PAYS-BAS
SDU Uitgeverij Plantijnstraat
Externe Fondsen
Postbus 20014
2500 EA's-Gravenhage Tel. (070) 37.89.880
Voor bestellingen: Fax: (070) 34.75.778

NEW ZEALAND – NOUVELLE-ZÉLANDE
GPLegislation Services
P.O. Box 12418
Thorndon, Wellington Tel. (04) 496.5655
Fax: (04) 496.5698

NORWAY – NORVÈGE
NIC INFO A/S
Bertrand Narvesens vei 2
P.O. Box 6512 Etterstad
0606 Oslo 6 Tel. (022) 57.33.00
Fax: (022) 68.19.01

PAKISTAN
Mirza Book Agency
65 Shahrah Quaid-E-Azam
Lahore 54000 Tel. (42) 735.36.01
Fax: (42) 576.37.14

PHILIPPINE – PHILIPPINES
International Booksource Center Inc.
Rm 179/920 Cityland 10 Condo Tower 2
HV dela Costa Ext cor Valero St.
Makati Metro Manila Tel. (632) 817 9676
Fax: (632) 817 1741

POLAND – POLOGNE
Ars Polona
00-950 Warszawa
Krakowskie Przedmieácie 7 Tel. (22) 264760
Fax: (22) 268673

PORTUGAL
Livraria Portugal
Rua do Carmo 70-74
Apart. 2681
1200 Lisboa Tel. (01) 347.49.82/5
Fax: (01) 347.02.64

SINGAPORE – SINGAPOUR
Gower Asia Pacific Pte Ltd.
Golden Wheel Building
41, Kallang Pudding Road, No. 04-03
Singapore 1334 Tel. 741.5166
Fax: 742.9356

SPAIN – ESPAGNE
Mundi-Prensa Libros S.A.
Castelló 37, Apartado 1223
Madrid 28001 Tel. (91) 431.33.99
Fax: (91) 575.39.98

Mundi-Prensa Barcelona
Consell de Cent No. 391
08009 – Barcelona Tel. (93) 488.34.92
Fax: (93) 487.76.59

Llibreria de la Generalitat
Palau Moja
Rambla dels Estudis, 118
08002 – Barcelona
(Subscripcions) Tel. (93) 318.80.12
(Publicacions) Tel. (93) 302.67.23
Fax: (93) 412.18.54

SRI LANKA
Centre for Policy Research
c/o Colombo Agencies Ltd.
No. 300-304, Galle Road
Colombo 3 Tel. (1) 574240, 573551-2
Fax: (1) 575394, 510711

SWEDEN – SUÈDE
CE Fritzes AB
S–106 47 Stockholm Tel. (08) 690.90.90
Fax: (08) 20.50.21

Subscription Agency/Agence d'abonnements :
Wennergren-Williams Info AB
P.O. Box 1305
171 25 Solna Tel. (08) 705.97.50
Fax: (08) 27.00.71

SWITZERLAND – SUISSE
Maditec S.A. (Books and Periodicals - Livres et périodiques)
Chemin des Palettes 4
Case postale 266
1020 Renens VD 1 Tel. (021) 635.08.65
Fax: (021) 635.07.80

Librairie Payot S.A.
4, place Pépinet
CP 3212
1002 Lausanne Tel. (021) 320.25.11
Fax: (021) 320.25.14

Librairie Unilivres
6, rue de Candolle
1205 Genève Tel. (022) 320.26.23
Fax: (022) 329.73.18

Subscription Agency/Agence d'abonnements :
Dynapresse Marketing S.A.
38, avenue Vibert
1227 Carouge Tel. (022) 308.07.89
Fax: (022) 308.07.99

See also – Voir aussi :
OECD Bonn Centre
August-Bebel-Allee 6
D-53175 Bonn (Germany) Tel. (0228) 959.120
Fax: (0228) 959.12.17

THAILAND – THAÏLANDE
Suksit Siam Co. Ltd.
113, 115 Fuang Nakhon Rd.
Opp. Wat Rajbopith
Bangkok 10200 Tel. (662) 225.9531/2
Fax: (662) 222.5188

TRINIDAD & TOBAGO
SSL Systematics Studies Limited
9 Watts Street
Curepe
Trinadad & Tobago, W.I. Tel. (1809) 645.3475
Fax: (1809) 662.5654

TUNISIA – TUNISIE
Grande Librairie Spécialisée
Fendri Ali
Avenue Haffouz Imm El-Intilaka
Bloc B 1 Sfax 3000 Tel. (216-4) 296 855
Fax: (216-4) 298.270

TURKEY – TURQUIE
Kültür Yayinlari Is-Türk Ltd. Sti.
Atatürk Bulvari No. 191/Kat 13
Kavaklidere/Ankara
Tel. (312) 428.11.40 Ext. 2458
Fax: (312) 417 24 90
Dolmabahce Cad. No. 29
Besiktas/Istanbul Tel. (212) 260 7188

UNITED KINGDOM – ROYAUME-UNI
HMSO
Gen. enquiries Tel. (0171) 873 0011
Postal orders only:
P.O. Box 276, London SW8 5DT
Personal Callers HMSO Bookshop
49 High Holborn, London WC1V 6HB
Fax: (0171) 873 8463
Branches at: Belfast, Birmingham, Bristol, Edinburgh, Manchester

UNITED STATES – ÉTATS-UNIS
OECD Washington Center
2001 L Street N.W., Suite 650
Washington, D.C. 20036-4922 Tel. (202) 785.6323
Fax: (202) 785.0350
Internet: washcont@oecd.org

Subscriptions to OECD periodicals may also be placed through main subscription agencies.

Les abonnements aux publications périodiques de l'OCDE peuvent être souscrits auprès des principales agences d'abonnement.

Orders and inquiries from countries where Distributors have not yet been appointed should be sent to: OECD Publications, 2, rue André-Pascal, 75775 Paris Cedex 16, France.

Les commandes provenant de pays où l'OCDE n'a pas encore désigné de distributeur peuvent être adressées aux Éditions de l'OCDE, 2, rue André-Pascal, 75775 Paris Cedex 16, France.

5-1996

OECD PUBLICATIONS, 2, rue André-Pascal, 75775 PARIS CEDEX 16
PRINTED IN FRANCE
(10 96 15 1) ISBN 92-64-15278-4 – No. 48961 1996
ISSN 0376-6438